More praise for *The Authentic Shakespeare*:

"This impressive collection of fifteen essays by Stephen Orgel, written over an astonishingly creative lifetime, enables us now to savor once again the revisionist delights of "The Spectacles of State," "Prospero's Wife," "Marginal Jonson," "Tobacco and Boys," and so many others that have changed our whole way of thinking about the Renaissance stage as architecture and as cultural institution, the acting profession, the task of the editor, and the poetics of spectacle. To revisit this achievement is to stand in admiration of the focus and the breadth of the author's investigation of English Renaissance drama. This book is truly Stephen Orgel's own best monument."

—David Bevington

"Whether writing of Shakespeare, Jonson, surprisingly on Marlowe, or on issues of authorship, authority, authenticity and plagiarism, Orgel is always pointed, pragmatic, skeptical and wise. All students of English poetry and drama should read it, no matter what their period of concern."

—John Hollander

"*The Authentic Shakespeare* is engrossing from the first page, not least because it's a compelling account of crucial developments that have occurred in our understanding of the early modern stage, written by one so largely responsible for them. So insightful, informative, and astute are these essays I dare to say that there's no reader who won't learn from—indeed be changed by—them. Here is dissenting intellect, critical sensitivity, and formidable scholarship in a rare and precious blend."

—Jonathan Dollimore

THE AUTHENTIC SHAKESPEARE

THE AUTHENTIC SHAKESPEARE

AND OTHER PROBLEMS OF THE EARLY MODERN STAGE

STEPHEN ORGEL

ROUTLEDGE

NEW YORK AND LONDON

Published in 2002 by
Routledge
29 West 35th Street
New York, NY 10001
www.routledge-ny.com

Published in Great Britain by
Routledge
11 New Fetter Lane
London EC4P 4EE
www.routledge.co.uk

10 9 8 7 6 5 4 3 2 1

Library of Congress Cataloging-in-Publication Data

Orgel, Stephen.
The authentic Shakespeare, and other problems of the early
modern stage / Stephen Orgel.
    p. cm.
Includes bibliographical references and index.
    ISBN 0-415-90013-1 (hardback: alk. paper) — ISBN 0-415-91213-x (pbk.: alk. paper)
1. Shakespeare, William, 1564–1616—Stage history—To 1625. 2. Shakespeare, William,
1564–1616—Criticism, Textual. 3. Theater—England—History—16th century.
4. Theater—England—History—17th century. 5. Playwriting—History—16th
century. 6. Playwriting—History—17th century. I. Title.
PR3095.O73 2002
822'.309—dc21
003625   2002

to
Randall Nakayama
and
Bill Germano

CONTENTS

LIST OF ILLUSTRATIONS

A RETROSPECTIVE PREFACE

This is a collection of fifteen interrelated essays about the theater of Renaissance England. The proposal for a volume of my essays on this subject was first broached to me over twenty-five years ago by Bill Germano, surely among the most patient (and tenacious) editors of all time. Written over a thirty-year period for a variety of forums, and often frankly revisionist in intent, they share with my books *The Illusion of Power* and *Impersonations* a broad general argument about the nature of theater as a social and aesthetic phenomenon in Early Modern England. They deal with the major dramatists of the time; with the development of the stage both as an architectural concept and a cultural institution; with the changing status of the acting profession; with the changing use and significance of settings and costume; with the complex and changing interaction of theater with the political life of the age; and with the transformation of the performing scripts of the Elizabethan stage into the books and editions that are, for our time, English Renaissance drama. Many of these pieces were originally written at the invitation of friends and colleagues who had read work of mine and wanted particular aspects elaborated. The selection—from a list of over fifty—is largely Bill's. All have undergone some revision, to avoid repetition, include cross references, and correct errors.

The earliest of the essays is "The Poetics of Spectacle," written in 1969. This argues against the prevailing critical orthodoxy that took Ben Jonson's side in his famous quarrel with Inigo Jones—that poetry, not stagecraft, was the essential element in the masque—and maintained, on the contrary, that the illusionistic scenery and splendid costumes and decor created by Inigo Jones for the Stuart court were not mere spectacle, but had a serious and recoverable philosophical basis—that, indeed, the idea that there was anything "mere" about spectacle in the Renaissance was anachronistic and misguided. The essay, in short, articulated the theory behind Jones's practice. This argument developed logically out of my early work on Ben Jonson and the masque in *The Jonsonian Masque* and my edition of the Jonson masques in the Yale Ben Jonson, and I take a particular pleasure in its continued currency because at the time it was written the masque was still the most esoteric of subjects. Indeed, my promotion to tenure at Berkeley was initially rejected because a significant number of my colleagues maintained that the masque was not a topic worthy of serious study—an opinion that was successfully countered, thanks to an indignant and sympathetic chair, by letters solicited from an even more significant group of scholars elsewhere. The essay subsequently became the first chapter of my book *Inigo Jones*, written in collaboration with Sir Roy Strong. *Inigo Jones* is a splendid piece of bookmaking that, because of its sumptuousness, has probably been more admired than read; but it has made the corpus of Jones's theatrical work comprehensible, and "The Poetics of Spectacle" still seems to me to distill its essence.

The masque, in fact, is probably a better index to the complexities of Renaissance theater than literary and theatrical history has been aware. Understanding it requires us to take seriously not only plot, character, style, and the constraints and economics of the theater business, but also the often arcane but nevertheless ubiquitous forms of Renaissance philosophy and symbolism, the demands of patronage, the nature of artistic collaboration, and most important, the presence of an active and specific audience. Dealing with these celebratory works only through their texts, moreover, constantly reminds us of how much in this quintessentially Renaissance form is lost to us: spectacle, music, choreography; most of all, the participation of identifiable performers who also constitute, in a real sense, what is being celebrated. My thinking on these matters gained immeasurably from a year and a half at the Warburg Institute in the late 1960s, where J. B. Trapp and the late D. P. Walker were the most generous of colleagues and hospitable of hosts (the late Frances Yates, however, proved elusive and distinctly uncommunicative). The social context and cultural implications of the masque are pursued in two other essays in this volume. Richard Trexler invited me to deliver the paper that became "The Spectacles of State" at a conference of social historians at SUNY Binghamton in 1982. I was flattered to be included; but such is the parochialization of academic disciplines that the volume in which it appeared has for the most part not reached literary and theatrical historians, and I doubt that many people interested in my work will know it. And "Marginal Jonson," concerned with the complex interaction between Jonson's invention and the patronage of Queen Anne, was written for a collection of new essays on the politics of the Stuart masque edited by David Bevington and Peter Holbrook.

The three brief pieces that open this volume are about how we construct

the literature of the past in general, and its drama in particular; and specifically, what the historical materialization of manuscripts and play scripts as
books implies. "What Is a Text?" was written at the invitation of David Berg-
eron for a panel on the editing of Renaissance texts at the Modern Language
Association in 1980, and when it was subsequently published in the annual
Research Opportunities in Renaissance Drama the title, with its allusion to
Foucault, was supplied by him. It is a nice title which has done the essay nothing but good; but though "What Is an Author?" is certainly relevant to the
argument, the essay owes more to D. F. McKenzie and Jerome McGann than
to Foucault. "What Is a Character?" was delivered at the Society for Textual
Studies in 1993, and "What Is an Editor?," under the title "The Postmodern
Variorum," at an MLA symposium on the future of the Variorum Shakespeare, also in 1993.

"Acting Scripts, Performing Texts" was written for a 1988 Toronto conference on textual studies organized by the most radical and original voice of the
new bibliography, Randall McLeod, and in its final form owes much to his
brilliance and intellectual generosity (and something as well to his finicky
objections and endless editorial fussing). "The Renaissance Poet as Plagiarist"
was presented (under the title "The Renaissance Artist as Plagiarist") in 1975
at an English Institute session on imitation organized by Tom McFarland, a
good friend and a formidable scholar. Both "Prospero's Wife" and "Gendering
the Crown" were written for Renaissance conferences organized by Margaret
Ferguson, Maureen Quilligan, and Nancy Vickers, the first at Yale in 1982, the
second at the University of Pennsylvania in 1992. "Shakespeare and the Kinds
of Drama" started life as a talk at a 1975 Princeton symposium on genre organized by Earl Miner; and many years later Peter Stallybrass, who was putting
together a panel for the 1993 English Institute on the history of Aristotelian
catharsis, asked if I wanted to extend my brief remarks in that essay on the
subject; the result was "The Play of Conscience." "Macbeth and the Antic
Round" was delivered at the *Scaena* conference at St. John's College, Cambridge, in 1997, and *Tobacco and Boys* was written at the invitation of Sara
Munson Deats for a meeting of the International Marlowe Society held at
Marlowe's college, Corpus Christi College, Cambridge, in 1998. "The Authentic Shakespeare" began as the James McAuley Memorial Lecture at the University of Tasmania in Hobart in 1987, an invitation that I owe to two dear
antipodean friends, Adrian Colman and Margaret Scott.

In a volume that covers as long a period as this, acknowledgments can only
be invidious; most of my friends and many of my students should be cited. I
name, therefore, only a very small number to whom I feel I shall always owe a
continuing and special indebtedness: the late Andrew Chiappe, D. J. Gordon,
Reuben Brower, Jonas Barish, and David Kalstone; and Jonathan Goldberg,

Marion Trousdale, Leonard Barkan, Stephen Greenblatt, David Halperin, David Kastan, Terry Castle, Peter Stallybrass, Ann Rosalind Jones, Margreta de Grazia; and three recent students, Sean Keilen, Anston Bosman, and Bradin Cormack. I owe a special debt of thanks to my uniquely talented student Elena Shvarts for her delightful versions of the two portraits in "Tobacco and Boys" that a peremptory owner and a dark photograph left us unable to reproduce. For her efforts in the Augean Stables of illustrations and permissions, I not only name Sara Brady, but avow that the volume would absolutely not exist without her. The dedication to Bill Germano gratefully and affectionately acknowledges many years of friendship and that this book is in essential ways his; the dedication to Randall Nakayama records a more personal indebtedness as well.

These essays first appeared in print as follows:

1. What Is a Text? *Research Opportunities in Renaissance Drama* 24 (1981).
2. What Is a Character? *Text* 8 (1996).
3. What Is an Editor? *Shakespeare Studies* 24 (1996).
4. Acting Scripts, Performing Texts. *Crisis in Editing: Texts of the English Renaissance*, ed. Randall McLeod (New York: AMS Press, 1994).
5. The Poetics of Spectacle. *New Literary History* 2 (1971).
6. The Spectacles of State. *Persons in Groups*, ed. Richard C. Trexler (Binghamton, NY, 1985).
7. The Renaissance Poet as Plagiarist. *ELH* 48:3 (fall 1981).
8. Gendering the Crown. *Subject and Object in Renaissance Culture*, eds. Margreta de Grazia, Maureen Quilligan, and Peter Stallybrass (Cambridge, 1996).
9. The Play of Conscience. *Performativity and Performance*, eds. Andrew Parker and Eve Kosofsky Sedgwick (New York: Routledge, 1995).
10. Shakespeare and the Kinds of Drama. *Critical Inquiry* 6:1 (fall 1979).
11. Macbeth and the Antic Round. *Shakespeare Survey* 52, 1999.
12. Prospero's Wife. *Representations* 8 (fall 1984).
13. Marginal Jonson. *The Politics of the Stuart Court Masque*, eds. David Bevington and Peter Holbrook (Cambridge University Press, 1998).
14. Tobacco and Boys. *GLQ* 6:4 (2000).
15. The Authentic Shakespeare. *Representations* 21 (winter 1988).

I

WHAT IS A TEXT?

MODERN SCIENTIFIC BIBLIOGRAPHY began with the assumption that certain basic textual questions were capable of correct answers: that by developing rules of evidence and refining techniques of description and comparison the relation of editions of a work to each other and to the author's manuscript could be understood, and that an accurate text could thereby be produced. Behind these assumptions lies an even more basic one: that the correct text is the author's final manuscript, which is sometimes (though usually not in Renaissance bibliographical practice) interpreted to mean the last printed edition published during the author's lifetime.

We assume, in short, that the authority of a text derives from the author. Self-evident as it may appear, I suggest that this proposition is not true: in the case of Renaissance dramatic texts it is almost never true, and in the case of non-dramatic texts it is true rather less often than we think.

What scientific bibliography has taught us more clearly than anything else is that at the heart of our texts lies a hard core of uncertainty. I want to consider the implications of this not so much for editorial practice as for our whole notion of the nature of the materials we are dealing with—the structuralist's question "what is a text?" has a particular force when it is applied to the texts of Renaissance plays. The two works that bear most directly on my subject are E. A. J. Honigmann's *The Stability of Shakespeare's Text* (1965) and G. E. Bentley's *The Profession of Dramatist in Shakespeare's Time* (1971), books whose implications seem to me far more radical and far-reaching than has generally been recognized.

I shall start with the second of these books. Bentley makes it clear how much the creation of a play was a collaborative process, with the author by no means at the center of the collaboration. The company commissioned the play, usually stipulated the subject, often provided the plot, often parceled it out, scene by scene, to several playwrights. The text thus produced was a working model, which the company then revised as seemed appropriate. The author had little or no say in these revisions: the text belonged to the company, and the authority represented by the text—I am talking now about the *performing* text—is that of the company, the owners, not that of the playwright, the author. This means that if it is a performing text we are dealing with, it is a mistake to think that in our editorial work what we are doing is getting back to an author's original manuscript: the very notion of "the author's original manuscript" is in such cases a figment.

Shakespeare might seem to be an exception, since he was not simply the playwright but also an actor and shareholder in the company—he was literally his own boss. But I do not think he is an exception: I think he was simply in on more parts of the collaboration. I shall return to this and to its implications shortly, but first I want to clarify it with a contrasting example. Ben Jonson provides an excellent control for our notions of Renaissance dramatic texts. Jonson makes a large point out of insisting that the printed versions of his plays are substantially different from the versions that were staged. He complains of the actors' cuts—other playwrights (including Shakespeare) report interpolations or revisions, with varying degrees of resentment. *Sejanus* constitutes what we might think of as a classic example for our purposes. The play was first written in collaboration with another playwright; that was the version the actors performed. But in preparing the play for publication, Jonson took control of the text: he replaced his collaborator's scenes with ones of his own, and added a good deal of new material, consisting largely of historical documentation. He is lavish in praise of his collaborator, but he also (pointedly I would think) doesn't mention his name, and since there are no other records, we can only speculate about who he was. Jonson here has succeeded in suppressing the theatrical production, and has replaced it with an independent, printed text, which he consistently refers to, moreover, not as a play but as a poem.

This example is, in Jonson's canon, extreme but not uncharacteristic. Why does he rewrite his plays for publication? Precisely because he hasn't sufficient *authority* in the theatrical versions. The only way for Jonson to assert his authority over the text was to alter it and publish it: his authority, that is, lies in the publication.

But even here, we would have to say that the author is a curiously shadowy figure. Let's move away from drama for a moment, to a situation where the issues might seem to be more clear-cut: the work of professional poets. For the Elizabethan age Spenser is the prime example, and yet Spenser continually asserts that the *authority* of his text derives not from his genius but from the poem's subject and patron, the queen. Our tendency is to dismiss this claim as flattery. Flattery it may be, but it cannot be dismissed on that account. As Jonathan Goldberg's book on Spenser *Endlesse Worke* (1981) quite brilliantly demonstrates, the question of authority in Spenser's text is both crucial and profoundly problematic. Similarly, when Ben Jonson says in *The Masque of Blackness* that he "apted" his invention to the commands of Queen Anne, he is distinguishing the *invention* of the text from its *authority*. Spenser and Jonson are the first writers in English to declare their status as professional poets—"laureate poets," in Richard Helgerson's excellent term—and it is therefore very important for them to locate the *authority* of their texts. They both locate it not in themselves, but in their patrons. (Jonson is a more ambiguous case than Spenser, but ambiguous here only means that he wants it both ways.)

It may seem that I am now working with a notion of authority that no longer involves what we ordinarily mean by it when we use it in relation to literature—that the text represents the poet's mind, voice, intentions (though we tend to be wary about the last of these), and that when we write about, say, *The Faerie Queene,* we are writing about Spenser. It would be perverse to argue that this is not true, but that is precisely what I am arguing. Let us take another analogy: Michael Baxandall, in *Painting and Experience in Fifteenth-Century Italy*, discusses the documents relating to one of Filippo Lippi's commissions. Not only is the contract for the painting quite detailed about what is to be included, but a correspondence survives from which it is clear that Lippi sent sketches to the patron for instructions about the composition and colors. Here is another example, from my own work: I was always puzzled about why Inigo Jones regularly did his costume designs in a brown or grey wash, and indicated the colors with annotations—wouldn't it have made more sense simply to do the paintings in color, so that both masquers and dressmakers could actually see what the costume was going to look like?—out of several hundred surviving drawings, there are only seven in which the color of the costume appears. The answer became clear when I got a look at the notes and letters accompanying the drawings: Jones would do his designs, and then submit them to the queen. The queen chose the colors, and made whatever alterations she wished in the design.

Now: when we write about a Lippi painting or an Inigo Jones drawing, are we really writing about Lippi or Jones? Aren't we, at the very least, writing about a complex collaboration in which the question of authority bears precisely on our notions of the nature of the artist's invention?

Let us return to literature and drama. I said that the only way for Jonson to assert his authority over his texts was to publish them, and for Jonson this was a genuinely effective strategy. For most writers, however, the situation was quite different. The authority of the published text was, for the most part, that of the publisher: he owned it; the author's rights in the work ended with his sale of the manuscript. The publisher was fully entitled to alter the manuscript if he saw fit—the manuscript was his. In this respect the publisher was precisely analogous to the theatrical company or to the recipient of a verse epistle or a manuscript poem; or, to carry the analogy further, into an area where the situation has remained largely unchanged since the Renaissance, precisely analogous to the owner of a painting. Once the painting has been sold, we do not believe that the artist has any further rights in it. The owner may cut it down to fit a particular place in his house or a frame he happens to like, may have it repainted to suit his taste, may even (as Lady Churchill did with Graham Sutherland's very famous portrait of her husband) destroy it, and we do not acknowledge that the artist has any say in the matter. In this last case, I would think the question of authority in the work was especially critical: to believers in the autonomy of the artist, the painting was a Sutherland; but to Churchill, the painting was a version of himself, and he didn't like it. The authority in this case belonged to the subject/patron just as Spenser says it does in *The Faerie Queene*.

Now let us consider a text. We have two versions of the first sonnet of *Astrophil and Stella*. The 1590 quarto version reads as follows: "Loving in truth and fain in verse my love to show, / That the dear she might take some pleasure of my pain. . . ." The Countess of Pembroke's folio version reads: ". . . That she (dear she) might take some pleasure of my pain." How shall we interpret this variation? Is Q's printer misreading the manuscript? It seems unlikely—those parentheses would be difficult to miss. Is the Countess then revising? She claims to be printing authentic texts, from her brother's own papers—does the concept of authenticity perhaps involve making improvements? Or was "she (dear she)" in the original manuscript, and did it seem too irregular or advanced for Q's editor, and did *he* improve it? Or were there, perhaps, as in the case of so many Donne poems, two (or more) versions of this sonnet, both Sidney's, both final, both authentic? The reason it is a mistake to believe we can answer this question is not merely that we cannot in fact do so; it is that it places an anachronistic emphasis on the author.

We return now to Shakespeare. E. A. J. Honigmann, in *The Stability of Shakespeare's Texts*, shows quite persuasively that the notion of final or complete versions assumed by virtually all modern editors of Shakespeare is inconsistent with everything we know not only about Renaissance theatrical practice, but about the way writers in fact work. Poets are always rewriting, and there is no reason to think that many of the confusions in Shakespeare's texts don't involve second thoughts, or amalgams of quite separate versions of a play. I'd want to go a great deal further than this, but the idea of the basic instability of the text seems to me an absolutely essential one.

I have argued that most literature in the period, and virtually all theatrical literature, must be seen as basically collaborative in nature, and I have said that Shakespeare can be distinguished from most other playwrights only because he was in on more parts of the collaboration. Editors who get this far usually want to go on to argue that Shakespeare's company wouldn't have presumed to alter Shakespeare's text—the play was, after all, written by the boss. I would argue, on the contrary, that all this means is that Shakespeare would have been in on the revisions. Or *might* have been: think about the text of *Macbeth*. We believe the opening scenes have been truncated, we know the witches' songs are by Middleton, and the Hecate scene and a later passage seem also to be non-Shakespearean interpolations for a court performance: if all this is true, where is Shakespeare's authority? If the changes were made after Shakespeare's retirement or death, why did the company think that was the right text to include in the folio? I suggest that the case of *Macbeth* is only an extreme example of the normal procedure. The text we have was considered the best (or "correct") text of the play at the time the folio was prepared. And if we think of the texts of Marlowe's *Doctor Faustus,* we shall see an even more extreme example, in which the author has become a curiously imprecise, intermittent, and shifting figure, even on the title page. He is referred to in the 1604 first quarto as "Ch. Marl.", and in the 1616 quarto as "Ch. Mar.", which, in the one surviving copy, has been expanded by an early owner to read "Marklin."

To summarize, then: when we make our editions, of Shakespeare or any other dramatist, we are *not* "getting back to the author's original text." We know nothing about Shakespeare's original text. We might know something about it if, say, a set of Shakespeare's working notes or rough drafts ever turned up, or if we ever found the text that Shakespeare presented to the company as their working copy. But if we did find such a manuscript, that would be something different from the play—just as different as the printed text of *Sejanus* is from Jonson's play. It is a difference in the opposite direction, but I would argue that the degree of difference is probably about the same.

2

WHAT IS A CHARACTER?

IN "WHAT IS A TEXT?" I argued for the radical instability of Renaissance dramatic texts, and ended by observing that the dramatic text in its own time was not the play: the text was a script, and it was only where the play started; the play, and its evolution into the texts that have come down to us, was a collaboration between author and actors, with the author by no means the controlling figure in the collaboration. The playwright in the Renaissance theater was an employee of the company, who wrote to order and was paid for piecework. Shakespeare may seem to be an exception, in the sense that he was, almost uniquely, his own boss, an actor and shareholder in the company as well as its leading playwright; but this probably only means that he was in on more parts of the collaboration than other playwrights were.

Renaissance plays are inevitably, for us, books, and they therefore have the air of finality that publication, in this case quite incorrectly, carries with it for our age. My claim, however, was not limited to drama, but was ultimately a claim about the Renaissance attitude toward texts as a whole, and part of the argument depended on observations about printing house practice, which practically guaranteed that no copy of any Renaissance book would be identical with any other copy: since proof corrections were made while printing was in progress, and both corrected and uncorrected sheets were indiscriminately bound up together in the book, there was never any single 'final' copy. The assumption that dramatic texts were unstable, therefore, is related not only to Renaissance theatrical practice, but also to assumptions about texts in general, and particularly about books, which, to summarize very briefly, did not require them to represent the true, or final, or accurate, or authentic text of the work they presented. This may seem like an exaggerated claim, but that is because we come to the matter with post-enlightenment assumptions of correctness—it would, after all, have been perfectly simple for Renaissance printers to stop the press for the ten minutes it took to proofread a single sheet; the fact that this was not considered necessary or even desirable is relevant to the basic question of what a book was conceived to be. This is not to say that there was no concept of textual authority, but only that the book was not assumed to be embodying that.

This argument has implications for the concept of character in drama as well. One way of thinking of character is simply as part of the text. This of course is the original meaning of the word: both a written account of a person, and the letters—characters—in which the account is written. When I was a student learning how to deal with literary texts, William Empson vanquished the sentimental hordes at one blow by pointing out that we cannot dispose of 'As flies to wanton boys are we to the gods: / They kill us for their sport' (4.1.36–7) by remarking that it represents the view of the crude and prosaic Gloucester, rather than that of the sensitive and perceptive Cordelia or Lear. Plays, Empson observed, have linguistic and poetic structures, and characters are not independent of those structures. The notion that the gods make fools of us is one that runs throughout *King Lear*, and is not dependent on the view of any particular character.[1] Characters, that is, are not people, they are elements of a linguistic structure, lines in a drama, and more basically, words on a page. This argument had, for some graduate students at Harvard in the 1950s, a wonderfully liberating effect.

It is, of course, very difficult to think of character in this way, to release character from the requirements of psychology, consistency and credibility, especially when those words on a page are being embodied in actors on a stage. But it is arguably a difficulty that drama itself accepts, indeed, embraces, and even explicitly at critical moments acknowledges. When Coriolanus angrily rejects Rome with the words 'There is a world elsewhere' (3.3.136), he imagines a space outside his play, a world he can control. He declares his intention, in effect, of writing his own script, invokes to himself the imagination of the playwright and the authority of the actors. The remainder of the play is in every sense designed to prove him wrong, designed to prove that no character can escape his play.

It may seem self-evident that in drama, the character is the script, though it is a truism that drama nevertheless also takes pains to articulate from time to time: Laertes calls Ophelia 'a document in madness' (4.5.178), Hamlet's fight with the pirates consists of Horatio reading aloud from a letter about it (4.6.12ff.): what actors do, after all, is not perform actions but recite lines, and the character is the lines. Even when the lines are incomprehensible or patently incorrect, they remain of the essence: characters are stuck with them, unless actors or editors revise them; in which case, the characters are stuck with the revisions. Thus Malvolio contemplating a love letter supposedly from Olivia sees in the lines of the forgery Olivia's character, in both senses:

By my life, this is my lady's hand. These be her very C's, her U's
and her T's; and thus makes she her great P's. It is, in contempt of
question, her hand. (2.5.80–2)

The unacknowledged and uncharacteristic obscenity—out of character for
either Malvolio or Olivia—is in fact elicited from Malvolio by Maria's hand,
not Olivia's (it is certainly in character for Maria); but Malvolio is being gulled
here much more significantly by the playwright than by the mischievous
maid: the salutation that is his text, 'To the unknown beloved, this, and my
good wishes,' contains neither C nor P, something many critics but no Malvolio have ever been able to point out. The real forgery in this instance, the
deliberate textual misrepresentation, is not the letter but the script, and
thereby the character himself. But Malvolio has no more options about the
letter than he has about his name; and indeed the overdetermination of character is the essence of drama.

Malvolio is one of a large number of Renaissance dramatic characters
whose nature is defined, encapsulated, determined by their names—Lussu-
rioso, Black Will, Sir Epicure Mammon, Sir Beauteous Ganymede, the
immortal Supervacuo: the point is obvious, the list extensive. The role of
Hamlet may be said to imply an inner life—the character certainly claims to
have one—but to attempt to understand Malvolio through notions of psychology, of stimuli, acculturation, development, childhood trauma, is
defeated at the outset by the mere *dramatis personae*: Malvolio, or Volpone, or
Subtle are not what they are because of something in their childhoods; what
they are is their names, which constitute, in the most platonic way, their
essence.

This might, of course, turn out to be true for all characters if we knew
more about the psychology of playwrights. The fact that Shakespeare had a
son named Hamnet and a younger brother named Edmund has not been lost
on psychoanalytic critics. Drama was obviously undertaking to free itself
from the constraints of nomenclature when it started calling its characters
things like Claudius instead of things like Everyman. But even here, the effects
of nomenclature are often more textual than dramatic. For example, Claudius
has no name in *Hamlet*; nowhere in the dialogue, in any of the three texts, is
he ever called anything except the king. He is also called 'King' throughout the
speech headings, and none of the original texts includes a cast list. The name
Claudius appears only once, in the second quarto and folio texts, in the stage
direction for his first entrance: 'Enter Claudius King of Denmark'; it is never
used again. For audiences *hearing* whatever text, he has no name; indeed,
even for actors working from the first quarto he will be only the king. Why

then is he Claudius? For whose benefit was the name included in that single stage direction? The answer can only be, for Shakespeare's; but why?

Similarly, Viola is unnamed until she transforms herself to a youth. Before this she is only called Lady, and thereafter she is called Cesario. The name Viola appears only at the play's end, in the recognition scene with her brother, who greets her with the words, 'Thrice welcome, drownèd Viola' (5.1.225). Doubtless one can make a case for the dramatic significance of the production of this particular name at the play's climax, drawing together as it does all the talk of music and instrumentality into the character who has been love's instrument; but it does raise questions about the relation of characters to their names, or more simply, about what constitutes their characters.

Changes of character are commonly accompanied by changes of name, even when these seem quite unnecessary. Viola's transformation into Cesario is dictated by a gender change (though one could speculate about the choice of the particular name Cesario, as I have done in *Impersonations*),[2] but why does her brother Sebastian become Roderigo? What *is* in a name? The answer here would seem to be, everything. What, then, is the point of playing Malvolio sympathetically, as Alec McCowan did so brilliantly in the otherwise disappointing BBC *Twelfth Night*? This is not a rhetorical question, and the issue it raises seems to me to bear directly on the question of the whole nature of dramatic texts. To argue that McCowan should not have played a character named Ill-Will sympathetically is to argue against the only good thing in a mediocre production; but it also needs to be said that the history of performance is largely a history of the subversion of the text. Actors are the original poststructuralists, assuming, throughout the history of theater, that the author does not control the play, the interpreter does; and that, indeed, there is, for the purposes of performance—which are, after all, the purposes of drama—no author, only an infinitely mutable script.

Editors have their own ways of identifying and fixing (in both senses) the characters of drama. A good deal of the commentary in editions since Pope's has been concerned with explaining why the characters say what they say, justifying lines that look obscure or inconsistent. Here again, the character is conceived to be something different from the lines; but how completely textual and anti-theatrical the editorial enterprise can become when dealing with character is illustrated in a recent edition by the moment when Sebastian/Roderigo describes his sister to Antonio:

> A lady, sir, though it was said she much resembled me, was yet of many accounted beautiful; but though I could not with such estimable wonder overfar believe that, yet thus far I will boldly

publish her: she bore a mind that envy could not but call fair.
(2.1.18)

The New Cambridge editor Elizabeth Story Donno explains that 'Sebastian's locution serves both to call attention to Viola's beauty and to depreciate it with becoming modesty, the audience having seen that brother and sister are identical in appearance.' Needless to say, no audience has ever seen anything of the sort: the audience has merely been told that Sebastian's sister is his twin. The two are sometimes made to look somewhat similar by giving them identical costumes (Viola says she is dressing as her brother used to dress); but they are indistinguishable only in the text.

Here is another example: at the end of Hamlet's scene with his mother, the following exchange takes place:

> *Ham.* I must to England, you know that?
> *Queen.*   Alack,
>   I had forgot. 'Tis so concluded on.

And in the second quarto, Hamlet continues,

> There's letters sealed, and my two schoolfellows,
> Whom I will trust as I will adders fanged—
> They bear the mandate. . . . (3.4.202ff.)

But the writing of the letters and the mandate to Rosencrantz and Guildenstern are things that have not happened yet; 'the "commission,"' as the Arden editor Harold Jenkins and innumerable editors before him note, 'was still to be prepared.' Jenkins continues, 'As to how Hamlet knew of it, since the text . . . is silent, speculation is invalid. The "difficulty" passes unnoticed in the theatre. . . .'

All this is doubtless true enough, but also disingenuous: most of what editors busy themselves with passes unnoticed in the theatre, and a director concerned about the difficulty, even one determined not to rewrite or misrepresent the text, can resolve it simply by using the folio version of the play, in which the exchange ends with 'I had forgot. 'Tis so concluded on.' The question of how Hamlet knows about the yet-nonexistent sealed letters is obviously not a question about character; it is about the nature of the text and the relation between its versions. But this editor assumes that if the question of how Hamlet knows something is not a question about character, then 'speculation is invalid.' Character is all there is to speculate about.

Historically, much editorial energy has been expended on the question of consistency in character. This is an issue that might appear to be more the performer's problem than the editor's: it is the actor or actress who must transform the lines into a credible simulacrum of human behavior, and the performing tradition has always claimed the broadest latitude in adapting the text to the demands of psychology. In Olivier's 1948 film, the melancholic and withdrawn Hamlet of the opening court scene is wonderfully persuasive; it depends, however, on the omission of about a third of the text; whereas Derek Jacobi, in the BBC production, does all the lines, and consequently comes across (no less persuasively, for me) as quite loony from the outset. Editors, at least after the time of Bowdler, have rarely felt free simply to cut large chunks of the text as Olivier did, but editorial revision is nevertheless common enough. From Dryden to Kittredge, Miranda's attack on Caliban, 'Abhorrèd slave, / Which any print of goodness wilt not take,' etc. (1.2.350ff.), was regularly reassigned to Prospero, being considered inappropriate to the character of Miranda—it is now rarely reassigned in printed editions, but is nevertheless often still given to Prospero in performance. This is a very clear case of the character being considered both prior to and independent of her lines, but it also clearly springs not from the play but from notions of how fifteen-year-old girls ought to behave. It bears no relation whatever, needless to say, to any notion of how they really do behave, and to that extent it is a change that makes Miranda less rather than more credible.

In any case, the psychologically credible is hardly a constant. Garrick made Hamlet's fear of the ghost believable by employing a pneumatic wig, which stood his hair on end when the spirit appeared. This was widely admired; a modern audience would find it merely hilarious. Burbage's Lear was characterized by a contemporary, in a funeral elegy for the actor, with the single adjective 'kind': 'kind Lear.'[3] Doubtless one could read the play that way—he gave his daughters all—but for us, self-centered, arrogant, enraged, suffering, and the like, all would seem more suitable choices if we needed to sum the role up in a single adjective. The credible in dramatic character is no more stable than the credible in life. For us, a husband of substantial means who lived apart from his family for twenty years and at his death bequeathed his wife nothing but his second-best bed would be, if not a cad and a bounder, at the very least unhappily married; but S. Schoenbaum assures us that there was nothing unusual in such a bequest in 1616, and that it did not imply that Shakespeare was unconcerned to provide for his widow's welfare. Character is no more stable than texts, and like texts, depends utterly on interpretation.

The notion that the characters are not a mere function of the script, but are, as Coriolanus imagines himself to be, somehow trapped in it, and might therefore free themselves, enter or create 'a world elsewhere,' contrive to act independently of the playwright, is one that underlies all my examples. It often forms, indeed, a basic metadramatic conceit. 'All the world's a stage, / And all the men and women merely players' assumes a drama with roles but no playwright, and the conceit is at the heart of Prospero's epilogue to *The Tempest, Rosencrantz and Guildenstern Are Dead, Six Characters in Search of an Author*. In an extreme example, Woody Allen's film *The Purple Rose of Cairo*, the characters begin to take control of the script and even reveal themselves capable of leaving the screen, thus making the Frankenstein story a model for theater.

This dramatic fantasy is the *reductio ad absurdum* of the notion that art imitates life, that theater holds the mirror up to nature. But figures like Hamlet and Falstaff have, almost from the beginning, had a life outside their plays; and there was a time when supplying Shakespeare's heroines with girlhoods was not only a reasonable undertaking, but a recipe for a best-seller. These are, for us, unthreatening examples, from which we have, for the past fifty years or so, managed to keep a comfortable distance. They are, however, more deeply implicated in the history of drama, and more particularly of the editing of drama, than we are willing to admit.

3

WHAT IS AN EDITOR?

I HAVE OBSERVED in "What Is a Text?" and "What Is a Character?" that the idea of a book embodying the final, perfected state of a literary work was not a Renaissance one, and what the Renaissance practice produced was an edition in which it was unlikely that any copy of a book would be identical to any other copy. Every copy was unique. In this respect, the difference between book culture and manuscript culture so essential to the Renaissance as constructed by Marshall McLuhan, Walter Ong, and Elizabeth Eisenstein is much smaller than has been claimed. Charlton Hinman tried to get around The Truth About Renaissance Books by producing, in his Norton facsimile of the Shakespeare first folio, an ideal copy, which he took to be a copy in which every page was in its final, corrected state. It would have been perfectly simple for Jaggard and Blount, the publishers of the real first folio, to produce such a book; the fact that they chose not to do so, that no copy of the book exists in this state, that no reader ever read the book in this form, and most of all, that no printer had any interest in publishing such a book, are of no account in Hinman's construction of what constituted an ideal Shakespeare folio. The text in flux, the text as process, was precisely what Renaissance printing practice—whether for economic or philosophical reasons—preserved.

Other traditional assumptions of modern bibliography have become increasingly questionable. The idea that spelling and punctuation have no rules in the period, and are a function of the whim of the compositor, the whole concept of *accidentals*—a class of textual elements (punctuation, capitalization, diacritical marks, typography) that we may alter without altering meaning—has come under heavy scrutiny. Behind these assumptions is an unacknowledged subtext: that the printing process is transparent and what we want from the editorial process is an unmediated access to the mind of the author; that, moreover, we can get closer to the author than the printer with a manuscript (which may or may not have been authorial) before him could; that there are elements of a text that are inessential or merely conventional, that they don't affect the meaning and we can therefore safely change them, and that all we are doing thereby is to translate them into our own equivalent conventions—that, indeed, we *have* equivalent conventions. Behind all this is a still deeper assumption, that not only the meaning of the text, but the text itself is somehow independent of its material embodiment. Historians of the book, from Stanley Morison to D. F. McKenzie, have effectively demolished this notion, but their work has had little effect on the practice of editors. As I have written in another context, the basic assumption of most editorial practice is that behind the obscure and imperfect text is a clear and perfect one, and it is the editor's job not to be true to the text's obscurity and imperfection, but instead to produce some notional platonic ideal.

It is quite easy to show how problematic such assumptions are. The undeniable fact that moving around commas really does affect meaning means that commas aren't "accidentals." There is no way of modernizing the notorious crux in Shakespeare's Sonnet 129, "A blisse in proofe and proud and very wo," not because there is no way of knowing whether the crucial letter in "proud" is a u or a v but because for a Renaissance reader it could only be both; and this means that there is no way of detaching that particular text from its material presence and its historical moment. The rationalizing and neatening of this text, moreover, as of so much of Shakespeare, belies its genuine difficulty—elucidation is, after all, a denial of the essential reality of obscurity. But it is also difficult to see how any number of close analyses of "Th'expense of spirit in a waste of shame" are going to have any significant effect on editorial practice—we all have too much invested in our own construction of the book to abandon it to the insights of deconstruction, or even of history.

But suppose we did want to take all this into account: what would a postmodern editorial praxis look like? Jerome McGann has been one of the most incisive and articulate theorizers of post-Bowers bibliography, but his wonderful, informative, beautifully edited Byron looks, after all, very much like everyone else's Byron: it's just better. I am the first to admit that my own practice in my Oxford *Tempest* and *Winter's Tale* hasn't done much to take into account my own arguments in "What Is a Text?" and "The Authentic Shakespeare," beyond a determination in the commentary to be true to the genuine obscurity, even incomprehensibility, of some of the text, and a stubborn refusal to emend if I can get any sense at all out of the folio. This does leave me open to the charge of fetishizing the text, and I suppose in one sense I should be arguing that since Renaissance dramatic texts are designed to be unstable, we are in fact not being true to them by religiously preserving what happened to come from the printing house. But my basic feeling as an editor is that texts aren't ideas, they are artifacts, and I want to preserve as much as I can of their archaeology.

Producing a modernized text is unquestionably not the best way of doing this, but I also want a Shakespeare accessible to the modern reader, and these two requirements are really not reconcilable. One way of attempting to take such issues into account, however, and in fact in its way a striking example of radically postmodern editorial practice, is the editorial conception embodied in the Victorian Variorum Shakespeare: an unedited text with an infinite commentary, the editor acting only as referee. The impulse behind this, of course, had nothing to do with some proleptic inkling of Barthes and Derrida, but rather with an application of Bentham and Mill to literary criticism, the conviction that if all critical opinions are given an equal voice, the truth will manifest itself. I have a tremendous admiration for H. H. Furness, though the project certainly didn't produce The Truth About Shakespeare; but that is because of a flaw in the reasoning of Bentham and Mill, not in the efforts of Furness. The problem is only partly that any Truth about Shakespeare will be true at most for a generation; it's also that criticism very rarely does what we want it to do.

A brief example: when Richard Knowles' *As You Like It*, the first volume of the new Variorum Shakespeare appeared, I took it up with particular interest. Curious to know what criticism had contributed to clarifying the text in the past hundred years, I started by looking up what are for me two cruxes neither of which the old Variorum had had much to say about. First, the choice of the name Ganymede for Rosalind in disguise: the new Variorum merely confirmed my impression that this is something critics haven't wanted to touch with a ten-foot pole (or perhaps a six-inch rod), and the edition was therefore on this subject nothing more than an epitome of three centuries of silence. Then I tried the most baffling moment in the play, when Rosalind, at the conclusion, appears from the woods with a figure identified in the speech headings as the god Hymen. My students always ask me who that is, and I tell them I don't know; we aren't told, and it must be significant that we aren't told—that in this most rationalized of Shakespeare's comedies, the resolution depends on a mystery; there is finally something in Rosalind's plans that we aren't let in on. So I was curious to see what Truth would emerge from the liberal democratic convictions of the new Variorum. Richard Knowles had assembled in fact a fairly modest array of opinion; there has apparently been less comment on this moment than one would have expected. Of the experts consulted, however, about two-thirds declared that the figure is some rustic who has been dressed up as Hymen for the occasion, and the rest assumed it was the god himself, and pointed to the analogous appearance of deities in wedding masques. What struck me here was that not a single one of the critics cited acknowledged that we don't know, we aren't told; not one saw it as a piece of dramaturgy rather than something to be explained away in the plot.

The first thing that all my students, year after year, notice about that moment in the play, is, according to the Variorum, something that no critic has ever concerned herself with. Nor does Knowles, as the scrupulously neutral referee, introduce any disturbing caveat into the commentary, any sense that in these two cases, criticism has been avoiding something.

Suppose, however, we went a step beyond the Variorum, produced just an unedited text, with the materials for Doing It Yourself on some endless hypercard—all the variants, all the commentary, all the analogues and sources (these provided, of course, with no mediating principle of selection). Such a project is now, with current computer technology, perfectly feasible. Ah, but what is an unedited text? The most brilliant and radically postmodern of textual scholars, Randall McLeod, proposes that we use only facsimiles, and thereby force ourselves and our students to confront the material reality of Renaissance literature, the Renaissance text in its genuine cultural context.

Fair enough. But of course the proposal rests on the premise that the camera is a neutral observer. It is not: it turns flyspecks into punctuation marks, conceals the impression made by uninked type, will not distinguish inks (so that a handwritten correction is undetectable), knows nothing of watermarks or chainlines, those essential distinguishing features of pre-modern paper—in fact, reading a photographic facsimile is nothing at all like reading a Renaissance book: we are absolutely not here confronting the material object. The camera is misleading in a more serious way, too, precisely in the way that Walter Ong and Elizabeth Eisenstein have misled us: every facsimile is identical to every other one, and in this respect facsimiles falsify the essential nature of the Renaissance book. When we read a Shakespeare play in facsimile, we are all reading the identical text. But Renaissance readers with different copies of a text were almost certain to be reading different texts.

I want to emphasize, moreover, that I am not talking simply about things we think we can ignore, the small errors that were tidied up in proofreading. How is editorial practice to take into account McLeod's astounding, essential work on the text of Holinshed? Through the use of his ingenious collator he has discovered tremendous variations in the text of the book, whole sections that were removed, and their removal concealed by the adjustment of catchwords and renumbered pages. What this means is that censorship and revision were at work not at the manuscript stage, but during the actual course of printing; and that, more startlingly, it was not considered necessary for the offending material to be expunged from every copy of the book, but only from those sheets that came off the press last. Within a single edition, therefore, different copies will have differing amounts of censored and uncensored material. This is a case where a modern facsimile of a single copy of Holinshed, which is then published in an edition of a thousand and read in several hundred libraries by many thousands of students, will totally misrepresent the unstable reality of the book.

In all my examples, it will be observed that the author has little or nothing to do with the case, and it is arguable, as Foucault has shown us, that the author, in the modern sense, is an anachronistic concept in the early modern period. But just to make it clear that even this will not lead us to a usable generalization, I want to conclude with a striking counter-example discovered by my student Steven Lally in the course of editing Thomas Phaer and Thomas Twyne's Elizabethan translation of the *Aeneid*,[1] an immensely influential book in its own time, but one that literary history has declared of no interest whatever. For modern readers the book is undeniably not an easy read, not least because it is printed in the murkiest of black letter typefaces; but Lally became fascinated by its typography and orthography. Phaer died in 1560, having completed nine books of the translation; these were published in 1562. In 1573 all twelve books appeared, including Twyne's completion of Phaer's translation and a partial revision of Phaer's text; and in 1584 Twyne's much more elaborate revision of the work was published. Lally observed that both Twyne editions contain a number of idiosyncratic spellings, as well as an elaborate array of mysterious diacritical marks—all, be it noted, so-called *accidentals*. It did not take long to realize that both these features of the text were entirely consistent throughout, and constituted a complete quantitative metrical system—Twyne, improving on Phaer's work, had devised a precise equivalent to Vergilian metrics, and had developed a legible notation for it. The notation was maintained, moreover, without variation, throughout both editions—it starts to break down in the editions after 1596, when the rights to the work moved to another printer. This implies the most complete and continuous authorial control over the printing of the text—a much greater degree of control than anything we believe we know about Renaissance printing-house practice would allow, and, indeed, greater than all but a very few modern writers have had over the printing of their own texts. We need cases like this to remind us that the author function is, after all, not something that was invented in the eighteenth century. Horace conceived himself to be building a monument more lasting than bronze fifteen hundred years before print culture; in the Middle Ages there were poets who were embedding their names within their poems and numbering the lines to defeat appropriation, expansion, revision: even in societies without copyright laws and notions of authorial privilege, there have always been writers who undertook to counteract the cultural vagrancy of literary texts. Foucault's argument is not about the invention of the concept of the author, it is about the extent of the cultural investment in it. Maybe its particular attraction for postmodern criticism lies in its construction of the pre-enlightenment world as a textual golden age, a world of textual free play: in some very basic way, it lets us, as editors and critics, off the hook.

4

ACTING SCRIPTS, PERFORMING TEXTS

IN AN ESSAY called "The Authentic Shakespeare"[1] I observed that it is a commonplace to remark the discrepancy between the performing time always given for Elizabethan plays—"the two hours' traffic of our stage"—and the actual length of the texts, but that no one has ever confronted the implications of the obvious conclusion that the plays Shakespeare's company performed were shorter than the plays Shakespeare wrote for them. The text, then, was not the play, and all plays would have been cut for performance. This observation, to my surprise, caused a great deal of consternation, and even indignation, among my scholarly colleagues, though I am hardly the first to assume that performing texts were cut texts. In one of the basic handbooks of modern bibliography, Fredson Bowers remarks of the text of *Anthony and Cleopatra* that it "may well have been set from . . . Shakespeare's own manuscript, *probably without cutting for the stage representation*";[2] and even plays we believe were printed from theatrical promptbooks clearly contain more than two hours' traffic.

Humphrey Moseley's introductory epistle to the 1647 Beaumont and Fletcher folio explains the matter:

> When these *Comedies* and *Tragedies* were presented on the Stage,
> the *Actours* omitted some *Scenes* and Passages (with the *Authour's*
> consent) as occasion led them; . . . But now you have both All that
> was *Acted*, and all that was not; even the perfect full Originalls
> without the least mutilation; So that were the *Authours* living . . .
> they themselves would challenge neither more nor lesse then
> what is here published. . . . [3]

A printed text, in Moseley's account, is a conflation of author's and players' versions. The implication is that cuts were determined by the occasion: actors varied their performances according to their sense of the audience; they might change from season to season, from playhouse to playhouse, even, if occasion required, from performance to performance. The play before the king was not the same as the play at the Globe, and neither of them was the text that came from the author's pen. But most editors and critics go to extraordinary lengths to avoid dealing with the notion that our printed texts are not what Shakespeare's actors spoke. It is often claimed, for example, that two hours is an approximate figure, which in the sixteenth century could mean anything up to four hours; that if you read very fast you can get through the text of most Shakespeare plays in around two hours; even that the Elizabethans spoke twice as fast as we do. The last may sound like a desperate argument, but at least it acknowledges the reality of the difficulty.

But if the text was not the play, what was the relationship between the two? What kind of authority did Shakespeare's manuscript have, and what kind of responsibility did playhouse practice feel toward it? Shakespeare seems, in *Hamlet*, to be especially concerned about the dangers of improvisation:[4]

> let those that play your clowns speak no more than is set down for them. For there be of them that will themselves laugh, to set on some quantity of barren spectators to laugh too, though in the meantime some necessary question of the play be then to be considered. (3.2.42ff.)

But in Hamlet's first scene with the ghost, Hamlet's own behavior, the jokes about the voice in the "cellerage" and all the rushing about the stage to avoid the "old mole" beneath, will look to an audience without access to the script like a particularly disruptive kind of comic improvisation. This is Shakespeare making the anti-textual textual, but it also puts Shakespeare the actor in league with the audience against Shakespeare the playwright, and it strikingly reveals a divided loyalty.

My subject is the tension between text and performance, and my contention is that as editors and critics, we share, in profound and unexamined ways, that original divided loyalty. There is, of course, very little evidence that will reveal to us the nature of a performing text in Shakespeare's theater; but there is a little. There are the "bad" quartos, whose evidence, in this respect, is not bad, but excellent, as Gary Taylor's remarkable *Henry V* has demonstrated. If we were less exclusively concerned with establishing texts and more concerned with the nature of plays, these would be the good quartos. More direct evidence survives in three pre-Restoration promptbooks, of *Macbeth*, *Measure for Measure*, and the two parts of *Henry the Fourth*.[5] The first two are marked up texts from a folio now in the library of the University of Padua, the third is a scribal transcription based on the quartos. The *Henry IV*, which dates from the early 1620s, was prepared for a private production at a country

estate. It underwent far more radical revision than the other two, amalgamat-
ing the two plays and reducing their approximately 6000 lines to roughly
3500, but also including additional original material. It reveals a great deal
about both the sophistication of amateur theater and the way a popular
Shakespearean text was regarded in the early seventeeth century; but it also
represents a special case, and is therefore less useful for my purposes than the
other two. These have been dated between 1625 and 1635, and were prepared,
according to G. Blakemore Evans, by a professional hand for a professional
company.[6] About their actual use we can say nothing, but they allow us at least
to see what a performing text of Shakespeare looked like within a decade or
two of the playwright's death.

2

The Padua *Macbeth* has small and apparently arbitrary cuts in the first act.
Moments in the text that have troubled later editors, such as the notorious
muddle of the Captain's account of the battle, are left intact; indeed, the only
cut before I.7 is Macbeth's "Present fears / Are less than horrible imaginings"
after he and Banquo meet the witches. Here is Macbeth's first soliloquy as it
appears in the promptbook—no bank and shoal of time, no bloody instruc-

Scena Septima.

Ho-boyes.   Torches.
Enter a Sewer, and diuers Seruants with Dishes and Seruice
ouer the Stage. Then enter Macbeth.

Macb. If it were done, when 'tis done, then 'twer well,
It were done quickly: If th'Affassination
Could trammell vp the Consequence, and catch
With his surcease, Succesle: that but this blow
Might be the be all, and the end all. Heere,
But heere, vpon this Banke and Schoole of time,
Wee'ld inmpe the life to come. But in these Cases,
We still haue iudgement heere, that we but teach
Bloody Instructions, which being taught, returne
To plague th'Inuenter. This euen-handed Iustice
Commends th'Ingredience of our poyson'd Challice
To our owne lips. Hee's heere in double trust;
First, as I am his Kinsman, and his Subiect,
Strong both against the Deed: Then, as his Host,
Who should against his Murtherer shut the doore,
Not beare the knife my selfe. Besides, this *Duncane*
Hath borne his Faculties so meeke; hath bin
So cleere in his great Office, that his Vertues
Will pleade like Angels, Trumpet-tongu'd against
The deepe damnation of his taking off:
And Pitty, like a naked New-borne-Babe,
Striding the blast, or Heauens Cherubin, hors'd
Vpon the sightlesse Curriors of the Ayre,
Shall blow the horrid deed in euery eye,
That teares shall drowne the winde. I haue no Spurre
To pricke the sides of my intent, but onely
Vaulting Ambition, which ore-leapes it selfe,
And falles on th'other.   *Enter Lady.*
How now ? What Newes?
La. He has almost supt: why haue you left the chamber ?

tions, no poisoned chalice, no spur to prick the sides of my intent, no vault-ing ambition.[7] In the ensuing exchange (at the point indicated by (1) in the margin of the extract), a large chunk of Lady Macbeth's persuasive rhetoric is deleted. I want to pause over a particularly interesting smaller cut. At the bot-tom of this excerpt (indicated by the marginal (2)) the Padua text reads,

> Who dares no more, is none.
> *La.* What Beaſt was't then
> That made you breake this enterprize to me?
> When you durſt do it, then you were a man:
> And to be more then what you were, you would
> (1) Be ſo much more the man. Nor time, nor place
> Did then adhere, and yet you would make both:
> They haue made themſelues, and that their fitneſſe now
> Do's vnmake you. I haue giuen Sucke, and know
> How tender 'tis to loue the Babe that milkes me,
> I would, while it was ſmyling in my Face,
> Haue pluckt my Nipple from his Boneleſſe Gummes,
> And daſht the Braines out, had I ſo ſworne
> As you haue done to this.
>   *Macb.* If we ſhould faile?
> (2)   *Lady.* We faile?
> But ſcrew your courage to the ſticking place,
> And wee'le not fayle, when *Duncan* is aſleepe,
> (Whereto the rather ſhall his dayes hard Iourney
> Soundly inuite him) his two Chamberlaines
> Will I with Wine, and Waſſell, ſo conuince,

> *Macbeth.* If we should fail?
> *Lady Macbeth.* We fail?
> When Duncan is asleep. . . .

What has been deleted here, after Lady Macbeth's "We fail?", is "But screw your courage to the sticking place / And we'll not fail." The cut represents both an editorial and a dramatic solution to the famous crux. This early seventeeth-century editor understood the mark of punctuation in "We fail?" as an ironic question mark, and not, as numerous editors from Rowe onward have done, as an exclamation point. In this production, Lady Macbeth would not acknowledge the possibility of failure.

Wholesale cutting begins in Act 2. All of the Porter's speech goes (as it often has done since); with it go most of the exchange between Macbeth and the murderers, the whole of III.6 between Lenox and the Lord, most of Mal-colm's interview with Macduff, in which Malcolm tests Macduff by claiming to practice monstrous vices. In all, 292 of the play's 2084 lines are cut, almost 15 percent. I want to pause over three other deletions.

When told that Macduff has fled to England, Macbeth here says:

> Time, thou anticipat'st my dread exploits.
> The mighty purpose never is o'ertook
> Unless the deed go with it.
> The castle of Macduff I will surprise. . . . (IV.1.144ff.)

That is, the passage about the firstlings of my heart and the firstlings of my hand has been omitted.

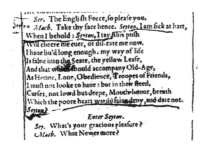

Macbeth's simplified response to the news that the English forces are in sight ("Seyton, I am sick at heart / When I behold—Seyton, I say—") omits what has become one of the most famous passages in the play (V.3.19–28):

And Macbeth's reply to Seyton's report of the death of Lady Macbeth reads this way in the Padua text:

What is for us a characteristically Shakespearean bit of self-referentiality, the poor player who struts and frets his hour upon the stage and then is heard no more, is deleted.

The cutting of the Padua folio's *Measure for Measure* seems far more systematic. Long speeches are shortened, debates are tightened and simplified, and—especially—poetic complexity is removed. A certain quality of continuous explanation in the play (a quality that most modern readers would call essential) disappears too: gone are the Duke's opening speech ("Of government the properties to unfold . . . "), the first fifteen lines of his charge to

Angelo ("There is a kind of character in thy life / That to th'observer doth thy history / Fully unfold," etc.), and, more strikingly, Claudio's exculpatory account of why he and Juliet never formalized their marriage:

> **Cla.** Thus ſtands it with me : vpon a true contract
> I got poſſeſſion of *Iulietas* bed,
> You know the Lady, ſhe is faſt my wife,
> Saue that we doe the denunciation lacke
> Of outward Order. This we came not to,
> Onely for propogation of a Dowre
> Remaining in the Coffer of her friends,
> From whom we thought it meet to hide our Loue
> Till Time had made them for vs. But it chances
> The ſtealth of our moſt mutuall entertainment
> With Character too groſſe; is writ on *Iuliet.*
> *Luc.* With childe, perhaps ?

Indeed, as the extract shows, even Claudio's revelation of Juliet's pregnancy was originally cut, but this was subsequently restored with a marginal "stet." Much of the Duke's explanation to the Friar of why he left his throne has gone (the extent of the cutting can be seen in the facsimile on p. 27)—unquestionably to the benefit of his logic, if not to the complexity of his character. In Isabella's first interview with Angelo (see p. 28), the arguments on both sides are effectively eviscerated; indeed, the omission from this production of what were to become the most famous passages in the play is notable. Gone are Isabella's "There is a vice that most I do abhor" speech (marginal number 1), her passage about "No ceremony that to great ones 'longs" (2), her observation that "all the souls that were were forfeit once" (3), and Angelo's reply that "It is the law, not I, condemn your brother" (4). Gone too (see p. 29) is Isabella's "Could great men thunder / As Jove himself does . . . " (5), including the famous passage (6)

> man, proud man,
> Dressed in a little brief authority,
> Most ignorant of what he's most assured,
> His glassy essence, like an angry ape,
> Plays such fantastic tricks before high heaven
> As makes the angels weep, who with our spleens
> Would all themselves laugh mortal. (II.2.117–23)

After this it is no surprise to find Angelo's final soliloquy (7) reading this way:

> What's this? what's this? is this her fault or mine?
> The tempter or the tempted, who sins most, ha?

Enter Duke and Frier Thomas.

Duk. No : holy Father, throw away that thought,
Beleeue not that the dribling dart of Loue
Can pierce a compleat bofome : why, I defire thee
To giue me fecret harbour, hath a purpofe
More graue, and wrinkled, then the aimes, and ends
Of burning youth.

Fri. May your Grace fpeake of it?

Duk. My holy Sir, none better knowes then you
How I haue euer lou'd the life remoued
And held in idle price, to haunt affemblies
Where youth, and coft, witleffe brauery keepes.
I haue deliuerd to Lord *Angelo*
(A man of ftri&ure and firme abftinence)
My abfolute power, and place here in *Vienna*,
And he fuppofes me trauaild to *Poland*,
(For fo I haue ftrewd it in the common eare)
And fo it is receiu'd : Now (pious Sir)
You will demand of me, why I do this.

Fri. Gladly, my Lord.

Duk. We haue ftri& Statutes, and moft biting Laws,
(The needfull bits and curbes to headftrong weedes,)
Which for this fourteene yeares, we haue let flip,
Euen like an ore-growne Lyon in a Caue
That goes not out to prey : Now, as fond Fathers,
Hauing bound vp the threatning twigs of birch,
Onely to fticke it in their childrens fight,
For terror, not to vfe : in time the rod
More mock'd, then fear'd : fo our Decrees,
Dead to infli&ion, to themfelues are dead,
And libertie, plucks Iuftice by the nofe ;
The Baby beates the Nurfe, and quite athwart
Goes all decorum.

Fri. It refted in your Grace
To vnloofe this tyde-vp Iuftice, when you pleaf'd :
And it in you more dreadfull would haue feem'd
Then in Lord *Angelo*.

Duk. I doe feare : too dreadfull :
Sith 'twas my fault, to giue the people fcope,
'T would be my tirrany to ftrike and gall them,
For what I bid them doe : For, we bid this be done
When euill deedes haue their permiffiue paffe,
And not the punifhment : therefore indeede (my father)
I haue on *Angelo* impos'd the office ;
Who may in th' ambufh of my name, ftrike home,
And yet, my nature neuer in the fight
To do in flander : And to behold his fway
I will, as 'twere a brother of your Order,
Vifit both Prince, and People : Therefore I prethee
Supply me with the habit, and inftru& me
How I may formally in perfon beare
Like a true Frier. Moe reafons for this a&ion
At our more leyfure, fhall I render you ;
Onely, this one : Lord *Angelo* is precife,
Stands at a guard with Enuie : fcarce confeffes
That his blood flowes : or that his appetite
Is more to bread then ftone : hence fhall we fee
If power change purpofe : what our Seemers be.   *Exit.*

F 2   *Scæna*

Not she, nor doth she tempt; but it is I.
What dost thou, or what art thou, Angelo? . . . (162ff.)

What has been omitted is, for the modern reader, the most distinctive
moment in the speech (8):

[it is I]
That, lying by the violet in the sun,
Do as the carrion does, not as the flow'r,
Corrupt with virtuous season. Can it be

Meaſure for Meaſure.   67

Scena Secunda.

Enter Prouoſt, Seruant.

Ser. Hee's hearing of a Cauſe; he will come ſtraight,
I'le tell him of you.

Pro. 'Pray you doe; Ile know
His pleaſure, may be he will relent; alas
He hath but as offended in a dreame,
All Sects, all Ages ſmack of this vice, and he
To die for't?

Enter Angelo.

Ang. Now, what's the matter Prouoſt?

Pro. Is it your will Claudio ſhall die to morrow?

Ang. Did not I tell thee yea? hadſt thou not order?
Why do'ſt thou aske againe?

Pro. Leſt I might be too raſh:
Vnder your good correction, I haue ſeene
When after execution, Iudgement hath
Repented ore his doome,

Ang. Goe to; let that be mine,
Doe you your office, or giue vp your Place,
And you ſhall well be ſpar'd.

Pro. I craue your Honours pardon:
What ſhall be done Sir, with the groaning Iuliet?
Shee's very neere her howre.

Ang. Diſpoſe of her
To ſome more fitter place; and that with ſpeed.

Ser. Here is the ſiſter of the man condemn'd,
Deſires acceſſe to you.

Ang. Hath he a Siſter?

Pro. I my good Lord, a very vertuous maid,
And to be ſhortlie of a Siſter-hood,
If not alreadie.

Ang. Well: let her be admitted,
See you the Fornicatreſſe be remou'd,
Let her haue needfull, but not laviſh meanes,
There ſhall be order for't.

Enter Lucio and Iſabella.

Pro. 'Saue your Honour.

Ang. Stay a little while: y'are welcome: what's your will?

Iſab. I am a wofull Suitor to your Honour,
'Pleaſe but your Honor heare me.

Ang. Well: what's your ſuite.

Iſab. There is a vice that moſt I doe abhorre,
And moſt deſire ſhould meet the blow of Iuſtice;
For which I would not plead, but that I muſt,
For which I muſt not plead, but that I am
At warre, twixt will, and will not.

Ang. Well: the matter?

Iſab. I haue a brother is condemn'd to die,
I doe beſeech you let it be his fault,
And not my brother.

Pro. Heauen giue thee mouing graces.

Ang. Condemne the fault, and not the actor of it,
Why euery fault's condemnd ere it be done:
Mine were the verie Cipher of a Function
To fine the faults, whoſe fine ſtands in record,
And let goe by the Actor.

Iſab. Oh iuſt, but ſeuere Law:
I had a brother then; heauen keepe your honour.

Luc. Giue 't not ore ſo: to him againe, entreat him,
Kneele downe before him, hang vpon his gowne,
You are too cold: if you ſhould need a pin,

You could not with more tame a tongue deſire it:
To him, I ſay.

Iſab. Muſt he needs die?

Ang. Maiden, no remedie.

Iſab. Yes: I doe thinke that you might pardon him,
And neither heauen, nor man grieue at the mercy.

Ang. I will not doe't.

Iſab. But can you if you would?

Ang. Looke what I will not, that I cannot doe.

Iſab. But might you doe't & do the world no wrong
If ſo your heart were touch'd with that remorſe,
As mine is to him?

Ang. Hee's ſentenc'd, tis too late.

Luc. You are too cold.

Iſab. Too late? why no: I that doe ſpeak a word
May call it againe: well, beleeue this
No ceremony that to great ones longs,
Not the Kings Crowne; nor the deputed ſword,
The Marſhalls Truncheon, nor the Iudges Robe
Become them with one halfe ſo good a grace
As mercie does. If he had bin as you, and you as he,
You would haue ſlipt like him, but he like you
Would not haue beene ſo ſterne.

Ang. Pray you be gone.

Iſab. I would to heauen I had your potencie,
And you were Iſabel: ſhould it then be thus?
No: I would tell what 'twere to be a Iudge,
And what a priſoner.

Luc. I, touch him: there's the vaine.

Ang. Your Brother is a forfeit of the Law,
And you but waſte your words.

Iſab. Alas, alas:
Why all the ſoules that were, were forfeit once,
And he that might the vantage beſt haue tooke,
Found out the remedie: how would you be,
If he, which is the top of Iudgement, ſhould
But iudge you, as you are? Oh, thinke on that,
And mercie then will breathe within your lips
Like man new made.

Ang. Be you content, (faire Maid)
It is the Law, not I, condemne your brother,
Were he my kinſman, brother, or my ſonne,
It ſhould be thus with him: he muſt die to morrow.

Iſab. To morrow? oh, that's ſodaine,
Spare him, ſpare him:
Hee's not prepar'd for death: euen for our kitchins
We kill the fowle of ſeaſon: ſhall we ſerue heauen
With leſſe reſpect then we doe miniſter
To our groſſe-ſelues? good, good my Lord, bethink you;
Who is it that hath di'd for this offence?
There's many haue committed it.

Luc. I, well ſaid.

Ang. The Law hath not bin dead, thogh it hath ſlept
Thoſe many had not dar'd to doe that euill
If the firſt, that did th' Edict infringe
Had anſwer'd for his deed. Now 'tis awake,
Takes note of what is done, and like a Prophet
Lookes in a glaſſe that ſhewes what future euils
Either now, or by remiſſeneſſe, new conceiu'd,
And ſo in progreſſe to be hatch'd, and borne,
Are now to haue no ſucceſſiue degrees,
But here they liue to end.

Iſab. Yet ſhew ſome pittie.

Ang. I ſhew it moſt of all, when I ſhow Iuſtice;
For then I pittie thoſe I doe not know,
Which a diſmiſs'd offence, would after gaule

And

That modesty may more betray our sense
Than woman's lightness? Having waste ground enough,
Shall we desire to raze the sanctuary
And pitch our evils there? Oh, fie, fie, fie!

The whole play is treated in this way. Indeed, the only major scene that is left even relatively intact is Isabella's interview with her brother in prison—even the notorious "prenzie Angelo" remains in III.1.94 (see below), which suggests that in the 1620s it made sense, and we ought to stop trying to emend it. In all, the reviser cut 579 of the play's 2660 lines, or about 22 percent—a larger proportion than the *Macbeth* cuts, but still leaving a longer play.

G. Blakemore Evans remarks of the *Measure for Measure* text that the cuts are for the most part designed simply to shorten the major roles, not, apparently, to adapt the play to any special circumstances.[8] Thus there is no attempt to reduce the number of characters or to alter sections that, in later revisions, were felt to be indecorous; and Evans observes that "not infrequently, as one might expect, the heart has been cut out of some of the most poetically famous speeches in the play." This is certainly true; but I'd like to pause over the claim that it is "as one might expect." A great deal of what modern readers would call "Shakespearean" has been deleted from these texts, what for us, and for almost three centuries before us, has made Shakespeare distinctive, remarkable, even recognizable. I don't think this is "as one might expect," and it certainly contradicts vast areas of modern critical and textual assumptions about early attitudes toward Shakespeare and toward the integrity of his texts, at least after the publication of the folio. I want to consider some of its implications.

Clearly for this reviser, the Shakespearean text has no particular integrity. This doesn't mean that he doesn't care about Shakespeare, or doesn't think the plays are good: if it didn't matter that these were Shakespeare plays, he wouldn't be revising them. But obviously by the 1630s (to put the date no earlier than we have hard evidence for), the concept of *Macbeth*, or of *Measure for Measure*, included broad areas of possibility and difference, and was not at all limited to the text of "the true original copies." What the reviser is producing are apparently not, moreover, conceived of as adaptations of Shakespeare. There were a number of adaptations of Shakespeare in the seventeeth century, but they represent themselves as new plays with new titles and new authors, not as versions of an original: *All for Love, The Law Against Lovers, The Fairy Queen*. In contrast, consider the title page of Davenant's *Macbeth* (figure 4.1): Macbeth, a Tragedy: with all the Alterations, Amendments, Additions, and New Songs. As it is now acted at the Duke's Theatre.

No author's name is, or need be, supplied; it is clear that, for all the amendments, additions, and new songs, the essential *Macbeth* is still thought to be here. Similarly, Dryden is unabashed to say, in the Preface to *The Tempest, or the Enchanted Island,* on which he collaborated with Davenant, that "it was originally Shakespear's." Since this text looks to a modern eye like a particularly radical case of revision—new characters and a good deal of new plot are supplied, and scarcely a third of the folio's dialogue is retained—one might logically take "it was originally Shakespear's" to imply that it is his no longer. But this was the form in which the play held the stage as Shakespeare's *Tempest*, with only a brief interruption thanks to Garrick, until 1832. Similarly, Nahum Tate's notorious *King Lear* (figure 4.2) is advertised on its title page as "Reviv'd with Alterations": not rewritten, but brought back to life.

These all suggest that the text of a play was thought of as distinctly, essentially, by nature, unfixed; always open to revision. This idea makes us very uncomfortable, and even critics who are willing to acknowledge the necessary instability of playhouse scripts in the Renaissance would probably want to

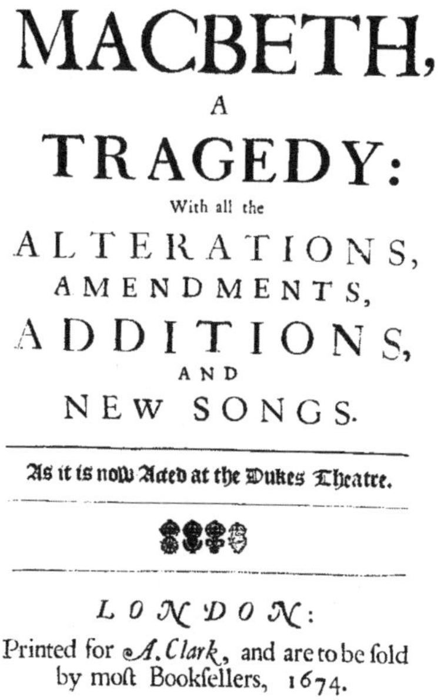

MACBETH,

A

TRAGEDY:

With all the

ALTERATIONS,

AMENDMENTS,

ADDITIONS,

AND

NEW SONGS.

As it is now Acted at the Dukes Theatre.

✿✿✿✿

L O N D O N:
Printed for *A. Clark,* and are to be sold
by most Booksellers, 1674.

Figure 4.1. Title page to Davenant's *Macbeth*, 1674.

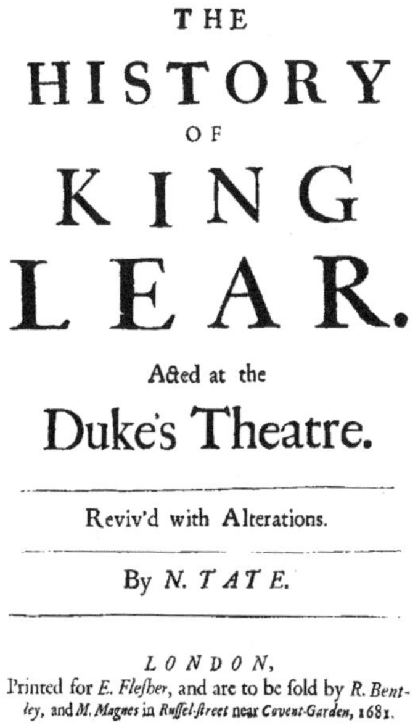

THE

HISTORY

OF

KING

LEAR.

Acted at the

Duke's Theatre.

Reviv'd with Alterations.

By *N. TATE.*

L O N D O N,
Printed for *E. Flesher,* and are to be sold by *R. Bentley,* and *M. Magnes* in *Russel-street* near *Covent-Garden,* 1681.

Figure 4.2. Title page to Tate's *King Lear*, 1681.

argue that, at least after Shakespeare's death, the "real" Shakespeare play was always what is preserved in the printed text, because all productions ultimately exist in reference to that. This makes perfectly good sense, but it seems to me that it makes sense only because of certain anachronistic assumptions we have about texts; and I therefore want to argue here first that it isn't correct, and second—more subversively—that when the chips are down we don't really believe it at all.

3

How do we know what the relation was between whatever texts have come down to us and what playgoers saw in Shakespeare's theater? Since our claims about the effects of Shakespearean drama are based almost entirely on the surviving printed texts, it would seem essential to consider this question, and not simply to assume that we can read backward from the latter to the former. I do not, of course, pretend that we are in any position to supply an answer; but I also think that the question is a larger one than we have made it, and that it is necessary to understand its full implications before we try to move beyond it.

I want to start with two well-known, certainly flawed, perhaps perverse, pieces of evidence, Simon Forman's accounts of *Macbeth* and *The Winter's Tale*, both of which he saw at the Globe in the spring of 1611. These have been examined often, and found tantalizingly, maddeningly unforthcoming. Both give significantly different versions of the plays from those we know, omitting some things we would call essential, including others that are not part of our texts and that look to us irrelevant or even impossible, and which, in any case, have no known source outside the play and defy any simple explanation. I am going to indicate briefly how Forman's Shakespeare differs from ours. I am doing this not because I believe we can thereby reconstruct the plays that Shakespeare's contemporaries saw, or to try to show how differently the Jacobean playgoer saw Shakespeare, but precisely because I don't believe we see Shakespeare differently from Forman, and I want to use his accounts as models, in the largest sense, of critical and even editorial practice.

Forman's version of *Macbeth* opens not with the witches and the report of the battle, but with:

> Mackbeth and Bancko, 2 noble men of Scotland, Ridinge thorowe a wod, the[r] stode before them 3 women feiries or Nimphes, And saluted Mackbeth, sayinge 3 tyms vnto him, haille Mackbeth, king of Codon; for thou shalt be a kinge, but shall beget No kinges, &c.[9]

Forman then recounts the prophecy that Banquo will beget kings. Arriving at Duncan's court, Macbeth is made "forth with Prince of Northumberland"—note that at this point in the play (or at least in the surviving text in the folio) it is *Malcolm* who is dubbed Prince of *Cumberland,* "a step," Macbeth says, "On which I must fall down, or else o'erleap, / For in my way it lies" (1.5.48–9). There follows in Forman's account a very powerful scene that also does not exist in our play:

> And when MackBeth had murdred the kinge, the blod on his hands could not be washed of by Any means, nor from his wiues handes, which handled the bloddi daggers in hiding them, By which means they became moch amazed and Affronted.

There is no mention in Forman's *Macbeth* of the apparition scene, or of the prophecies relating to Birnam Wood and the man not born of woman, or of the moving forest, though Forman does record, as an afterthought, Lady Macbeth's sleepwalking scene.

Forman's *Winter's Tale* is much closer to ours. His notes are, in fact, with one exception, a reasonably accurate summary of the play as we know it.[10] The exception, however, is a startling one: Forman either fails to mention or did not see Hermione's resurrection, the statue coming to life.

Some of these discrepancies have been accounted for by assuming that Forman consulted Shakespeare's sources. Macbeth and Banquo cannot have been "riding through a wood" on the stage of the Globe, but a woodcut in Holinshed depicts them on horseback (figure 4.3),[11] and reference to Holin-

Figure 4.3. Macbeth and Banquo meeting the witches, in Holinshed's *Chronicles,* Part 2, *The Historie of Scotland* (1577), p. 243.

shed would also account for Forman's characterization of the witches as
"feiries or Nymphes": in the *Chronicles* they are "Nimphes or Feiries." But the
source in this case also raises new problems, because if we assume that Forman checked Holinshed to refresh his memory of the play, how can we
explain his version of Macbeth's title, "king of Codon," which looks like an
auditory error for Cawdor (Holinshed spells the name "Cawder"), and, more
striking, the creation of Macbeth Prince of Northumberland, where Holinshed, like the folio, has Malcolm created Prince of Cumberland? And of
course there is no known source for Forman's scene of Macbeth and Lady
Macbeth "moch amazed and Affronted" at their inability to wash Duncan's
blood off their hands.

Did Forman's admittedly lively imagination simply add this to his recollection of the play? The answer may very well be yes: Forman would then be
conflating Macbeth's "multitudinous seas incarnadine" speech with Lady
Macbeth's desperate handwashing pantomime in the sleepwalking scene, to
produce the kind of clear moral emblem he found so attractive. Certainly it is
difficult to imagine Lady Macbeth speaking lines like "What's done is done"
and "This is the very painting of your fear" after such a scene as Forman
describes. In fact, we *must* argue Forman's evidence away unless we are willing to conclude that the King's Men in 1611 were presenting a radically different *Macbeth* from the one that has survived—a possibility, certainly, but one
that few editors will care to entertain. The scene, of course, need not be considered entirely imaginary: Forman may be memorializing a particularly
effective piece of stage business when the Macbeth of 1611 asked, "Will all great
Neptune's ocean wash this blood / Clean from my hand?"

As for the absence from Forman's *Winter's Tale* of Hermione's statue, it is
also absent from the story in Greene's *Pandosto*; but did Forman simply substitute the source for the play? This is harder to argue away than the handwashing scene in *Macbeth*. The statue scene has been, for at least two centuries, not only the emotional culmination of the drama, but an absolutely
essential element of the plot. It is difficult for us to imagine a spectator either
failing to recall it or thinking it not worth mentioning. Here we inevitably
take refuge in *ad hominem* arguments: Forman is our only witness, and he is
hardly a reliable one, and we would certainly be overstepping the bounds of
his very shifty evidence if we used it to assert that there was a version of the
play in 1611 that did not include the restoration of Hermione.[12] The most we
can assert—it is in fact a great deal—is that this contemporary spectator preserved for himself a version of *The Winter's Tale* quite different from one that
we believe any of us in his place would have taken away from a performance
of the play.

What more can we say of these, the only eyewitness accounts we possess of two of Shakespeare's most perennially compelling plays in Shakespeare's own theater? We assume the accounts cannot be correct because they are contradicted by the surviving texts. We dismiss them by saying that they are unreliable because they are influenced—or "contaminated"—by other works, experiences, emotional and psychological demands, some of which (e.g., the sources) we think we can identify, but most of which we cannot even begin to imagine. I am not arguing that we are wrong to deal with Forman in this way; but the problems we face with his versions of Shakespeare seem to me at most somewhat exaggerated instances of the problems we face with all versions of Shakespeare, from good and bad quartos and the folio on down through the whole history of editorial and critical practice. And our appeal to the texts as the bottom line is far more problematic than, historically, we have been willing to allow.

4

What texts? It hardly needs to be remarked that none of our texts is original, that every word we possess by Shakespeare has been through some editorial process. And even if a Shakespeare manuscript were discovered tomorrow, if we suddenly found those magical foul papers to whose elusive authority all editorial claims are ultimately referred, it would not simply declare its secrets to us. We would have to edit it before we could draw conclusions about it, and the editorial process would involve all the familiar decisions about what was really written, or intended, or meant, and these would inevitably be based on the editor's own assumptions about what the text ought to look like, and different editors would produce different texts. The conclusions, that is, really come first, not last; and whatever secrets Shakespeare's foul papers reveal to us will inevitably be perceived through the distorting glass of our own secrets. This is the respect in which Simon Forman is the appropriate model for the editor and critic: it is a mistake to believe that our sense of Shakespeare, whether we are scientific bibliographers or casual playgoers, is not "contaminated," and indeed determined, by a myriad of other texts.

Indeed, Shakespeare's own working conditions, the requirements of his playhouse and the fact that his texts were to be spoken by actors, may be considered a form of contamination. In any case, the fact that they are, and have always been so considered, can, I think, be demonstrated. Take, for example, the question of whether a particular passage is verse or prose. This is an issue that will be of much more significance to the editor and typographer than to the actor, who will speak the lines, however they are printed, as s/he sees fit. Editors have taken, however, historically, much less trouble over this question than it seems to warrant. Here are two speeches of Caliban's that appear as prose in the folio, but have been, since the time of Pope, represented as verse (II.2.154–66):

> *Cal.* I'le fhew thee the beft Springs: I'le plucke thee'
> Berries: I'le fifh for thee; and get thee wood enough.
> A plague vpon the Tyrant that I ferue;
> I'le beare him no more Stickes, but follow thee, thou
> wondrous man.
>   *Tri.* A moft rediculous Monfter, to make a wonder of
> a poore drunkard.
>   *Cal.* I'prethee let me bring thee where Crabs grow;
> and I with my long nayles will digge thee pig-nuts;
> fhow thee a Iayes neft, and inftruct thee how to fnare
> the nimble Marmazet: I'le bring thee to cluftring
> Philbirts, and fometimes I'le get thee young Scamels
> from the Rocke: Wilt thou goe with me?

These have, since Pope, appeared to be simple cases—they do, after all, have the rhythm of blank verse—but they become less simple if we stop to ask why we prefer treating them as verse to treating them as prose that has the rhythm of verse. Clearly some judgment about the true nature of Caliban's language is involved. Conversely, a group of verse speeches by Stephano and Trinculo in III.2 have appeared since Pope to be just as obviously prose:

> *Ste.* Trinculo; if you trouble him any more in's tale,
> By this hand, I will fupplant fome of your teeth.

> *Ste.* How now fhall this be compaft?
> Canft thou bring me to the party?

> *Ste.* Do I fo? Take thou that,
> As you like this, giue me the lye another time.

> *Ste.* Giue me thy hand, I am forry I beate thee:
> But while thou liu'ft keepe a good tongue in thy head.

> *Ste.* At thy requeft Monfter, I will do reafon,
> Any reafon: Come on *Trinculo*, let vs fing.

Here is the final exchange in the scene between the three conspirators as the folio prints it (III.2.142–50):

> *Ste.* This will proue a braue kingdome to me,
> Where I fhall haue my Muficke for nothing.
>   *Cal.* When *Profpero* is deftroy'd.
>   *Ste.* That fhall be by and by:
> I remember the ftorie.
>   *Trin.* The found is going away,
> Lets follow it, and after do our worke.

> *Ste.* Leade Monſter,
> Wee'l follow : I would I could ſee this Taborer,
> He layes it on.
>   *Trin.* Wilt come?
> Ile follow *Stephano.*   *Exeunt.*
>   *Scena.*

The layout of these passages has been explained by the compositor's pur-
ported need to lose space at the end of the scene, though no editor who sub-
scribes to this explanation has gone on to consider the implications of the
claim that in 1623 Shakespeare's prose could become verse for reasons that
had nothing to do with either authorial intention or metrics. But no compos-
itorial exigencies will account for the folio setting of a speech of Stephano's in
Act V, which since Pope has been printed as prose (V.1.256–8):

> *Enter Ariell, driuing in Caliban, Stephano, and*
>   *Trinculo in their ſtolne Apparell.*
> *Ste.* Euery man ſhift for all the reſt, and let
> No man take care for himſelfe ; for all is
> But fortune : *(oragio* Bully-Monſter *Corasio.*

Why do we declare this to be prose, rather than bad poetry?

   If the question seems perverse in the face of what are, for us at least, such
clear-cut examples, let us turn to a case that looks, on the face of it—to everyone, that is, except editors—significantly less clear-cut, and where the question will look more like a real one. What shall we do about a passage in the
opening scene that the folio prints this way?

> Though euery drop of water ſweare againſt it,
> And gape at widſt to glut him. *A confuſed noyſe within.*
> Mercy on vs.
> We ſplit, we ſplit , Farewell my wife, and children,
> Farewell brother : we ſplit, we ſplit, we ſplit.

Can a confused noise be blank verse? Editors have resoundingly answered yes.
Pope believed not only that this was verse, but also that it must originally have
been better verse than it is: he emended the final line to "Brother farewell, we
split, we split, we split." Capell was the first editor to perceive a difficulty, and
printed the whole thing as a stage direction, with the clauses separated by
dashes—as confused noise, that is.

> Though every drop of water ſwear againſt it,
> And gape at wid'ſt to glut him.—Mercy on us !
>   [*A confus'd Noiſe within.*__We ſplit, we ſplit !
>   __Farewel my wife and children !__ Farewel,
> brother!__ We ſplit, we ſplit, we ſplit !

This seemingly sensible emendation, however, failed to persuade the vast
majority of subsequent editors, who almost without exception, have adhered
to the folio lineation. In recent years, only Anne Barton in the New Penguin
edition and the notoriously quirky editor of the New Oxford *Tempest* have
treated the passage as prose.

Antony and Cleopatra provides a reverse instance. Here, from the folio, is
an exchange between Cleopatra and the messenger who brings the news of
Antony's marriage to Octavia (III.3.6–10):

> *Mef.* Moft gratious Maieftie.
> *Cleo.* Did'ft thou behold *Octavia* ?
> *Mef.* I dread Queene.
> *Cleo.* Where?
> *Mef.* Madam in Rome, I lookt her in the face; and
> faw her led betweene her Brother, and *Marke Anthony.*

Since the Johnson-Steevens-Reed edition of 1793, the passage has almost
invariably been printed like this (the last two lines in this extract begin the
next page):[13]

> MES. Moft gracious majefty,—
> CLEO.   Didft thou behold
> Octavia?
> MES.   Ay, dread queen.
> CLEO.   Where?
> MES.   Madam, in Rome
>
> M m 2
>
> 532   ANTONY AND CLEOPATRA.
>
> I look'd her in the face; and faw her led
> Between her brother and Mark Antony.

What is involved in deciding that such examples are "really" not verse but
prose, or not prose but verse? The last two instances, the confused noise and
Cleopatra's exchange with the messenger, are very clear cases of the playhouse's being conceived as a contaminating medium: editors have decided
with overwhelming unanimity that whatever the drowning sailors, Cleopatra
and the messenger, will sound like on stage, they are nevertheless speaking
blank verse. There is an aesthetic assumption here, with strong moral over-
tones, an editorial syllogism that goes: verse is better than prose, Shakespeare
is the best poet, therefore anything that can be made to look like decent verse
should be. The other examples, Caliban's blank verse, Stephano's and Trinculo's prose, may seem to have more to do with judgments about stylistic consistency, but here too, it is doubtful whether their underlying assumptions are
merely metrical. They are surely also moral and even political, having to do
first, as I have suggested, with decisions about how we want the particular

character to be perceived. Caliban has been systematically ennobled by revising his prose into verse wherever possible—ironically, even as Prospero's character has been sweetened and sentimentalized by the critical tradition, the editorial tradition has consistently taken Caliban's side against him. Conversely, Stephano and Trinculo are declared too vulgar and inconsequential for verse, even for doggerel. But more deeply, the editorial assumptions have to do with questions of Shakespeare's own nature: *can* our greatest poet have written doggerel? Didn't he really, most of the time, *think* in blank verse?

If we turn to manuscript sources, to the sort of text the folio compositors would have been working from, such assumptions begin to look very suspect. What kind of evidence have we about the distinction between verse and prose in Shakespeare's time? One of the things we are quite sure we know about the text of *The Tempest* and several other Shakespeare plays is that they were prepared for the press by the scrivener Ralph Crane, a number of whose manuscripts survive. Trevor Howard-Hill remarks, with characteristic caution, that "often it cannot be decided whether Crane realised that he was transcribing verse because he did not extend lines of prose uniformly to the right-hand margins of his transcript."[14] Another way of putting this is that in dramatic transcripts, Crane did not make much of a distinction between prose and verse. Was this a scrivener's idiosyncrasy, or does it reflect a feature of the manuscripts he was copying? There is no Shakespeare holograph for us to compare with the folio text of *The Tempest,* but Crane made three copies of Middleton's *A Game at Chesse*, of which a manuscript in Middleton's own hand and another partly in his hand also survive. In Middleton's texts as in Crane's, the form is often ambiguous. The most familiar prosodic marker of verse to us, capitals at the beginning of the lines, is absent in all transcripts—such capitalization was commonly a printing convention, not a manuscript one (R. C. Bald's edition of Middleton's holograph misrepresents the manuscript by substituting initial capitals throughout, thereby removing the ambiguity).[15] The following passage, however (quoted here from M. A. Buettner's edition), looks unambiguously like verse in all three of Crane's texts:

> they'had need haue given you a whole Bag by your self,
> This Fat Black-Bishop, hath so over-layd me
> so squelchd, and squeezd me, I haue no veriuyce left in me;
> you shall find all my Goodnes (if you looke for't,)
> in the bottom of the Bag. (V.3.205–9)[16]

But in both Middleton's holographs, the corresponding passage is just as unambiguously prose (the relevant section is indicated by the marginal line):[17]

Nevertheless this is, predictably, printed as verse in Bald's edition. For this editor, not even the evidence of two autograph manuscripts outweighs the prejudice in favor of verse.

Trevor Howard-Hill, commenting on this passage, takes an uncharacteristically traditional line. Observing that we don't know what manuscript Crane was copying, he suggests that there may have been yet another Middleton original in which the passage was, as he puts it, "correct as verse."[18] That is, if the holographs we have don't say what we want, we can invent a ghost holograph that does. Howard-Hill is clearly very uncomfortable with this speculation; he proposes it cautiously and does not pursue it. But I think Occam's Razor is a better guide here than the editorial tradition, and the creation of a fictitious text will only prevent us from understanding the evidence we actually have.

Let us consider an alternative example.

Here, from the Huntington manuscript, which is partly in a scribe's hand and partly in Middleton's, is how the scribe renders a passage that must be prose.[19] The passage is labeled, at the far right, "The Letter," and is in two sections because it extends onto the following page. In its arrangement on the page it is indistinguishable from verse. I don't think this layout can be accounted for by proposing that the scribe didn't know he was transcribing prose: the passage is a letter being read aloud; in the manuscript it is indicated as such, and therefore (unlike the speech we have just considered) it would be assumed to be prose; and indeed, on the next manuscript page the last few lines of the same letter *are* written as prose. Moreover, Middleton made a number of corrections and additions to this manuscript, and there is no indication that he considered the scribe's work in this passage an error. I think it is more likely that here, as in a number of instances in Crane's dramatic transcriptions, we see one normal way of presenting prose in dialogue: the shape of the text is dictated not by metrics, but by what the scribe wants his page to look like. The rule in dramatic manuscripts would seem to be that if it looks like prose, it is; and if it looks like verse, it may or may not be.

To realize that this is not verse, one would have to be sensitive to the prosody; but confusion on the question would have been largely immaterial to anyone except a compositor, who had to translate the manuscript into the quite different conventions of printing. How difficult it was to establish the differentiation between prose and verse in such cases is clear from the early printed editions, which must have been set up from just this sort of copy. In the first line of the letter in the first of the two examples illustrated on page 42,[20] the compositor realizes he is setting prose, but misses the fact that the letter continues beyond the Black Knight's aside, and prints the last few lines as verse. In the second example, however, another compositor, in a different edition, understands where the letter begins and ends, and has the whole prop-

> *B. Kt.* There where thou ſhilt be
> Shortly, if arte faile not.
>
> The Letter.
>
> Right Reuererend and noble (meaning me) our true kinſman
> in affeltion, but alienatedin blood, your vnkind diſobedience
> to the mother cauſe , proues the onely cauſe of your ill fortune at
> this time : My preſent remooue by generall eleltiou to the Papall
> dignity, had now auſpiciouſly ſetled you in my Sede vacante (how
> had it ſo) which at my next remooue, by death might proued, your
> ſtep to ſupremacy.
> (Hah, all my bodies blood mouuts to my face,
> To looke vpon this letter.)
>   *B. Kt.* The pill workes with him,
> Thinke on't ſeriouſly it is not yet too late then,
> Through the ſubmiſſe acknowledgment
> Of your diſobedience,
> To be brotherly receiued into the louing
> Boſome of the Conclaue.

> *Bl. Kni.* There where thou ſhalt be ſhortly : if Art faile not.
>   *Hee reades the Letter.*
> *Fat B. Right reuerend and noble* (meaning me) *Our*
> *Kins-man in blood , but alienated in affeltion ; your*
> *Vnkinde diſobedience to the Mother-cauſe, proues*
> *At this time the onely cauſe of your ill fortune :*
> *My preſent remooue by generall Eleltion ,to the*
> *Papall dignitie , had now auſpiciouſly ſettled you*
> *In my Sede vacante* (how? had it ſo?) *which at my next remoue*
> *By death , might haue proued your Step to Supremacie.*
> *Hah ? all my Bodies blood mounts to my face*
> *To looke vpon this letter.*
>   *Bl. Kni.* The Pill workes with him.
> *Fat Biſh. Thinke on't ſer'iouſly ,it is not yet too late*
> *Through the ſubmiſſe acknowledgement of your*
> *Diſobedience , to be louingly receaued into the*
> *Brotherly Boſome of the Conclaue.*
>   E2   This

erly in italics; but he also misunderstands his copy to the extent of setting it as verse.

All this suggests that the question of poetry versus prose was a far less pressing one to Jacobean playwrights, and to those concerned with the transmission of their texts, than it has been to the subsequent editorial tradition. It was, for purely practical reasons, of most immediate concern to the typographer. Many speeches could be either; no character's nobility was impugned if he was detected speaking prose, nor was any dramatist's excellence vitiated if he was found to have written it. And if *The Tempest* had come down to us as a play by Middleton, we would have hard evidence that the grounds for deciding whether Caliban's prose is really verse or Stephano's verse is really prose are very shaky indeed.

5

The quarto and folio texts are our evidence for most of what we know about Shakespeare; but what are the texts evidence of? As R. C. Bald's handling of Middleton's holograph indicates, the editorial tradition has in fact allowed texts, even those in the author's own hand, to be evidence of very little. The political agenda of editorial practice, at least from the time of Pope, has remained curiously unchanged: to deny differences and make Shakespeare as much like us as possible; and in this enterprise, ambiguities of sense and syntax have always been much more tolerable than ambiguities of form. The former can be elucidated away or celebrated for their poetic complexity, but the latter undermine our whole sense of taxonomy. That this enterprise should be a constant, despite all the radical shifts in taste over the past three centuries, says much for the continuity, indeed for the stubborn tenacity, of scholarly assumptions.

I want to conclude by considering the history of a small but significant emendation in *The Tempest* (1.2.374ff.). I am particularly interested here in what has constituted an explanation for the necessity of emending. There is a minuscule but perennially troublesome crux in the punctuation of Ariel's first song:

> *Enter Ferdinand & Ariel, inuisible playing & singing.*
> *Ariel* Song. *Come vnto these yellow sands,*
>   *and then take hands :*
> *Curtsied when you haue, and kist*
>   *the wilde waues whist :*
> *Foote it featly heere, and there, and sweete Sprights beare* -
>   *the burthen.*   Burthen dispersedly.
> *Harke, harke, bowgh wawgh : the watch-Dogges barke,*
>   *bowgh-wawgh*

Davenant and Dryden in their revision of the play, followed by Rowe in his 1709 edition, introduced a comma after "kist", thereby making "the wilde waues whist" a nominative absolute—the sense became "when you have curtsied and kissed, the wild waves being silent," not "when you have curtsied and kissed the wild waves into silence." This reading was generally accepted throughout the eighteenth and nineteenth centuries, with a number of editors intensifying the absolute construction by enclosing "the wild waves whist" between parentheses or dashes. No eighteenth-century editor saw any need to justify the emendation, and indeed few thought of it as a change at all. By the middle of the nineteenth century, however, the kiss began to require an explanation, and it was accounted for, first by Staunton and Halliwell, as a standard element of formal dances, which were said to have commenced with the taking of hands, curtsying and kissing. This assertion continues to be repeated in modern editions, though it has been revealed as a pure figment of the editorial imagination; kissing, as Alan Brissenden has shown, was not a customary part of the beginning of dances.[21] But the claim served to justify the comma: if the kiss is part of the dance, it is not the waves that are being saluted. A very few voices were raised in protest: Knight argued that "this is one of the many instances of a poetical idea being utterly destroyed by false punctuation," and the old Cambridge editors were the first to draw support for the folio reading from the text itself, observing that Ferdinand's lines:

> This music crept by me upon the waters
> Allaying both their fury and my passion

indicate that the waves are acted upon in the way the original punctuation suggests.[22] Dover Wilson accepted the explanation of the kiss as part of the dance, but nevertheless let the passage stand without emendation, observing laconically, "No stop in F." Kermode, in his 1954 Arden *Tempest*, was the first editor to question the dancing kiss. He followed the folio punctuation, but nevertheless felt a need to argue with it:

> To take hands and curtsy . . . were the first two steps in all dances, but the kiss normally came when the dance was finished [this too, according to Brissenden, is an error]. . . . Yet although this suggests that "kiss'd" must govern "waves", the notion is disagreeable, being grotesque in a context which does not require grotesquerie. The syntax should perhaps be allowed to be ambiguous.

The problem, however, is that as the passage stands in the folio, the syntax is not at all ambiguous. The only ambiguity in it has been editorial. Editors since Kermode, for the next thirty years or so, for the most part continued to opt for the comma, almost invariably without explanation. Northrop Frye's old Pelican, Blakemore Evans' Riverside, David Bevington's Scott Foresman texts all have it; while more recent editions such as Anne Barton's Penguin, Peter Holland's new Pelican, the new Folger and my own Oxford *Tempest*, which argues energetically against it, do not.

Which brings me to Stanley Wells and Gary Taylor. For this crux, the New Oxford *Complete Works*, and the Norton, which is based on it, go back not to the folio, but to the middle of the nineteenth century, and place "the wild waves whist" between dashes, rendering it firmly parenthetical. The Oxford *Textual Companion* explains the matter this way:

F would have to imply that the waves themselves are kissed into silence. This sense is not only excessively conceited; it is also practically incommunicable in a song. Kissing partners as a preliminary to a dance may be unconventional but it is quite plausible for imagined spirits.[23]

Kermode's complaint that the imagery is "disagreeable" because "grotesque" has been honed a little; the imagery is now "excessively conceited," and this has become a reason to emend; but no attempt has been made to refer what are obviously matters of taste to any seventeenth-century standards. If we do undertake to do so, we will find it impossible to separate the grotesque and conceited from the elegant and classical in early modern sensibilities, as even a cursory look at contemporary iconologies (or paintings, or architecture, or even clothing) makes clear. I offer here, in figures 4.4 and 4.5, random examples from an absolutely inexhaustible store. Why the Oxford editors find it "plausible" for spirits of nature to kiss each other but not to kiss the waves is no doubt vain to enquire; but one man's excess is another's sufficiency. Long ago Steevens noted a parallel in Milton's "Nativity Ode":

Figure 4.4. Vincenzo Cartari, *Imagini de i Dei . . .* (Venice, 1571), p. 82.
The Egyptian Jove, or Serapis.

Figure 4.5. Cartari, *Imagini*, p. 97. Mercury, with a ram's head,
and Phoebus Apollo.

> The winds with wonder whist
> Smoothly the waters kissed.

This is obviously an allusion to Ariel's song. Clearly the reader of 1629
admired what Kermode and Wells and Taylor three centuries later find so disagreeable—there's no accounting for tastes, but there's also no denying them.
The "Nativity Ode" is certainly conceited, to the modern eye excessively so,
but that has never been invoked as a reason to emend it. As for the sense being
"practically incommunicable" in a song, this would depend on the setting (the
original is lost), but it should be added that Shakespeare songs are not invariably models of communication:

> Hark, hark, the lark at heaven's gate sings,
> And Phoebus 'gins arise,
> His steeds to water at those springs
> On chaliced flowers that lies.

Much critical energy has been expended on explaining the excessively conceited and syntactically baffling third and fourth lines of this song from *Cym-*

beline, but no editor has suggested that their obscurity ought to be cured by rewriting them. In fact, in the surviving Jacobean setting of the song, which has been ascribed to Robert Johnson or John Wilson, the puzzling lines are simply omitted.[24] This is evidence, if we need it, that incommunicability is far more likely to be a feature of the original text than of the play in performance.

What I have been arguing, then, is that the instability of the texts, which the editorial tradition has consistently undertaken to control, is in fact what licenses it. Without recognizing that instability as evidence of anything at all, editors repeat precisely what they claim to guard against. The testimony of the text, in editorial practice, dissolves when contradicted by modern assumptions about verse and prose, by wholly anachronistic principles of taste and decorum, by notions of the disagreeable, the excessively conceited, the implausible, the incommunicable. As editors, we stage the plays we contemplate, and in the process they become our own. We are closer to the Padua scribe or to Simon Forman than we may care to admit.

5

THE POETICS OF SPECTACLE

1

THE THEATER OF INIGO JONES was created for that most ephemeral of Renaissance genres, the court masque. Hymns of praise, instances of royal magnificence, spectacular fantasies, the form was, even in its own time, ambiguously regarded. "These Things are but Toyes," said Bacon, "to come amongst such Serious Observations."[1] Nevertheless, to Ben Jonson, classicist and moralist, masques were the vehicles of the most profound ethical statements, creating heroic roles for the leaders of society, and teaching virtue in the most direct way, by example. Every masque moved toward the moment when the masquers descended and took partners from the audience, annihilating the barrier between the ideal and the real, and including the court in its miraculous transformations. We may even feel in the Caroline masques of Aurelian Townshend, Thomas Carew, and Sir William Davenant a kind of mimetic magic, as if by the sheer force of poetry and spectacle incipient war and dissolution could be metamorphosed into harmony and peace.

What remains of the form to us is a diminished thing. Ben Jonson undertook to translate the momentary visions of permanence into a literary form, but most of a masque was not literature. If we can take the masque at all seriously, it is largely through Jonson's efforts; his text appears the center about which the work of other artists—designer, composer, choreographer—revolved. This is an accident of time; for Jonson, a happy accident, considering his famous quarrel with his foremost collaborator. But to a contemporary spectator, the experience of a masque allowed no easy distinction among the creators of so elaborately composite a form. The "device" was the poet's, but it required for its expression nearly every other art known to the age: painting, architecture, design, mechanics, lighting, music of both composer and performer, acting, choreography, and dancing both acrobatic and formal. Indeed, by far the largest part of a masque was taken up with the dancing, which could consume much of the night in a production whose text lasted barely an hour.

Nevertheless, to a certain extent the spectator's view misled him, for the Stuart masque as a form was largely the creation of a unique collaboration in the history of the English stage, that of Inigo Jones and Ben Jonson. That their views often diverged is evident, and that Jones's greatest triumphs were achieved after he and Jonson had parted company is undeniable. But the masque, whether as spectacle or poem, was the form in which both artists found their richest and most continuous means of expression, and for over twenty years, despite their quarrel, their joint creation displayed a remarkable degree of consistency and coherence. It is impossible, indeed, to understand the development of Inigo Jones's theater apart from his collaboration with Jonson.

We might begin, then, with a consideration of how each artist viewed his work. The antithesis of spectacle and poem is an obvious one; but it becomes less clear and its implications grow more complex as we look at it in a Renaissance context. Let us start with two assertions about the nature of the masque. For Ben Jonson in 1631, "all representations, especially those of this nature in court, public spectacles, either have been or ought to be the mirrors of man's life."[2] On the contrary, "these shows," said Inigo Jones in 1630, "are nothing else but pictures with Light and Motion."[3] Jonson and Jones at the bitter end of their collaboration seem at last to be enunciating the terms of their dispute with a classic antithesis; Jonson's ethical assertion is set against Jones's aesthetic vision, the revelation of moral truth against the manipulation of spectacular effects, the mirrors to instruct the spirit against the pictures to delight the eye.

It has been customary to view the collaboration in this way, and to say that the Caroline masque, freed of Jonson's moral pressure, degenerated into spectacle for its own sake, the unbridled exercise of Jones's scenic ingenuity pandering to the tastes of a decadent court. But let us now consider Jones on the *effect* of one of his pictures: his elaborate costume for Queen Henrietta Maria in Townshend's *Tempe Restored* has been devised, he says, "so that corporeal beauty, consisting in symmetry, color, and certain unexpressable graces, shining in the Queen's majesty, may draw us to the contemplation of the beauty of the soul, unto which it hath analogy."[4]

Jones's aesthetics, then, derive from good Platonic doctrine and have clear moral ends. And Jonson's moral mirror, even with its weight of medieval allegorical usage behind it, appears increasingly pictorial the more closely we examine it. Somewhere far behind Jonson's statement, certainly at least half-consciously, is Aristotle's assertion that drama is an imitation of an action. Linguistically we do not distinguish between action and its imitation: the verb for both is *act*. But Jonson has made a distinction, because an imitation of an action is not the same as a mirror of man's life. Imitation is an action, a mirror is not. In its way, Jonson's formulation is as aesthetically oriented as Jones's, and it exhibits, moreover, the Ramistical tendency to translate actions into things. Mirrors are not actions but things we look at; imitation requires an *actor*, someone to do the imitating: even Hamlet's mirror requires an actor to hold it up to nature. But Jonson's mirror requires only a viewer; or more precisely, the viewer and the actor are the same: what a man sees in it is his own life.[5] The remark is a very precise statement of how Jonson conceived the masque to work. In such representations, he asserted, the court saw not an imitation of itself, but its true self; and so every masque moved toward the moment when masquer and spectator merged, joining in the great central dance, affirming thereby the identity of fictive and real.

Jones and Jonson, then, despite their famous quarrel, were working toward similar ends. Indeed, as D. J. Gordon has shown, the basic issue of the quarrel was not that their positions were antithetical but that they were so much the same. Each looked beneath the finished coalition of language and spectacle to claim the primacy of invention for himself. Moreover, Renaissance critical terminology did not distinguish the poet's kind of invention from the designer's.[6] Nor did the Renaissance critic assume that such a distinction could be made: *ut pictura poesis,* he asserted, unambiguously (if inaccurately) applying Horace's dictum. If pictures and words were inseparable in so simple a medium as verse, then to attempt to separate the visual elements from the verbal in any structure as complex as a Renaissance entertainment must clearly involve us in a considerable historical fallacy. The nature of the difficulty is exemplified simply in the stage set for such a work. The modern viewer tends to think of the stage as a frame enclosing backgrounds for dialogue and action. But Jones's masque machines are not stage sets in this sense. On the contrary, for the most part they are themselves the "action," providing the crucial developments and transformations, and it is the dialogue that is clearly ancillary, elucidating or moralizing the spectacle.

But in a larger sense, in order to understand the spectacles of Inigo Jones we must remember that the antithesis between visual and verbal experience did not exist in the Renaissance, even for Jonson, in the way it does for us. "Whosoever loves not Picture," said the poet in *Timber*, "*is* injurious to Truth: and all the wisdome of Poetry" (1522).[7] There was for Jonson a basic connection between the image and the word, and truth was lost when picture was rejected.

For the Renaissance artist, the relation between verbal statements and visual representations was direct and unquestioned. On the one hand, every picture was a symbol. One might admire the sensuous qualities of a painting, but the significance of the work lay in its meaning, and this was invariably expressed in allegorical or symbolic terms. Pictures, that is, expressed in a visual fashion a meaning that was conceived verbally. Hence the age's intense interest in hieroglyphs: the oldest language, closest to the fount of wisdom, united the image and the word. On a less arcane level, the ubiquitous emblems and devices presented the Renaissance reader with verbal pictures of an exemplary moral nature. Initially, these were intended to consist only of words; the first emblem writer, Andrea Alciato, defined an emblem as a pictorial epigram, a verbal image, and the first edition of his famous *Emblemata* (1531) was not designed to include illustrations. The pictures were added by Alciato's German publisher, and though they were a logical enough development of the original idea, they remained very much an addition: the pictorial part of the emblem is a function of the verbal part, and to interpret the picture correctly one must know how to "read" it.

But on the other hand, the concern with images is an aspect of Renaissance psychological theory shared by both Aristotelians and Platonists; and words, particularly to the latter, had a very dubious function in the intellectual process. Even for Aristotle, the mind knows only forms, and thought consists of forms which are received by the mind as images.[8] Nevertheless, Aristotelian philosophy in the logical and metaphysical writings, and later as practiced by the Schoolmen, laid considerable stress on syntactic structures as the primary vehicles of meaning. Truth, to an Aristotelian, consisted of assertions, which could be dialectically defended or logically tested. Platonists had no such conviction, and in dealing with the relation of the mind to external reality emphasized not language but forms and Platonic Ideas, and these they invariably conceived as images. Hieroglyphs were first expounded in the service of neoplatonism; indeed, the word to a Platonist was not part of an assertion, but rather the name of an Idea, or image, or thing, and out of this grew a conviction that everything could be represented pictorially or schematically.[9] The conviction was institutionalized in the work of the notorious Petrus Ramus, whose dichotomies and diagrams reduced the action of the intellect to a mere reflection of a world that had itself been reduced to a mere collection of things. Nevertheless, the Ramist's insistence on pictorializing language by schematizing it is essentially the same as the impulse of Alciato's publisher to add illustrations to the *Emblemata*: pictures are the age's way of conceptualizing abstractions. This is how the mind worked; "the conceits of the mind are Pictures of things, and the tongue is the Interpreter of those pictures," said Jonson again in *Discoveries* (2128) . The assumption behind this is that there is a direct relation between reality, pictures, and thought. We know through images. Indeed, Jonson's Platonism carried him even further. As a poet, he was bound to assert that "the Pen is more noble, than the Pencill" (1514) . But he continues almost at once, "Picture is the invention of Heaven: the most ancient, and most a kinne to Nature" (1523). Paradoxically, Jonson claims for the visual arts precisely that divinity that had constituted, for Sidney, the chief defence of poetry. The quarrel with Inigo Jones takes on a new coloring when we realize the extent of Jonson's admiration for the marvels of picture. His testimony, though qualified, is unambiguous: "it doth so enter, and penetrate the inmost affection (being done by an excellent Artificer) as sometimes it orecomes the power of speech, and oratory" (1526).

What this means is that we cannot consider Jones's spectacles apart from his poets' texts. Jonson's argument in their debate is essentially that of an emblem writer; not that the spectacle has no meaning, but that it is properly the *expression* of the meaning, the body of the work as the poetry is the soul. Jones, with a respectable array of philosophical and psychological opinion behind him, was maintaining in effect that it is visual experience that speaks most directly to the soul, that it is *images* that *mean*, and words that explain their meaning. It is probably fortunate that he did not have access to Jonson's commonplace book, for he could, as we have seen, have cited the poet against himself.

The issues raised by the quarrel of poet and designer relate to the more special question of the function of visual experience in theatrical performances. Critical opinion in the Renaissance ranges from the assertion that spectacle was a mere distraction to the conviction that it was in fact the substance of theater. The latter view may appear perverse, but it became on the whole the dominant one. For example, it is simply assumed by Prospero when he opens the production of his masque with the admonition "No tongue. All eyes. Be silent."[10] The attention he commands is not aural but visual, that of eyes, not ears. The terms of the controversy can best be understood by a brief look at its Italian counterpart, in which the theoretical issues were more clearly enunciated, largely because the problems involved were more directly practical. Dramas in sixteenth-century Italy were normally produced with *intermezzi* between each act. These were grotesque, comic, or spectacular, and were regularly, until late in the century, unrelated to the main drama. The most elaborate scenic machinery was employed for the *intermezzi*, not for the play itself. The charge, therefore, that spectacle detracted from the seriousness of the drama was in Italy directly, though rarely explicitly, related to the fact that the two really were providing separate and competitive entertainments. Arguments in favor of spectacle tended perforce to ignore the question of the *intermezzi*, and to imply by the term "spectacle" simply the visual element of the drama itself what we would call the "production." And here they found good classical support, in Aristotle for theory, in Vitruvius for practice. From the *Poetics* they learned that "the fearsome and the piteous may arise from the spectacle" (1453b). The claim is modest enough, and Aristotle at once goes on to say that producing the catharsis in this way is inferior to producing it through the construction of the action. Nevertheless, this passage served for many critics as a considerable authority. Francesco Robortello's influential commentary on Aristotle (1548) is indicative. Robortello points out that spectacle ("*apparatus*") is the essence of drama, since it is the necessary expression of the work, and therefore must contain all the other parts defined by Aristotle—melody, diction, thought, character, plot.[11] Moreover, the effect of drama for Robortello derives from its power to evoke wonder or admiration through its depiction of the marvelous. All of this can be justified by reference to Aristotle, for whom wonder is the end of poetry, and drama is a form of poetry. Indeed according to the *Poetics*, "the marvelous is required in tragedy" (1460a), and all things—even impossibilities—that render the work more astounding are appropriate because of the wonder they evoke.[12] Nevertheless, Robortello's formulation, with its emphasis on spectacle, has clearly moved very far from Aristotle's assumption that the construction of the action is the central element in drama.

Similarly, Castelvetro in 1570 assumes that the marvelous, with its ability to produce wonder, is the essence of drama, though this is not a point in its favor: it is only what makes drama appeal to the vulgar taste of the mob.[13] And by 1594 Giovambattista Strozzi could argue that because tragedy effects the catharsis "through the marvels of representation and spectacle"—this is not argued, but simply assumed—it is therefore inferior to epic, which relies on poetry.[14]

On the practical side, Vitruvius provided the necessary assurances that classical drama had employed scenic machinery; and certainly the classicizing aspect of spectacular devices contributes a great deal to their fascination for the Renaissance. Thus there is a direct and paradoxical connection between the insistence that drama must observe the unities, becoming thereby rational and realistic, and the devotion to astonishing and fantastic stage effects. Vitruvius' chapter on theaters, however, proved disappointingly uninformative. It is for the most part concerned not with settings, but with acoustics, dimensions, the necessity for colonnades, and the like. The only scenic devices it discusses are the *periaktoi*, triangular pillars with a different scene painted on each side. "When the play is to be changed," says Vitruvius, "or when the gods enter to the accompaniment of claps of thunder, these may be revolved and present a face differently decorated."[15] The fact that there was more complex machinery on the ancient stage is suggested only later, in a chapter on machines and engines. Vitruvius remarks, in a tantalizing aside, that such devices are used "in accordance with the customs of the stage . . . to please the eye of the people."[16]

Periaktoi, then, were apparently used not to indicate changes of scene, but a new play; possibly to suggest the genre of the drama being performed, so that the pillars would show a different face for tragedy, comedy, or satire. They were also employed in some way as a spectacular device, increasing the wonder of the appearances of gods. It is important to observe that initially, moveable settings did not contribute to the realistic aspects of the drama. To use them realistically (for example, to indicate a change of place in a new scene) was a Renaissance innovation, though doubtless based on a misreading of the Vitruvian account. But it must be stressed that for the Renaissance spectator, the realistic and the marvelous—that which produced wonder, the end of drama—were neither antithetical nor, on the whole, even distinguishable. What was marvelous about spectacular machinery was precisely the realism of its illusions.

The idea that the function of stage machines was "to please the eye of the people" was elaborated by Sebastiano Serlio in 1545 in such a way that settings and machinery appear almost to take on an independent existence:

> Among all the things that may bee made by mens hands, thereby to yeeld admiration, pleasure to sight, and to content the fantasies of men; I think it is placing of a Scene, as it is shewed to your sight, where a man in a small place may see built by Carpenters or Masons, skilfull in Perspective worke, great Palaces, large Temples, and divers Houses, both neere and farre off; broad places filled with Houses, long streets cross with other wayes: tryumphant Arches, high Pillars or Columnes, Piramides, Obeliscens, and a thousand fayre things and buildings, adorned with innumerable lights. . . . There you may see the bright shining Moone ascending only with her hornes, and already risen up, before the spectators are ware of, or once saw it ascend. In some other Scenes you may see the rising of the Sunne with his course about the world: and at the ending of the Comedie, you may see it goe downe most artificially, where at many beholders have bene abasht. And when occasion serveth, you shall by Arte see a God descending downe from Heaven; you also see some Comets and Stars shoot in the skyes . . . which things, as occasion serveth, are so pleasant to mens eyes, that a man could not see fairer made with mens hands.[17]

For all its uncritical enthusiasm, Serlio does make some attempt to account for the effect of scenic machinery on the viewer: it produces admiration, or abashes the beholders. This is perfectly appropriate; the end of drama is wonder. The claim that scenes "content the fantasies of men" is worth pausing over. The Italian reads "*contento d'animo*"; Serlio's term is the general one for any of the intellectual or spiritual faculties. The English "fantasies" is both more technical and more precise. The fantasy is the faculty that receives images; it is also the power to create them. It thus combines the meanings of both perception and imagination; in contenting his fantasy, the spectator is both passive and active.

We should note that there is little suggestion in all this that the effectiveness of scenery is related to its use in a particular drama, or that it functions as an expression of the text. And where Vitruvius had merely implied that it was proper for public officials to provide people with shows and plays, for which machines are useful, such scenic displays take on for Serlio a significant social and political role, for they are the outward expressions of the magnanimity and liberality of princes:

> The more such things cost, the more they are esteemed, for they are things which stately and great persons doe, which are enemies to niggardlinesse. This have I seene in some Scenes made by Ieronimo Genga, for the pleasure and delight of his lord and patron Francisco Maria, Duke of Urbin: wherein I saw so great liberalitie used by the Prince, and so good a conceit in the workeman, and so good Art and proportion in things therein represented, as ever I saw in all my life before. Oh good Lord, what magnificence was there to be seene . . . but I leave all these things to the discretion and consideration of the judicious workeman; which shall make all such things as their pattrons serve them, which they must worke after their owne devises, and never take care what it shall cost.[18]

"This it is," said Jonson the moralist in *Hymenaei*, "hath made the most royal princes and greatest persons, who are commonly the personators of these actions . . . studious of riches and magnificence in the outward celebration or show, which rightly becomes them."[19]

Jones's work, then, is clearly a direct realization of the most serious Renaissance dramatic theory, and of all the implications of Serlio's account of stagecraft. Charges that he, or his audiences, were ever interested in spectacle "for its own sake" are ignorant of how complex a concept spectacle was in the period, and how central the idea of wonder was to all Renaissance discussions of art in general, and of poetry in particular. The means of drama, the age asserted, was spectacle, its end was wonder, and the whole was an expression of the glory of princes. This is the theory behind all Jones's practice.

2

So far as we know, Jones's first stages were devised for Jonson's *Masque of Blackness* on Twelfth Night 1605, and for four plays produced in the hall of Christ Church, Oxford, during a royal visit eight months later. All of these had complex settings. The machinery for *Blackness* consisted of first a front curtain with a painted landscape, then an artificial sea with wave machines, the masquers being placed in a great shell "curiously made to move on those waters and rise with the billow," and for a final revelation, the appearance of the moon-goddess above the stage in a silver throne. These are the devices of *intermezzi*; for the plays in August Jones's practice were more classical. His texts were a neo-Latin pastoral called *Alba*, a new tragedy of *Ajax Flagellifer*, Matthew Gwynne's allegorical comedy *Vertumnus*, and Samuel Daniel's *Arcadia Reformed*, the only play in English.[20] The last was for the benefit of the queen, who did not understand Latin, and King James did not attend. The other three are Oxford's attempt to display its excellence in the three ancient genres. (The first, *Alba*, was the satyr play, and appropriately included "five or six men almost naked, which were much disliked by the Queen and Ladies.")[21] For these classical texts Jones created what he understood to be a classical stage, with *periaktoi* and other scenic machines, so that (a spectator records) "not only for spectacles on different days, but also within a single play, new façades for the whole stage were made to appear with diversity and speed, to the amazement of everyone."[22] Or practically everyone; a spy from Cambridge reported that Jones had been hired to furnish "rare devices, but performed very little, to that which was expected."[23] Disappointing or not, this was a new kind of stage in England, and Jones's sense of its potentialities may be gaged by comparing the settings for the tragedy and the comedy. In *Ajax Flagellifer* the scenes were first Troy and the Sigean shore, then woods, wilderness, dreadful caves and the dwellings of the furies, and last a view of tents and ships. In *Vertumnus*, however, in keeping with its allegorical mode, the stage contained representations of the four winds, and a palm tree in the center with twelve boughs, each bearing a light. Above this was the sun in a zodiac. There were two changes of setting—that is, three scenes—though no record remains of what they were. Jones used his *periaktoi* to create a realistic Italian stage for the tragedy and an emblematic Elizabethan one for the comedy. What was similar about them was the really crucial innovation, the use of perspective for both.

It is worth pausing for a moment to consider what an Oxford audience's expectations would have been for this sort of play. The association between classical drama and scenic machines had been made in England at least as early as 1546, when John Dee constructed a flying device for a Cambridge production of Aristophanes' *Peace*. This was so effective that there were dark mutterings of witchcraft, though it is difficult to see why, since such machines had been employed in Lord Mayors' pageants and similar entertainments for many years. If this was a Vitruvian experiment,[24] there is no evidence that it created a tradition. Nor is this especially surprising. University drama was essentially a verbal and rhetorical art providing for the spectator the same sorts of pleasures as formal debates and oratory—listening to debates was a favorite Elizabethan intellectual pastime. Obviously something about tastes was changing in 1605, since Oxford hired Jones to furnish the plays in the new fashion, and paid him the handsome sum of £50, which was more than he got from the court for the Christmas masque. But it was the court's tastes that were changing, not the university's, and the plays at Christ Church do not signal a new trend in Oxford drama. Indeed, so far as we know, the university did not see another drama on a perspective set with movable scenery until 1636, thirty-one years later, for another royal visit, and with Jones again, this time at the height of his success, creating the settings. For Oxford throughout the intervening years, drama remained basically a rhetorical form, and Jones's settings were thought of not as essential, but rather as providing their own additional and separate pleasures for the spectator. The university's commentators in 1605 did not conceive the new stage to have changed the character of the drama that was produced on it, or to be necessary, or even desirable, for future productions.

The special nature of such stages is worth emphasizing. They were employed only at court or when royalty was present; they were not used in the public or private playhouses. The implications of this deserve more attention than they have received. Jones's stage subtly changed the character of both plays and masques by transforming *audiences* into *spectators*, fixing the viewer, and directing the theatrical experience toward the single point in the hall from which the perspective achieved its fullest effect, the royal throne. There is a reason behind the fact that Oxford employed perspective settings only in the presence of royalty: such a stage was truly appropriate only to the court. Through the use of perspective the monarch, always the ethical centre of court productions, became in a physical and emblematic way the centre as well. Jones's theater transformed its audience into a living and visible emblem of the aristocratic hierarchy: the closer one sat to the king, the "better" one's place was, and only the king's seat was perfect. It is no accident that perspective stages flourished at court and only at court, and that their appearance there coincided with the reappearance in England of the Divine Right of Kings as a serious political philosophy.[25]

Jones's stage was a radical and unfamiliar phenomenon for English audiences. The assumption behind it was that a theater is a machine for controlling the visual experience of the spectator, and that that experience is defined by the rules of perspective. Moreover, it is not simply the optical realism of the setting that is important, but the ability to change the settings, and thereby continually to exercise the spectacle's control over the audience. It is important to remember that these are assumptions about theaters, not plays: in principle any play may be presented on such a stage, and the separation of the theatrical and dramatic experiences for the spectator is clearly implied in all the contemporary accounts—and indeed, well into the Restoration.[26] As Jones was employing them, changes of setting were not so much backgrounds for the action as they were *wonders* in plays. At Oxford in 1605 Jones was creating tiny spectacular *intermezzi* for his classical dramas.

The unfamiliarity of the principles behind Jones's stage may be measured by the bureaucratic difficulty that Oxford encountered when it attempted to apply them. In August, 1605, eight months after witnessing *The Masque of Blackness*, a group of court officials came to oversee the arrangements for the king's visit to the university. These functionaries "utterly disliked the stage at Christchurch, and above all the place appointed for the chair of Estate, because it was no higher, and the King so placed that the auditory could see but his cheek only." The university's vice-chancellor and his workmen undertook to explain the nature of illusionistic theater; they "maintained that by the art perspective the King should behold all better than if he sat higher." To the courtiers, however, the king was the spectacle—the spectators at a play were an "auditory," and the realities of the art perspective were irrelevant. "In the end, the place was removed, and sett in the midst of the Hall, but too far from the stage." Ironically, in the event, King James complained that he could not *hear* the play.[27]

From 1605 onward illusionistic stages were regularly used for the masque, but it was many years before the implications of this sort of theater were realized in the drama, or indeed, recognized at all. Not until the end of the 1630s do we begin to find assertions that spectacular settings affect the plays that are produced in them. In part such claims have an air of special pleading, the rationalizations of popular dramatists writing for the old-fashioned public stage. On the other hand, Peter Hausted, one of the least of the Sons of Ben, takes a firm Jonsonian line defending the lack of scenery in his adaptation of *Epicoene, The Rival Friends*, produced at Cambridge for a royal visit in 1632:

> Our offense was the same that was imputed to Cicero, . . . that it was *saucinesse* in him amongst so many *Patricians* of eminent blood, to dare to be *vertuous* or *Eloquent*. I doe confesse we did not goe such quaint wayes as we might have done; we had none of those *Sea-artes*, knew not how, or else scorn'd to plant our *Can-*

> *vas* so *advantagiously* to *catch* the *wayward breath* of the *Specta-*
> *tours*; but freely and ingenuously labour rather to *merit* then
> *ravish* an *Applause* from the *Theatre.*[28]

The terms of this are instructive: scenery, for Hausted, appeals to passion
rather than judgment, and the dangerous effectiveness of such an appeal is
amply indicated by his use of the word "ravish" to describe the experience.
Both neoplatonists and neo-Aristotelians could have objected that ravish-
ment is precisely the effect for which art is created: the response to beauty for
Plato, like the end of poetry for Aristotle, is not judgment but wonder. Hence
at court, in the same year, Mercury was admonishing the audience of the
Christmas masque, Townshend's *Albion's Triumph,* that they might "admire,
but censure not."[29] Hausted, in fact, is seeing the drama not as poetry but as a
form of oratory or debate, the end of which is rational persuasion. Most significant for our purposes, however, is not the philosophical basis of the passage, but the necessity for an apology: in 1632 a play presented before the king
was expected to have illusionistic scenery. William Strode at Oxford four years
later produced a genial compromise by asserting that his allegory *The Float-*
ing Island would, with Jones's scenes, provide two equal and alternative pleasures for its royal audience:

> Whether you come to see a play or hear,
> Whether your censure sit in th'Eye or eare,
> *Fancy or Judgement,* Carelesse of Event
> We aime at Service; cannot misse th'Intent.[30]

The radical charge that the new stage is positively anti-verbal is a rare and
very late one, and highly inaccurate if we consider the court dramas of the
1630s. Nevertheless, it does appear as a justification for the lack of illusionistic
scenery in the professional theaters. Thus the prologue to a Blackfriars play of
about 1640, William Cavendish's *Country Captain,* posits a necessary relation
between spectacular productions and incompetent poetry:

> Gallants, I'll tell you what we do not mean
> To show you here a glorious painted scene,
> With various doors to stand instead of wit,
> Or richer clothes with lace, for lines well writ;
> Tailors and painters thus, your dear delights,
> May prove your poets only for your sight,
> Not understanding. . . .[31]

All this testifies more than anything else to a considerable uncertainty about the relation between visual and verbal experience in the theater. Looking backward in 1664, Richard Flecknoe thought he detected a transformation in the very nature of theater, from an auditory to a spectacular phenomenon:

> Now for the difference between our Theatres and those of former times, they were but plain and simple, with no other Scenes nor Decorations of the Stage, but onely old Tapestry, and the Stage strew'd with Rushes, with their Habits accordingly, whereas ours now for cost and ornament are arriv'd to the height of Magnificence; but that which makes our Stage the better makes our Playes the worse perhaps, they striving now to make them more for sight than hearing.[32]

No doubt the audiences of Wycherley and Congreve would have been surprised to learn that modern drama was designed more for sight than for hearing; nevertheless, Flecknoe's perception of a new attitude toward the stage as a scenic machine is obviously valid. Davenant's *Playhouse to be Let* (c. 1660) may be taken as a prime example: it is an anthology of scenic possibilities, and its evident enthusiasm is an index to the novelty of the idea that something other than rhetoric might be the substance of drama. This is the heritage of Jones's theater, though it is not a theater he ever knew or contemplated, and it derives from the adaptation of masque stages to the production of plays.

After the Oxford productions of 1605, Jones does not seem to have produced another play for over twenty years. His stage was developed for masques. But his handling of the two forms was always very different, and it is important for us to keep the distinction of the genres clearly in mind. A masque was not, to the Renaissance, a kind of drama. John Chamberlain in 1613 reported widespread criticism of Thomas Campion's *Lords' Masque* for being "more like a play than a masque," and conversely, Sir Dudley Carleton was especially pleased with Sir Philip Herbert's wedding masque in 1604, "which for songs and speeches was as goode as a play."[33] The art of the stage designer is employed in both, but his function is not the same. The scenic machine is the setting for a play, and it may also provide its own momentary interludes of wonder as the drama pauses. But the scenic machine is the *action* of a masque, its metamorphoses, miracles, apotheoses. And despite the normal use of theatrical terminology in descriptions of masques—scene, stage, proscenium, etc.—the masquing hall was never referred to as a theater.

Plays are rhetorical structures and imitations of actions. Masques are, as Jones says in *Tempe Restored*, analogies: Ideas made apprehensible, visible, real. Our tendency to confuse the two, and to take Jonson's side in the debate with his designer, has lead us to assume, like Cavendish and Flecknoe, that the visual emphasis of Jones's theater made it also anti-verbal—in crude terms, that the taste for spectacle was what killed Shakespearean drama. But if we look at Jones's relation to his playwrights, and consider the dramas (not the masques) that were actually written to be produced on his stage—plays like Cartwright's *Royal Slave*, Montagu's *Shepherd's Paradise*, Carlell's *Passionate Lovers*, Strode's *Floating Island*—we shall find them not less but more rhetorical than plays for the public theater. Montagu's, indeed, despite at least nine changes of scene, was notorious for its long-windedness. The model for such dramas is the formal debate or the Platonic dialogue, and Jones's stage was considered an appropriate setting for them. The relation between this sort of drama and Jones's scenic machines must lie partly in the sophisticated rationality of the settings they provided; but it is even more profoundly involved with the continuing assumption that the true end of drama is the production of wonder. Aristotelian pragmatism blends here into Platonic mysticism, for wonder is the quality that, in Platonic theory, leads the mind to the apprehension of truth,[34] and Jones, as we have seen, is well aware of this. Illusionistic machinery for the dramatic stage first comes fully into its own, logically enough, when the drama becomes not only overtly philosophical but directly Platonic.

3

In a sense the possibilities and implications of a theater like Jones's had already been explored in late Shakespearean drama. It is a commonplace to observe elements of the masque in these plays: Prospero's marvels, Posthumus' dream, the emblematic procession of knights in *Pericles*, Hermione's statue, Henry VIII's disguising. Indeed, the resolutions of both *The Winter's Tale* and *The Tempest* are directly effected by illusionists, theatrical producers who control what the audiences within their plays see, and thereby believe. It is not accidental that the most palpable example we are shown of Prospero's art is a masque. The emphasis in all the late plays is on the awaking of wonder as the means to reconciliation and the restoration of losses, with a corresponding emphasis on visual and irrational experience. Pericles believes Marina not because of what he hears from her, but because of what he sees:

> I will believe thee,
> And make my senses credit thy relation
> To points that seem impossible, for thou look'st
> Like one I loved indeed. (V.i. 122–5)

This is illogical, but seeing is believing, and specifically, believing the impossible. Analogously, *The Winter's Tale* stresses the validity not of reasonable explanations but of fantastic stories; truth is "like an old tale still." Leontes' salvation lies in his ability to believe that his son's death is not the physical consequence of shock and grief, but a judgment sent from Apollo; that the restored Hermione has not simply been hidden for sixteen years but is a statue come to life. So the miraculous becomes fact, seeming becomes being, the ideal the real. Ben Jonson's dubiety about spectacle and the art of Inigo Jones is directly related to his feelings about plays like *Pericles*:

> No doubt a mouldy Tale,
> Like *Pericles*, and stale
> As the Shreives crusts, and nasty as his Fish,
> Scraps out of every Dish,
> Throwne forth and rak'd into the common Tub,
> May keep up the Play Club.[35]

Jonson for once was not a good enough Platonist to appreciate the central experience of wonder in *Pericles*. The old tale, with its appeals to the fantastic and irrational, strikes him as mindless and vulgar, rather than transcendent. Ironically, it is precisely the masque-like qualities of the drama that offend the greatest masque-writer of the age: such elements are inappropriate to plays, which for Jonson are still rhetorical structures or imitations of actions. But symbolic fables and miraculous resolutions are the substance of masques. Wonder, indeed, appears in person to control and define the miracles of Inigo Jones's metamorphoses in Jonson's *Vision of Delight*, becoming at last the agent of its idealizations and apotheoses:

> How better than they are are all things made
> By Wonder![36]

exclaims Fantasy, at which, on a midwinter night in 1617, the Bower of Zephyrus opened to loud music, and the masquers were discovered as the Glories of the Spring.

It is the wonder of the spectators that is being invoked at such a moment. Their response plays an active role in the masque, not only through its allegorical embodiment in the figure of Wonder, but more generally, in this as in all masques, through the audience's inclusion in the apotheosis. For it is the transformation of both masquer and spectator, of the whole court, that the masque as a form undertakes. The directing and ordering of the viewer's wonder is the means toward this transformation: "No tongue," says Prospero, "all eyes. Be silent." Around the heroic roles of Jonson's, Campion's, Davenant's poetry Jones created the palpable reality of a sensibly apprehensible world, and this, in turn, became the palace at Whitehall, the Banqueting House, the masquing room. When the spectators joined in dancing the revels, they were participating in the mimesis; and seeing beneath the disguise, recognizing the identity of the masquers, was the first step toward understanding the wisdom they embodied, because it revealed the relation between the idealization and the reality. This is the step that Ferdinand takes when, halfway through his masque, he asks Prospero, "May I be bold to think these spirits?"

Allegory, symbol, and myth are the substance of masques. Courtiers are seen as heroes, kings as gods, actions as emblems, and meaning in this form is, in both the figurative and literal senses, dependent on how things *appear*. The viewers' understanding of the masque, moreover, depended on their ability to read what they saw. If they could not interpret the symbolism, as must almost invariably have been the case, it had to be explained to them, either in the dialogue or more often in the printed text of the work, as in *The Masque of Blackness*, or *Tempe Restored*. The fact that even this procedure was exceptional only means that we must not underestimate the Renaissance's love of mysteries and enigmas. To find oneself in the presence of mystic and impenetrable truths afforded considerable pleasure. That Jones should have relied, in so profoundly symbolic a form, on the realistic properties of perspective is an important index to his sensibility and that of the age as a whole. It suggests to begin with that the 'realness' of perspective lay less in its naturalism than in its power to project something that was recognized to be an illusion. For such an effect to be successful, a certain sophistication is required of the viewer's perception as well as of the designer's skill: one must learn not only how to devise perspective scenes, but also how to read them. Straight lines on a page moving upward and converging will appear to recede to a vanishing point only if we have learned the rules for translating three-dimensional images into two dimensions and back again; otherwise the lines will simply appear to move upward and converge. The evidence indicates that Jones had to deal with an untrained audience who were not, moreover, quick learners.

We have already remarked that courtiers who had witnessed *The Masque of Blackness* in January 1605 were still unfamiliar with the principles of perspective at Oxford the next August. We might compare Jonson's description of Jones's marine setting for *Blackness* with that of a member of the audience. Jonson writes,

> an artificial sea was seen to shoot forth, as if it flowed to the land, raised with waves which seemed to move, and in some places the

billow to break, as imitating that orderly disorder which is common in nature. In front of this sea were placed six tritons in moving and sprightly actions. . . . Behind these a pair of sea-maids, for
song, were as conspicuously seated; between which two great sea-
horses, as big as the life, put forth themselves, the one mounting
aloft and writhing his head from the other, which seemed to sink
forwards. . . . The masquers were placed in a great concave shell
like mother of pearl, curiously made to move on those waters and
rise with the billow.[37]

Here is what Sir Dudley Carleton saw:

There was a great Engine at the lower end of the Room, which
had Motion, and in it were the Images of Sea-Horses with other
terrible Fishes, which were ridden by Moors: the Indecorum was,
that there was all Fish and no water. At the further end was a great
Shell in the form of a Skallop, wherein were four Seats; on the
lowest sat the Queen. . . .[38]

Doubtless we must make some allowances for Carleton's sense of humor;
nevertheless it is clear that this account cannot be treated, as commentators
have done, merely as a perverse joke. To begin with, the setting does not seem
to Carleton a stage; it is "an Engine at the lower end of the Room." Where
Jonson saw a sea so artfully devised that the great shell moved on it and rose
with the swell of the waves, what Carleton saw as "all Fish and no water." What
Carleton describes, in fact, is not an Italianate perspective scene, but a traditional English pageant car and a number of attendant devices that happen to
be grouped at one end of the hall. But also, what Carleton sees is precisely
what is there; only he does not interpret it as its designer intends it to be
interpreted.

Thirty-one years later, in 1636, here is what Antony à Wood reported that a
Cambridge spectator said he had seen at Jones's production of William
Strode's *Floating Island*:

It was acted on a goodly stage reaching from the upper end of the
Hall almost to the hearth place, and three or four openings on
each side thereof, and partitions between them, much resembling
the desks or studies in a Library, out of which the Actors issued
forth. The said partitions they could draw in and out at their
pleasure upon a sudden, and thrust out new in their places

according to the nature of the Screen, whereon were represented Churches, Dwellinghouses, Palaces, etc. which for its variety bred very great admiration.[39]

Clearly Wood's source is richly appreciative of the ingenuity of Jones's settings, and if the end of drama is wonder, the architect has done the poet's work well for him. Nevertheless, what the spectator is seeing is apparently not quite what he is intended to see. The side wings of Jones's perspective scene look, in this account, like "the desks or studies in a Library"; instead of reading the set as an uninterrupted receding perspective, the observer sees, like Carleton in 1605, exactly and only what is there: a number of individual flats arranged in two rows on either side of the stage.

But the mimetic effects toward which Jones was working depended not only on an audience with educated eyes. It depended as well on certain assumptions about the nature of the artist: that his power was the power to project illusions, but that these had meaning and moral force; that seeing was believing, and that art could give us a vision of the good and the true; that the illusion represented, in short, a Platonic reality. In the same way, the masque was for Jonson a form of idealizing poetry. The sorts of contexts and personae he provided for his masquers were realizations of those he created for the heroes of his society in works like the epistle to Sir Robert Wroth, *To Penshurst*, and the several addresses to the Countess of Bedford. The creation of exemplary roles for the leaders of the culture was one of the highest acts the Renaissance poet could perform, and in treating the masque as a poem Jonson was also preserving from oblivion the heroic virtues he had thus embodied. So much Jonson himself tells us in the preface to *Hymenaei*. But there is a more complex aspect of the masque, less rational and overt, that was, as we have seen, an equally large element in the form's meaning for the age. "Though their voice be taught to sound to present occasions," says Jonson, "their sense or doth or should always lay hold on more removed mysteries."[40] The emphasis on mystic symbols, on charms and incantations, and particularly on metamorphoses and miraculous transformations in seeming defiance of the laws of time or gravity suggests an ultimate vision that partakes of the magical. Nevertheless, we need a better word than magic to describe what Jones's theater was doing. It was not magic precisely because it required so completely the collusion of the observers: their wit and understanding made the miracles and metamorphoses possible. If anyone is deceived, the effect has failed. Even Dr. Dee, in 1546, had had only amused condescension for those who thought the ascent of his cloud machine was really magical.

The better word is, perhaps, scientific. For the masque is the form that most consistently projects a world in which all the laws of nature have been understood and the attacks of mutability defeated by the rational power of the mind. Nature in the masque is the nature envisioned by Baconian science; its pastorals embody not innocence but the fullest richness of experience, not contemplation but the widest range of action. The heroic dead return, humankind enters a golden age and moves with perfect ease from earth to heaven; and most to the point, this vision, at its climactic moment, includes us, the mortal spectators: we too are transformed by the power of knowledge and reason. Every masque is a ritual in which the society affirms its wisdom and asserts its control of its world and its destiny. The glories of the transformation scene express the power of princes, bringing order to human and elemental nature, partaking thereby of the divine. The court and the aristocratic hierarchy expand and become the world, and the king in turn is abstracted— to Pan the universal god, to the life-giving sun, to Hesperus the evening star, or even, in an extraordinary example, to a physical principle, pure potential, through whom the ultimate scientific mysteries of perpetual motion and infinite power are finally solved:

> Not that we think you weary be,
> For he
> That did this motion give,
> And made it so long live,
> Could likewise give it perpetuity.
> Nor that we doubt you have not more,
> And store
> Of changes to delight;
> For they are infinite,
> As is the power that brought those forth before.[41]

If this sort of claim appears extravagant, it will seem less so if we set it beside a philosophical assertion that is not involved with the patronage of kings and the society of courts. Here is Marsilio Ficino, discussing Archimedean mechanical models of the heavenly spheres:

> Since man has observed the order of the heavens, when they move, whither they proceed and with what measures, and what they produce, who could deny that man possesses as it were almost the same genius as the Author of the heavens? And who could deny that man could also make the heavens, could he only obtain the instruments and the heavenly material, since even now he makes them, though of a different material, but still with a very similar order?[42]

Jonson's assertion of the infinite power of the mind to create and control looks less like flattery in such a context.

The control is expressed on every level, through the rich formality of the celebratory verse, the harmony of music, the movement of dance; but most of all, through Inigo Jones's ability to do the impossible. The exchequer records testify to the extent of the crown's investment in such assertions; that they came at the season of renewal and epiphany is not accidental. Nor is it surprising that Jones's talents found their most receptive patron in King Charles, whose visions of a harmonious commonwealth were substantiated only in the realities of the theatrical machine. The illusionist's control over the way we look at things was an important instrument of royal policy—or at least the king was under the illusion that it was.

Other spectators had their doubts. A year after Charles's execution, the creator of the most famous English masque, Milton the iconoclast, undertook to demolish not only the late king's claims but even his "conceited portraiture," the literal *Eikon Basilike*, "before his book, drawn out to the full measure of a masking scene, and set there to catch fools and silly gazers" (figure 5.1.). In the picture prefixed to the royal apology the king kneels before an altar in the entrance to a chapel; he holds a crown of thorns called *grace*; his earthly crown, *splendid but heavy*, lies discarded. His gaze is on a third crown, *glory*,

Figure 5.1. William Marshall, frontispiece to *Eikon Basilike*, 1649.

appearing in the heavens. Outside, a distant landscape presents two personified winds, storm clouds, a raging sea. From the clouds a shaft of brightness, *more light out of darkness*, extends to the king's head. In the sea a rock stands, *unmoved, triumphant*. A nearby field contains two palm trees, emblems of peace; one is hung with weights, and its motto reads *Virtue grows greater under burdens.*

"But quaint emblems and devices," argued Milton, "begged from the old pageantry of some Twelfthnight's entertainment at Whitehall, will do but ill to make a saint or martyr."[43] This registers, certainly, a Puritan's distaste for Laudian Anglicanism with its emphasis on display and ceremony, outward and visible signs. But it also reveals that the author of *A Maske Presented at Ludlow Castle* had a clear and accurate sense of how masques worked and what they undertook to do. The mechanics of idealization are under attack here. What Milton decries as the Commonwealth triumphs is the art of Inigo Jones, the power to create a hero by controlling the way we look at a man.

6

———

THE SPECTACLES OF STATE

MY TITLE comes from Ben Jonson's poem *An Expostulation with Inigo Jones,* a long and vitriolic attack on his old artistic collaborator by whom Jonson felt betrayed. Neutral enough out of context, the phrase is in Jonson's verse bitterly ironic:

> O shows, shows, mighty shows!
> The eloquence of masques! what need of prose,
> Or verse, or sense t'express immortal you!
> You are the spectacles of state! (39–41)

The intensity of Jonson's outrage at what he sees as the soulless spectacle of the Caroline masque is a measure also of the real depth of his commitment to the masque as a form. Jonson's profound ambivalence, the deep ambiguities of that neutral-sounding phrase The Spectacles of State, may serve us as a cultural touchstone for his age.

I begin with a well-known painting of a group of people performing in a spectacle of state. Figure 6.1 shows Queen Elizabeth, in the last year or two of her reign, transported in triumph through an imaginary landscape combining both urban and rural visions, city palaces and country castles, surrounded by her courtiers and watched by her subjects. The picture is attributed to Robert Peake, and is usually called *Queen Elizabeth Going in Procession to Blackfriars in 1600.* It is traditionally said to commemorate the queen's attendance at an important dynastic marriage: the wedding at Blackfriars of one of her maids of honor, Lady Anne Russell, granddaughter of the Earl of Bedford, to Henry Somerset, Lord Herbert, son of the Earl of Worcester, and ultimately the inheritor of the title. Lady Anne and Lord Herbert are indeed participants in this ceremony, but it is clear that the identification of this scene with their wedding procession must be wrong.[1] To begin with, the setting, with its prospect of hills and castles, can hardly be Blackfriars, one of the most crowded sections of the City of London. Secondly, the only woman who could

Figure 6.1. Engraving after the painting attributed to Robert Peake,
Queen Elizabeth and the Earl of Worcester in Procession, c. 1601.

be the bride, in white in the right middle-ground, is not dressed for a wedding: Elizabethan brides wore their hair down, in token of their virginity.
Through an analysis of the iconography, history, and provenance of the painting, we arrive at a quite different interpretation.

Many of the male figures in the procession are identifiable, through personal iconography and other portraits. They include the most powerful aristocrats in the realm. In a group of Garter Knights in the left foreground we
can recognize the Lord Admiral, Lord Howard of Effingham; the Earl of
Cumberland; Lord Hunsdon, the Lord Chamberlain, among others. Most
important, we recognize the central figure just below the queen: Edward Somerset, Earl of Worcester, Elizabeth's last Master of the Horse, who succeeded
the Earl of Essex in that crucial ceremonial office after his disgrace and execution in 1601. Worcester is the father of the young man in white behind him:
this is Henry Somerset, Lord Herbert. The woman in white is Lady Anne Russell, now Lady Herbert, Worcester's daughter-in-law—not a fiancée going to
her marriage, but a wife of a year or more. The landscape probably depicts
Worcester's two castles of Chepstow and Raglan, and the town house would
be his mansion in the Strand. What the picture commemorates, in this analysis, is the triumph not of Elizabeth but of Worcester, and it must have been he
who commissioned it. In the drama presented here, the queen, though a central figure, plays a distinctly secondary role. She is the background, the neces-

sary context, the crucial prop; but the protagonist is Worcester. The painting celebrates his elevation to the position of Master of Ceremonies for this most ceremonial of courts. He continued in this office long after Elizabeth's time, serving as Earl Marshal for King James's coronation and again for his entry into London in 1604, and as late as 1610 overseeing the solemnities at the creation of James's son Henry as Prince of Wales.

This painting is a performance, and the central actor is also the primary spectator. What the picture records is not a moment of history but an assertion of status, the creation of a public self. This is the way the Earl of Worcester presents himself, the way he wants to be seen—above all, the way he wants to see himself. In such a performance, any distinction between actors and audience will be misleading. The protagonist *is* the audience, and other spectators, to view the spectacle correctly, must see it through his eyes. The persona he adopts, his mask, is not intended as a disguise but as a revelation: of the truest, essential, Platonic self.

Figure 6.2. Attributed to Robert Peake, *Henry, Prince of Wales*, investiture portrait, 1610. By courtesy of the National Portrait Gallery, London.

Let us now consider one example of the public self in the process of creation. Henry Prince of Wales is an excellent test case for our purposes because the iconographic documentation is so thorough and the time span so brief. Henry was born in 1594. He became Prince of Wales in 1610 at the age of 16, and died two years later, in 1612. He embodied, for that brief two years, all the militant idealism of Protestant England chafing under a pacifist king who was increasingly pro-Catholic. All the portraits I have included were done during that two-year period.

Figure 6.2 is the standard official portrait, with the subject aged about sixteen. The picture can be dated by the ostrich feathers on his hat: these are the emblem of the Prince of Wales, hence the date must be after his investiture. He is presented as a slim, boyish, splendidly appointed young man. Figure 6.3, by Isaac Oliver, was painted only a year or so later: it is basically the cameo portrait of a Roman emperor. In figure 6.4, another Isaac Oliver portrait, the face has become forceful and manly, and the iconography explicitly military: the prince wears elegant armor, and poses before an encampment of tents in the right background. Figure 6.5 shows the prince practicing at the lance, a very popular engraving that appeared as the frontispiece to Drayton's *Poly-Olbion* (1613), published in the year after Henry's death. The military idealization appears here, too, and we note the imperial Roman profile again. And figure 6.6, finally, shows how Inigo Jones presented him in Jonson's masque *Oberon* at New Year's, 1611, when the prince was sixteen—this drawing was done less than a year after the first portrait, of the slim youth. It hardly needs to be emphasized that the idealization here—the classic musculature, the commanding stance—is the work of the artist: this young man has not been

Figure 6.3. Isaac Oliver, *Henry, Prince of Wales*, 1610–11. Fitzwilliam Museum, Cambridge.

Figure 6.4. Isaac Oliver, *Henry, Prince of Wales*, c. 1611. The Royal Collection © 2001, Her Majesty Queen Elizabeth II.

lifting weights for the last six months, and the process of heroic definition is not a function only of court masques. Jones's way of presenting Prince Henry is fully consistent with that of the other artists the prince commissioned to depict him, and most to the point, fully consistent with the role that he imagined for himself. Had he lived, his plan was to follow his sister Elizabeth to Bohemia after her marriage to the Elector Palatine, and to lead the Protestant armies there.

What I have been suggesting is that the theatrical and ceremonial were crucial aspects of political life for the Elizabethan and Stuart crown. Such a claim will come as no surprise, and will scarely distinguish the English monarchy

Figure 6.5. William Hole, Prince Henry at the Lance, frontispiece to Michael Drayton's *Poly-Olbion*, 1613.

Figure 6.6. Inigo Jones, costume for Prince Henry in Ben Jonson's *Oberon*, 1611. Devonshire Collection, Chatsworth. Reproduced by permission of the Duke of Devonshire and the Chatsworth Settlement Trustees.

from any other, in almost any historical era whatever. But theater and ceremony as employed by Elizabeth, James, and their courts, are double-edged,
and have dimensions that are ambiguous, ironic, and often subversive. It is
this special quality that I want to identify and consider.

A logical place to begin is with the literally theatrical, the Elizabethan public theater. Figure 6.7 shows the closest thing we have to an eyewitness sketch,
an early copy of the Dutch traveler Johannes de Witt's drawing of the Swan
Playhouse in London in 1595. It shows an arena with a simple platform stage
and an architectural back façade containing two doors and a gallery above.
The apparent simplicity of the sketch, however, is belied by de Witt's accompanying description, which reports that the pillars were painted to look like
marble and the roof over the stage was richly decorated. Other accounts of
Elizabethan playhouses bear out de Witt's impression of visual splendor. The
splendor was conveyed through costumes and symbolic properties—rich
robes, crowns and thrones, badges of office, heraldic banners, shields and the
like. The splendor, that is, was an aspect less of the setting than of the persons
and their roles, and the theater itself constituted an appropriately lavish context for the action.

One of the chief attractions of the Elizabethan popular theater was clearly
this kind of pageantry, and it provided a ceremonial dimension that could be

Figure 6.7. Arend van Buchel after Johannes de Witt, The Swan Playhouse,
London, c. 1595. University Library, Utrecht, ms. 842 fol. 132r.

conceived in the broadest sense. Through it the stage was able to mirror the spectacle of courts and aristocratic enterprises to an urban, predominantly middle-class audience, in a society that had grown relatively mobile, and that contemporary critics feared had grown far too mobile. Ironically, the attraction was especially powerful when the pageantry was presented in the service of a nostalgic medievalism, expressing the traditional values of an established hierarchy and a chivalric code, since that was precisely the mythology of the Elizabethan court. The symbolism was evident, for example, in Elizabeth's coronation procession in 1558, a spectacle of knights, feudal trappings, heraldic paraphernalia. Tudor chivalry was a mythology consciously designed to validate and legitimate an authority that must have seemed, to what was left of the old aristocracy, dangerously *arriviste*. Indeed, it must have seemed so to Elizabeth herself, the granddaughter of a prosperous London merchant, faced with continual questions about the sources of her authority and the very legitimacy of her birth.

Both Elizabeth and her half-sister Mary Tudor were legally illegitimate. They were declared so on the birth of their father's male heir, the future Edward VI. Even without a formal declaration of bastardy, the dubious validity of Henry's first two marriages would have rendered the status of his daughters doubtful enough to leave their place in the line of succession open to challenge; and Elizabeth had the additional problem of her mother's conviction and execution on a charge of adultery. Mary herself maintained, at least in moments of anger, that Elizabeth was not the daughter of Henry VIII at all, but of Anne Boleyn's lutenist Mark Smeaton, who had confessed to the adultery, pleaded guilty at the trial, and was executed as the queen's lover (along with four other men who did not confess, including her own brother). Henry confused the issue even further by maintaining both his daughters' illegitimacy to the end, but at the same time including them in the line of succession, next after Edward, in his will. This legacy was the sole source of Elizabeth's claim to the throne. Her chivalric ceremonials have been described as a gradually developing Elizabethan phenomenon, but they are no such thing. They are present from the moment of her accession, and they are a conscious assertion of her rightful lineage through a powerful allusion to her father's and her grandfather's personal mythology.

The chivalric code, with its attendant social forms and public displays, had been a crucial element in Tudor policy from the beginning; and it always had to do with questions of legitimacy and authority. Gordon Kipling has shown how consciously Henry VII imported Burgundian chivalric models as the basis of a broad cultural program to project the image of a noble and honorable court.[2] The image, for this monarch, was everything, since Henry reigned without even a doubtful claim to the English throne: he ruled because he had invaded and conquered. Chivalry here was a mask for the inelegant realities of military power on the one hand, and the mundane details of administrative efficiency on the other. For his son Henry VIII, chivalry served as a mask for the lack of either, as quickly became apparent. The splendid fantasies of the Field of the Cloth of Gold were universally admired, but nobody, least of all the French king whom they were designed to impress, was deceived into thinking they represented real power.

What happened under Elizabeth was that Tudor chivalry was increasingly codified into a mode of ceremonial assertion and official behavior. Every year from about 1572 onward the anniversary of the queen's accession was celebrated with a tilting. Elizabeth redefined Tudor chivalry to make of the family mythology a drama that was peculiarly her own. In it, the essence of knighthood was service to a lady, and when the lady was a version of the queen, frustration was indissoluble from heroic achievement. The chivalric under Elizabeth thus merges with the Petrarchan; Spenser's epic, *The Faerie Queene*, sums up and embodies decades of royal image-making, accurately expressing not only the ideal but its powerful ambivalence—for example, in the endlessly delayed or aborted marriages (the Redcross Knight and Una, Scudamore and Amoret, Florimel and Marinell, Calidore and Pastorella), and summed up in the narcissistic paradox of the lady knight Britomart, trapped in her own chivalric disguise.

Chivalric ideals and their expression in courtly spectacle, in Accession Day tilts, royal entertainments and court protocol generally, constitute a good instance of the utility of ceremonial fictions—of pageantry and poetry in the largest sense—within a society. It is clear that Spenser grew increasingly dubious about the values inherent in his chivalric metaphor, and that Elizabethan society did so too. Recent criticism has tried to see in Elizabethan chivalry an effective cultural mediator, a social trope that allowed for the channeling and sublimation of potentially dangerous energies. Ceremonials and their attendant fictions certainly can function in this way, as the work of Clifford Geertz amply demonstrates, and Elizabeth clearly had something of the sort in mind; but it is also clear that, by the last two decades of the reign at least, a strong sense of impatience and disillusion with the royal mythology was being felt. The mythology had become increasingly private, a way for Elizabeth to see herself, and its rhetoric was adopted only by those who had a vested interest in mirroring her self-image. People whose livelihood did not depend on court patronage adopted quite a different tone in addressing her.

Consider, for example, the case of John Stubbs. Stubbs was a Puritan barrister who, in 1579, appalled by Elizabeth's apparent intention of marrying the Duc d'Alençon, published a pamphlet entitled *The Discovery of Gaping Gulf Wherein England is Like to be Swallowed* which energetically argued against the match. The pamphlet included nothing that was not a popular common-place, but it became notorious because of Elizabeth's explosive (and uncharacteristic) reaction to it, which was outraged, panicky, and vindictive. The queen wanted Stubbs and the publisher charged with seditious libel and hanged. This turned out to be legally impossible, but they were imprisoned (ironically, charged under a statute of Mary Tudor's providing penalties for those who libeled her husband Philip II of Spain) and their right hands were cut off by the public executioner. A reading of the pamphlet reveals no intention of either sedition or libel, but it does tell a good deal about Elizabeth's pathology on the subject of marriage—or perhaps simply on the subject of conducting her own affairs without interference. Stubbs is undeniably rude about Alençon, whom he despises as an adventurer and a Papist, but his attitude toward Elizabeth, while not exactly reverent, is unquestionably loyal and loving. The tone he takes might best be described as fraternal: scolding and impatient, but also affectionate and indulgent; above all, straightforward and commonsensical—about matters like Elizabeth's advanced age, for example. (What, Stubbs asks, does a young man like that want with an old woman like you? Young men only pursue older women for their money; and so forth. Such arguments are undeniably tactless, but scarcely seditious.) Stubbs's model for his relation to the sovereign is not the chivalric court, but the family. We surely err in taking the queen's version of herself as a working model for the life of the commonwealth. King James's son Prince Henry, in 1610, saw himself as the center of a chivalric revival: chivalry had to be *revived* in 1610, having been dead, in Henry's mind, not for the seven years since Elizabeth's time, but since the Middle Ages.

Let us look at Prince Henry again, in figure 6.4: those are tents and soldiers, an army camp in the background. He is surrounded by the trappings not of ceremonial tilts but of war. The program that Henry proposed, militaristic and aggressively Protestant, involved a very different notion of chivalry from that of Elizabeth. It is the same notion that thirty years earlier had informed Sir Philip Sidney's pleas for royal employment, and that was responsible for his aborted career. The cause was a Protestant crusade against the Catholic powers of Europe, something Elizabeth did not at all want to be involved in. Sidney's version of chivalry was antithetical to the queen's, and dangerous to it. Prince Henry's, in the same way, was energetically resisted by a powerful court faction, including both his father the king and his poet Ben Jonson.

Such reactions are not merely political or narrowly pragmatic. The age's complex attitude toward chivalry is exemplified in Book VI of *The Faerie Queene,* in which chivalric courtesy turns out to be the most dubious of moral principles. The age's attitude toward chivalry is part of a larger attitude toward poetry as a whole, toward the relation of symbolic fictions to effective action—and to real life. There is a remarkable touchstone for this in Book V of Spenser's epic, the Book of Justice, in the trial of Mary Queen of Scots, who is represented here as the beautiful and treacherous Duessa. After a prosecution by Zeal seconded by Artegall, the Knight of Justice, Duessa is declared guilty by the court, and Elizabeth, called here Mercilla, is appealed to for judgment. This is Spenser's account of what happened:

> But she, whose Princely breast was touched nere
> With piteous ruth of her so wretched plight,
> Though plaine she saw by all, that she did heare,
> That she of death was guiltie found by right,
> Yet would not let iust vengeance on her light;
> But rather let in stead thereof to fall
> Few perling drops from her faire lampes of light;
> The which she couering with her purple pall
> Would haue the passion hid, and vp arose withall. (V.9.50)

Allegorized as Mercilla, what else can Elizabeth do? Four stanzas into the next canto, after lavish praise of the queen's incomparable mercy, Spenser does face up to the facts: Mary was, after all, executed—though even here he cannot quite bring himself to say so. The death is referred to as Duessa's "willful fall," thereby effectively exonerating Elizabeth from making the decision. This was a clear mirror not of events but of the queen's mind. Elizabeth had devised a similar fiction for her own conscience, by signing Mary's death warrant but declining to send it. It was sent by her Privy Councillors—on her tacit instructions, of course, though being tacit they also had what in modern parlance is called deniability, and her advisers thereby bore the direct responsibility for Mary's execution. A less shrewd poet would have undertaken to justify Elizabeth's actions, and would have offended her as deeply as Spenser's account of Duessa's fall offended King James, who on the publication of *The Faerie Queene* demanded that Elizabeth arrest the poet and punish him for the insult this episode clearly offered to James's mother. (Elizabeth instead granted Spenser a pension.) As for the poet's own attitudes here, they remain utterly obscure: the poem is an expression not of the poet's mind, but of his patron's.[3] The moment, however, is a dangerous one—this is not merely flattery, and Spenser is not playing it safe. Obviously the queen cannot be criticized in an epic celebrating her greatness, especially in a section of the poem devoted to the theme of Justice; but why does Spenser want to include such an ambiguous episode at all? This is not an isolated example. In the latter books of *The Faerie Queene* Spenser repeatedly confronts the realities of his society with his poetic mythology and keeps making the same point: it doesn't work.

Figure 6.8. George Gascoigne, Self-Portrait before Queen Elizabeth, 1575.
ROY.18.A.xlviii. By permission of the British Library.

The choice of this particular myth, and its extraordinary elaboration under Elizabeth, are not difficult to understand. The idea that knighthood consists of service to a lady is surely the most disarming of fictions, and we find it asserted again and again in the official iconography of the age. Figure 6.8, for example, shows the soldier-poet George Gascoigne offering his works to the queen. His motto declares him "Tam Marti quam Mercurio," devoted as much to Mars as to Mercury (patron of the arts of language), but the image represents him as a suitor offering a love token. And in figure 6.9, even more strikingly disarmed, is the Queen's Champion George Clifford, Earl of Cumberland, soldier and privateer. He is dressed for a tilt as the Arthurian Knight of Pendragon Castle, but his shield, helmet, and gauntlets are laid aside, he wears a richly decorated coat and skirt, and he carries in his hat his lady's favor, Elizabeth's jeweled glove.

Spenser himself testifies to the ineffectiveness of this disarming mythology, even as an image of order, even within the courtly circle mirrored in the sixth book of *The Faerie Queene* with its quintessentially courtly hero Calidore, the Knight of Courtesy, or in that more personal and profoundly ambivalent image of the court, *Colin Clouts Come Home Againe*. Needless to say, it expressed even less the realities of Elizabethan society. And for Elizabeth's successor James I, chivalry was a positively dangerous myth. The king's favored

Figure 6.9. Nicholas Hilliard, George Clifford, Third Earl of Cumberland.
© National Maritime Museum, London.

personae were instead biblical or classical: Solomon, Aeneas, Neptune. When his son undertook to revive the chivalric mythology in the interest of his own military ambitions, he was firmly put down—disarmed—as much because he had got the point of the myth wrong as because, in the king's terms, it was the wrong myth.

Perhaps the richest example the English Renaissance affords of the social dimension of ceremonial fictions is provided by the Elizabethan theater. Expressions of communal fantasies, stage plays are consistently described, from the opening of the first public playhouse in 1576 till the closing of all the theaters in 1642, in violently antithetical terms. Educative and subversive, moral and licentious, theaters are seen—sometimes simultaneously—as a way for princes to maintain order and a continual threat to the stability of the commonwealth.

The ambiguities of chivalry, too, are insistently present. On Shakespeare's stage, we find it throughout the Lancastrian tetralogy, for example, epitomized most clearly, perhaps, in the character of Hotspur; or in the account of the Field of the Cloth of Gold that opens *Henry VIII*, which provides an enormously admiring description of the festivities, but then concludes that they weren't worth the expense; or in Hamlet's yearning for a time when kings settled their differences heroically, in single combat, and honored their compacts; or in the fairy-tale first scene of *King Lear*, with its lucid vision of the darkest sides of hyperbolic rhetoric and feudal relationships; or in the subversive career of the ill-made knight Bertram, the anti-hero of *All's Well that Ends Well*; or in that most profoundly anti-chivalric drama of love and war, *Troilus and Cressida*.

If the mythology is evident, the realities of courtly spectacle are insistently present too, whether chivalric, classical, or simply opulent. The richness of the costumes surprised and impressed foreign visitors, and in 1599 an inquisitive Swiss traveler named Thomas Platter investigated and found that they were real court clothes, the slightly used suits and dresses of genuine aristocrats. At a theater like the Blackfriars, where one could, for a relatively high price, buy a seat on the stage, the distinction between spectacle and spectator would have all but disappeared. At court masques, those quintessential instances of Renaissance pageantry, the audience was as much on display as the performers, and contemporary accounts tend to dwell at greatest length on the spectators, not on the players or the drama. This was, of course, entirely appropriate, since the center of the spectacle was not the entertainment but the entertained, the monarch.

The interchangeability of spectacle and spectator does not end here. Upon his accession in 1603, one of King James's first acts was to bring all the theatrical companies under royal patronage. Shakespeare's company, the Lord Chamberlain's Men, became The King's Men, and thereby took a giant step up in social status. The actors, traditionally on the fringes of society, and still, in Puritan rhetoric at least, stigmatized as mountebanks vagabonds, even male whores, were suddenly Gentlemen, the King's Servants, technically members of the royal household, and entitled to wear the royal livery. Thus clothed, they were in fact part of the pageantry of Jacobean royal power, outward and visible signs of James's sense of his office. Shakespeare himself registers the same ambitions as his upwardly mobile audience by reviving his father's application for a coat of arms. To do this was not simply to move up into—or in this case back into—the gentry. It was to become a part of that same courtly mythology of romantic medievalism, whereby the mark of a gentleman was a heraldic shield. And—fortuitously no doubt, but the fact must have pleased the Shakespeares—the shield designed by the College of Heralds bore a recognizably chivalric symbol, a lance, the spear of the family name, but one that looks, in the extant drawing, more ceremonial than serviceable. The motto, which would have been devised by Shakespeare, not by the heralds, asserted his right to the honor he claimed in an appropriately antique French: *non sanz droict.*

The spectacle of the Elizabethan stage went deeper than displays of courtly magnificence. At the beginning of the reign, two aristocratic political playwrights, Thomas Sackville, Lord Buckhurst, later Earl of Dorset, and Thomas Norton, the famous parliamentarian, entertained the queen with a historical drama that spoke directly to her own situation, the neo-Senecan tragedy *Gorboduc.* This was an exemplum designed specifically for Elizabeth. The play recounts how, in his old age, an ancient British king divided his kingdom between his two sons, and thereby plunged the realm into civil war and anarchy. The resemblance to the plot of *King Lear* is not accidental: Gorboduc was Lear's grandson. What the play expressed through its historical example was the urgent necessity for a clearly defined and legitimate succession.

For Elizabeth in 1561, the example of Gorboduc would have been doubly powerful, Janus-faced, looking both forward and back. The queen's claim to the throne, like that of the half-sister she succeeded, was profoundly ambiguous. Both Henry's daughters were legally illegitimate, and their place in the line of succession derived exclusively from their designation in their father's will. Such a proceeding was dubiously valid to begin with; but in any case, their half-brother Edward's will designated his cousin Lady Jane Grey as his successor, and if Henry VIII's will was valid on the question of the royal succession, so must Edward VI's have been. The two sisters' path to the throne, therefore, offered the commonwealth, not for the first time, a dangerous precedent. Like Henry IV and Henry VII, Mary and Elizabeth succeeded to the throne only after the deposition, and ultimately the execution, of a reigning claimant whose pedigree was, unlike theirs, impeccable, Lady Jane Grey. When Mary died in 1558, Elizabeth succeeded without difficulty because she was popular and Protestant, and perhaps most important, because there were no longer any other serious claimants; but she still embodied enough dangerous potential for Sackville and Norton to see in her accession the material for a classical tragedy. In her presence at the performance, the essential meaning of the play was made manifest, and the other spectators must have made the connection.

Like the monarch at a court masque, Elizabeth was not merely an audience for this spectacle, but the crucial element in it; and *Gorboduc* may be taken as a prototypical instance of royal theater. During the course of Elizabeth's reign, the association between the crown and the stage developed into a complex symbiosis. At Oxford in 1565, the scholars of Christchurch made the queen the visible center of their drama by placing her on the stage for the production of Plautus' *Aulularia* they had devised to entertain her. Twenty-five years later, at the climax of George Peele's *Arraignment of Paris*, she received from the Trojan prince the golden apple that mythology had intended for Venus. The conceit had already been used of her in a painting, dated 1569, perhaps by Hans Eworth (figure 6.10). By 1590 she had a drama that was truly her own.

The relationships I have been describing sound fairly cosy, but in fact they are distinctly uneasy and involve a good deal of tension. Theatrical pageantry, the miming of greatness, is highly charged because it employs precisely the same methods the crown was using to assert and validate its own authority. To mime the monarch was a potentially revolutionary act—as both the aging Elizabeth and the rebellious Earl of Essex were well aware.

Figure 6.10. Attributed to Hans Eworth: Queen Elizabeth and Three Goddesses, 1569. Hampton Court. The Royal Collection © 2001, Her Majesty Queen Elizabeth II.

In February, 1601, Essex undertook his final, desperate adventure, to lead an uprising and seize the throne. In order to marshal public opinion in his favor, he commissioned Shakespeare's company to revive the old tragedy of *Richard II*, a play about the overthrow of a vain, weak, and histrionic monarch. On the day after the performance he marched with his men through the streets of London, but the popular support never materialized, and he was arrested, tried, and executed in short order.

In August of the same year, Elizabeth had an interview with her archivist William Lambarde, who presented her with a summary of the royal documents he had catalogued. She paused at length over the reign of Richard II, and when Lambarde expressed his surprise, she explained, "I am Richard II, know ye not that?" Lambarde acknowledged that he understood this to be an allusion to the drama of the late Earl of Essex, and the queen continued, "He that will forget God will also forget his benefactors; this tragedy was played forty times in open streets and houses."[4]

The point here is not merely that Elizabeth understood how Essex was attempting to use the play, but that she and Essex shared the same assumptions about it. In her moving and baffling expostulation to Lambarde, she transformed the drama of *Richard II* into a piece of very dangerous civic pageantry, an allegory of her own reign performed, as she put it, "forty times in open streets and houses." Forty times is doubtless an accurate enough assessment of the old play's popularity (it uses forty in the biblical sense, meaning simply many), and the houses would include playhouses as well as, metaphorically, Essex's palace in the Strand. But the "open streets" are the queen's invention, a fantasy whereby the whole city became a stage for a continual performance in which, in the person of her ancestor, she was mimed and deposed.

In 1599, Ben Jonson mimed the queen openly in *Every Man Out of His Humor*. The play presents a complex debate which only the queen's presence can resolve; and in the first performance, at court, the denouement constituted an elegant compliment to the royal spectator. But on the public stage, the queen's presence had to be counterfeited, and here, understandably, the theater was considered to have overstepped its bounds, making the monarch subject to the whim of the playwright, a prop for his drama. Jonson alone among dramatists would have presumed so far, using—like the Earl of Worcester in the Procession painting—the power of royalty to establish the authority of his fiction; but the case is exceptional only because Jonson's ego is involved. Other plays—for example Jonson's tragedy *Sejanus*, and *Eastward Ho*, of which Jonson was a part-author—were presumed to be miming, and thereby undermining, the royal authority, even though Jonson protested (from prison in the latter case) that this time he had no such intention. Examples like these place that famous fraud, Richard Venner's *England's Joy*, in a rather different light from the one in which we are accustomed to view it. *England's Joy* was a pageant play about Elizabeth, and it was to be performed (so the advertisements asserted) not by professional actors but "only by certain Gentlemen and Gentlewomen of account." The prospect of seeing the gentry on stage attracted a very large audience; but at the last moment Venner was found to have decamped with the receipts, and there was no play—and probably never had been one. Venner's genius lay in claiming to have created a theater that would at last present not impressions of courtly life, but the real thing. The conception actualizes one of the deepest corporate fantasies of the Elizabethan stage and its audience.

In fact, in the period the alliance between court and theater works both ways. King James wanted the theatrical companies under royal patronage because he believed in the efficacy of theater as an attribute of royal authority; and no doubt when the actors, poets, designers, and musicians provided court masques celebrating his wisdom and glory, the investment looked like a good one. But the theater is too anarchic to be so confined, and often enough the protection of the crown was interpreted by the actors to be protection *from* the crown. Take, for example, the strange case of the Children of the Revels producing plays satirizing the king, his favorites, and his new Scottish knights. One particularly offensive production not only had a go at the knights, but depicted James himself, according to the French ambassador, "ivre pour le moins une fois le jour"—drunk at least once a day. This play so enraged the king—not surprisingly—that he swore he would never have the company play before him again and would make them "beg their bread."[5] In fact, the players were back at court within the year: the incident reveals how little we really understand what must have been a very complicated and ambivalent relationship.

Why did the company produce such plays to begin with? They pitted the prejudices of the Blackfriars audience, or at least of some segment of it, against the wishes and authority of their own patron: how was this in their interest? Why did they not anticipate the king's displeasure, or if they did, why were they willing to risk it—what was in it for them? Where was the censor: why did the Lord Chamberlain allow such a production? And surely most baffling of all, why did the king cool down? Consider a few dates: the play depicting the king drunk was produced in March, 1608—the French ambassador's letter about the king's fury is dated March 25. The boys next played at court on January 1 and 4, 1609, the Christmas season of the same year. But their *last previous* appearance at court had been in the season of 1604/5: they were not a company that regularly played before the king. The invitation to perform at New Year's 1609 was therefore extraordinary, a mark of special favor. The troupe's insolence had greatly advanced their standing.

What are we to make of all this? James was used to being attacked and insulted to his face by ministers preaching in his chapel, but surely neither he nor the players could have believed that theatrical companies, like preachers, served a higher law. Ben Jonson, characteristically, regretted the fact. He told his friend William Drummond that "he hath a mind to be a churchman, and so he might have favor to make one sermon to the King, he careth not what thereafter should befall him, for he would not flatter though he saw Death."[6] Like the Children of the Revels Jonson dreamt of attacking with impunity; and the target of the attack in both cases is not the playhouse audience but the king. The relationship between the Renaissance stage and the crown was a complex mixture of intimacy and danger. Given this context, Queen Elizabeth's statement to William Lambarde sounds less like a paranoid fantasy.

Sir Henry Wotten's remarks on the first performance of Shakespeare's *Henry VIII*, that celebration of kingship all of which, as the contemporary subtitle assures us, is true, may be taken as paradigmatic. The play was, he wrote, "sufficient in truth within a while to make greatness very familiar, if not ridiculous."[7] For this spectator, to mime nobility on the stage was to diminish it. And yet Elizabeth and James could not remain aloof, for this was precisely how they saw themselves: both regularly employed the metaphor of the player-monarch. "We princes," Elizabeth told the Lords and Commons in 1586, "are set on stages, in the sight and view of all the world duly observed."[8] Surely the queen imagined the threatening tragedy of *Richard II* being performed not at the Globe but in the public streets because she herself repeatedly took to the public streets, in splendid pageantry, to assert and confirm her authority. King James avoided the streets, but he fully concurred with Elizabeth's view of the royal situation. "A king," he told his son, "is as one set on a stage, whose smallest actions and gestures all the people gazingly do behold."[9] This is a central precept of the *Basilicon Doron*, James's treatise on kingship. "A king is as one set on a stage": a king is like an actor. But the passage as I have cited it comes from a second edition of the treatise, published after James ascended the English throne. In the first edition, published in Edinburgh several years earlier, the sentence reads, "A king is as one set upon a *scaffold*. . . ." The king's emendation of the ambiguous word surely reveals something of the danger James must have felt to be inherent in the royal drama. It was a danger that, needless to say, was not merely linguistic; and it could not be eliminated through judicious emendation. As Charles I learned, a king *is* as one set upon a scaffold. Elizabeth was undoubtedly a better performer than either of her successors; but whether the pageant constituted celebration or satire lay ultimately not in the power of the actor or the intentions of the inventor, but in the eye and mind of the beholder.

7

THE RENAISSANCE POET AS PLAGIARIST

In 1638 Inigo Jones and Sir William Davenant produced two masques for the English court. The first, *Britannia Triumphans*, danced by the king in January, celebrated, a little prematurely, the triumph of the royal scheme of Ship Money: the famous trial was about to reach its conclusion, with a narrow victory in the Star Chamber for the crown. Three weeks later, at Shrovetide, the queen danced in *Luminalia*, Jones's most elaborate scenic spectacle up to that time. The complexity of the engineering was the more impressive, Jones tells us, because it had to be devised very quickly:

> The King's majesty's masque being performed, the Queen commanded Inigo Jones . . . to make a new subject of a masque for herself, that with high and hearty invention might give occasion for variety of scenes, strange apparitions, songs, music, and dancing. . . . This being suddenly done and showed her majesty, and she approving it, the work was set in hand, and in all celerity performed in shorter time than anything here hath been done in this kind.[1]

Modern scholarly opinion has been very hard on *Luminalia*, and Enid Welsford believed that she had found the explanation for its poetic and dramatic deficiencies: "in no other masque," she writes, "is the plagiarism so blatant and so extensive. *Luminalia* is in fact nothing else but a clumsy adaptation of Francesco Cini's Notte d'Amore.[2]

Clumsiness is not, however, the only problem faced by the modern critic of *Luminalia*, because Jones's account of its sudden inception and hasty preparation, if we take it at face value, cannot be true. On November 9, and again on December 16, a courtier named George Garrard wrote from Whitehall that the queen was preparing a Shrovetide masque: the project had, therefore, been under discussion for many months. G. E. Bentley believes that this contradition, like the production's structural flaws, can be explained by invoking the concept of plagiarism:

> No doubt Jones was in a great fret, first getting his masquing hall finished, then cleaning it all away before he could set his men to work on the elaborate constructions for *Luminalia*, but he did not need to wait all this time to begin on the designs. . . . Perhaps his uneasiness about the plagiarism led him to magnify and advertise the pressure of time.[3]

Bentley's explanation seems to run this way: Jones was sufficiently uncomfortable about the plagiarism to want to cover himself by pleading extenuating circumstances; and he did so by inventing a lie which everybody who had been at court since November would have known to be a lie. This strikes me as very implausible. We have no way of determining what really happened, but with the same evidence I can devise a more credible hypothesis. All that Garrard's letters tell us is that the queen was planning a masque. He says nothing about what kind of masque it was, how elaborate the spectacle was to be, and how complex the engineering. But the king's masque in January, *Britannia Triumphans*, was an exceedingly elaborate spectacle, with wonderful visions of hell, the Palace of Fame, a sea-triumph of Galatea, the fleet in full sail. And Jones tells us that after the queen saw this masque, she commanded him "to make a new subject of a masque for herself, that with high and hearty invention might give occasion for variety of scenes, strange apparitions," and so forth. This account suggests to me that the queen wanted just what Jones says she wanted: "a new subject of a masque"—not the masque they had been planning, but a new and more elaborate one.

In this hypothesis, it will be seen that the question of plagiarism has become a red herring. And indeed, what Enid Welsford discovered about *Luminalia* is more usually referred to as finding a source than as uncovering plagiarism—there are few Stuart masques that are not similarly based on some earlier example of the genre. But without quibbling over definitions, we could probably all agree that if *Luminalia* constitutes plagiarism, so does Shakespeare's use of old plays like *Hamlet* and *Promos and Cassandra*, old tales like *Romeus and Juliet* and *Apolonius and Silla*, and new novels like *Rosalynde* and *Pandosto*. I doubt that Enid Welsford and G. E. Bentley found such examples as these reprehensible; and it is fair therefore to speculate about whether the charge of plagiarism here may not be doing service for something else—for those other qualities of Inigo Jones's (preferring spectacle to poetry, disliking Ben Jonson enough to get him fired) that displease the modern critic, but somehow seem not to be sufficiently actionable.

And now, having dismissed the charge, I wish to return to it; because in fact by any standard we may apply, Inigo Jones was a thoroughgoing—one might almost say blatant—plagiarist. Welsford and Bentley simply had the wrong example. There is scarcely a single stage design by Jones that is not copied. Most of the costume drawings come directly from costume books; the most inventive antic figures turn out to be cribbed straight from Callot; pastoral settings reproduce engravings by Antonio Tempesta; almost every Roman figure derives from a single handbook of classical antiquities by Panvinio; buildings are copied from architectural treatises: there is hardly a drawing in the collection that one could call genuinely original. I want to pause over a particularly curious example.

In 1633 Queen Henrietta Maria and her ladies appeared in a pastoral marathon called *The Shepherd's Paradise.* It was designed to take eight hours (in the event, it was presented in a cut version), and dealt exhaustively with the subject of Platonic love. Jones designed appropriate costumes for his noble shepherdesses, one of which is copied directly from a portrait (now at Knole[4]) of a lady in Spanish court dress, almost certainly the Infanta Maria, to whom Charles had been engaged in 1623. She wears a high ruff, an elaborate feathered headdress, a cape with wide, stiffened shoulders, a long v-shaped bodice surmounted by a heavy chain and pendant, and a skirt with a wide striped hem around the bottom and up the front. In her right hand she carries a fan; her left hand rests on a wooden balustrade. Behind her a heavy drapery is drawn aside to reveal a distant landscape. Jones did three versions of this figure. In the first, his copy is exact, including even the balustrade and drapery. These have disappeared in the second, and the lady has turned her head to the right. In the third, the fan has been removed. But in all three the costume is an exact copy of that in the portrait, down even to details of embroidery and jewels.

This portrait of Charles's fiancée must have arrived in England during the negotiations for the Spanish match in the early 1620s. It was presumably in the royal collection, and by 1633 would have been hanging there for about ten years (the engagement was broken off in 1624). What did Jones think he was doing? It is difficult to believe that he did not mean something by alluding to the painting, because the Infanta's dress is so obviously, even to a modern eye, out of fashion. All the other female costumes in the play show the high waists, decolletage, and sloping shoulders characteristic of the early 1630s; this costume alone is a dozen years behind the times. Now, masques of the period are full of arcane visual symbolism that only the contrivers and a few members of an intellectual elite could interpret: was this such an allusion? Did anyone recognize the costume and relate it to the portrait that had been hanging in Whitehall Palace for a decade? Did Charles himself recognize in the character

of Fidamira the figure of his former future wife? One can imagine this as a
very witty touch, a Caroline in-group joke; and indeed, there *is* a Spanish
princess in the play. But this is not her costume, and the function of the plagiarism is utterly obscure. We have no way of determining whether it was
designed for some dramatic effect to which we can no longer respond, or was
simply a very puzzling aspect of Jones's invention.

I have chosen this example because, like most instances of plagiarism in
the period, it is utterly ambiguous. But the difficulties it presents are only ones
of interpretation. Judging from Jones's practice in other stage designs, the
problem is not why Jones plagiarized, but why he copied this particular painting. For this Renaissance artist, invention was deeply involved with copying.
To a critic who charges Jones therefore with lack of originality, we might
begin by answering simply that it is in the nature of art to be imitative. The
concept of invention in the Renaissance retained its etymological meaning of
finding the subject, the theme. One cannot find something that is not there to
begin with. To be sure, the notion of artistic invention has generally been
more broadly defined than Jones appears to be doing here, and Jones's practice may legitimately raise certain questions about the validity, function,
philosophic implications of imitation and its relation to the larger issue of
representation; but such questions will also be profoundly time-bound. Different ages give very different answers to the basic question of what, exactly, it
is that art imitates: for example, nature, or other art, or the action of the mind.
Modern critics grow uncomfortable when it proves to be imitating other art
too closely, but clearly Jones has no such compunctions.

We know that for the Renaissance artist, the entire creative career was often
conceived to be imitative, the adoption of the role of an exemplar, usually
classic. Thus poets were regularly urged to begin by writing pastorals because
that is where Virgil began; and the assumption followed that any poet's
mature poem would be an epic, on the model of the *Aeneid*. We might want
to argue that there is a vast difference between adopting the role of a classic
poet and copying his words, but is there? The adoption of roles by Renaissance poets involved a good deal of direct imitation and allusion. Renaissance
Latin poetry in particular often seems merely a mosaic of classical frag-
ments—though "merely," of course, expresses only a modern prejudice in
favor of originality. Whether a critic describes this sort of thing as conser-
vatism or plagiarism depends on attitudes that have little to do with the facts.
Sir Thomas Browne, in a passage I shall return to, attacks Virgil himself for
plagiarizing Homer (the opprobrious term is Browne's). If, therefore, G. E.
Bentley had wanted to go on to attack Shakespeare for plagiarizing *Hamlet*,
Twelfth Night, The Winter's Tale, he would have been in good company—but
so, by the same token, would Shakespeare. The age, however, affords far more

blatant instances than any I have yet cited: Shakespeare's use of North's Plutarch, Jonson's of Sallust, Tacitus, and Athenaeus. In examples like these, we are surely concerned with more than the relation between the artist and his creativity, the sources of his invention, because works of art are not autonomous creations: they have patrons, audiences, readers, connoisseurs, owners; and if in plagiarizing the artist is cheating or lying, he is doing it *to them.*

So, to stay for the moment with simple cases, how would a Renaissance audience have responded to blatant plagiarism? Sometimes, obviously, simply as an allusion: a great deal of Renaissance art offered its patrons precisely the pleasures of recognition. Take, for example, the case of the contemporary spectator at *Volpone* recognizing in the song "Come my Celia" the most famous seduction poem in literature: did he condemn Jonson for plagiarizing Catullus? or did he, on the contrary, admire a particularly witty adaptation of the art of the past to the designs of the present? Even when there was no such directly allusive intent, familiarity in works of art was surely felt to be an advantage. To redo a popular old play was a good formula for success; and as examples from *Don Giovanni* and *The Marriage of Figaro* to *My Fair Lady, The Kiss of the Spider Woman, The Phantom of the Opera, Sunset Boulevard, The Producers* (and so on ad infinitum) demonstrate, it continued and continues to be so. Analogously, in the unlikely event that any members of the Whitehall audience at Shrovetide, 1638, recognized Francesco Cini lurking behind *Luminalia*, the fact doubtless only added to their pleasure.

Let us turn now to a more complex case. In 1933 D. C. Allen discovered a particularly flagrant example of plagiarism in that classic of Elizabethan criticism, Francis Meres' *Palladis Tamia.*[5] By some exhaustive scholarly detective work, Allen was able to show that the book was a pure pastiche, and that its material derived, moreover, not even from classic or obscure sources, but for the most part from absolutely standard Renaissance compilations of the sort that were used as school texts. This discovery convinced Allen of the meretricious worthlessness of the book, and became the basis of an attack not only on the ignorance of modern critics, who have taken Meres seriously, but also on the whole Renaissance educational system, which, grounded as it was exclusively in the practice of imitation, fitted a student like Meres precisely for nothing better than plagiarism.

The facts in the case are incontrovertible, and the line of argument sounds to a modern reader plausible. But what about the Renaissance reader: what did he see in *Palladis Tamia?* If Meres' material was cribbed from standard schoolbooks, were contemporary readers not aware that they had heard it all before? Why was the book popular? It went through three editions, the last as late as 1636. Were Renaissance readers simply being deceived? Or did they find in the book precisely the force of the *commonplace*, a term that suggests to us a thing not worth saying, but implied to the Renaissance a universal truth? The volume's full title is *Palladis Tamia, or Wit's Treasury*: did anyone buying a book called *Wit's Treasury* think he was paying for originality?

Modern critics are usually willing to allow Renaissance authors their sources provided they are sufficiently classical and seem to demonstrate some real learning on the borrower's part. If *Luminalia* had been based on Ovid, rather than on Francesco Cini, Enid Welsford and G. E. Bentley probably would not have felt they had a case. Even with classical borrowings, however, the idea of intermediate sources bothers us intensely. Allen attacks *Palladis Tamia* less because it is a pastiche of classical passages than because Meres did not go to original texts. He used contemporary handbooks and anthologies, and Allen therefore believed that his intent was to deceive the reader into thinking he was a scholar. E. W. Talbert used the same line of argument to level a grave charge against Ben Jonson. Talbert discovered that Jonson's citations are often copied from Renaissance dictionaries and encyclopedias; Jonson's learning, Talbert felt, was thereby impugned. On this basis he went on to accuse the poet of lying when he claims, in the dedicatory epistle to *The Masque of Queens*, that he wrote the work "out of the fullness and memory of my former readings."[6] But every age has its reference books, and a more scrupulous generation than ours may criticize us for failing to acknowledge our use of bibliographies, periodical indexes, and Internet search engines, as if we were thereby pretending to carry all the relevant scholarship in our heads.

Clearly different ages have very different notions of what constitutes a valid source for the artist. Behind Talbert's attitude lies a long critical history of discomfort with Jonsonian borrowing. In Jonson's own time, it was made the point of an attack by none other than the archplagiarist himself, Inigo Jones:

> I wonder howe you ever durst invay
> In Satire, Epigram, or Libell-play,
> against the manners of the tyme, or men
> in full examples of all mischiefes, when
> No ill thou couldst so taske dwells not in thee,
> and there the store house of your plottes wee see.
> . . . with like forme thou hast writt
> of good and badd things, not with equal witt.
> The reason is, or may be quickly showne,
> the good's translation, butt the ill's thyne owne.[7]

There is one real master-stroke of invective here, weighing the poet's egotism against his sense of tradition. The force of the attack is directed at what is original in Jonson: he writes best about vice because he is writing about himself. But both "translation" and what is "thyne owne" are virtues. Jonson is not being criticized for his borrowing—quite the contrary. Modern readers will doubtless wish to take "the good's translation" ironically, but it is not so intended—the architect concludes with a couplet that is quite unequivocal about the quality of his adversary's verse:

> From henceforth this repute dwell with thee then,
> The best of poettes, but the worst of men.

Even to Jones's jaundiced eye, neither plagiarism nor egotism made Jonson anything less than the best of poets.

By the time Dryden was writing *Of Dramatic Poesy*, however, Jonson's borrowings required a defense. Dryden refers to Jonson as a "learned plagiary," and says that if Horace, Lucan and the rest "had their own from him, there are few serious thoughts which are new in him." Dryden does finally rise to Jonson's defense, but the task requires some (admittedly magnificent) sleight of hand: "He has done his robberies so openly that one may see he fears not to be taxed by any law. He invades authors like a monarch, and what would be theft in other poets is only victory in him."[8]

This was written only forty-five years atter Jones's praise of Jonsonian "translation," and thirty years after Jonson's death. In that short time translation, imitation, borrowing, have become "learned plagiary," "robbery," "theft," and the admirer of Jonson had to come to terms with them as best he could. Other critics were less indulgent than Dryden, as his friend John Oldham, ten years later, testifies in his ode on Jonson:

> Beshrew those envious tongues who seek to blast thy bays,
> Who spots in thy bright fame would find, or raise,
> And say it only shines with borrowed rays. . . .[9]

Oldham is referring to critics like Aphra Behn, who invidiously compares the scholarly Jonson with the uneducated Shakespeare, and then goes on to impugn not only Jonson's aesthetic morals but his learning as well:

> Benjamin was no such rabbi neither, for I am informed his learning was but grammar high (sufficient indeed to rob poor Sallust of his best orations). . . .[10]

It is not clear here whether Behn means to imply that a genuine scholar would not have plagiarized, or that if Jonson had been a true scholar, the plagiarism would not have been a fault (which is the line Dryden takes); but in any case, her example is a very odd one. The Sallust orations appear in Jonson's tragedy *Catiline*. They are Catiline's speeches, and Jonson includes them for historical reasons, because according to the best authority, Sallust, they are what Catiline actually said. To accuse Jonson of plagiarizing from Sallust makes about as much sense as accusing Sallust of plagiarizing from Catiline. To be sure, most of Jonson's "translations" are not amenable to this line of defense, but in this particular instance he is in the clear, and it is apparent that for Behn, as two and a half centuries later for Enid Welsford and G. E. Bentley, plagiarism covered a multitude of sins.

Shakespeare provided a happy, if self-serving, contrast with Jonson for Behn's purposes. She argues that since the uneducated Shakespeare wrote better plays than the learned Jonson, and since the only intellectual advantage men have over women derives from their education, there is no reason why women cannot be as good playwrights as Shakespeare. Of course Behn was unaware of Shakespeare's own borrowings. These first began to come to critical attention only in 1691, with Gerard Langbaine's *Account of the English Dramatick Poets*. Langbaine's interests were primarily antiquarian; he noted the sources for a number of Shakespearean plots. It was Pope who first uncovered the myriad classical borrowings, which for him redounded to Shakespeare's credit by proving that he was educated after all. "The speeches copy'd from Plutarch in *Coriolanus*" are, says Pope, "an instance of his learning."[11] When Johnson pointed out that the speeches in question were not copied from Plutarch at all, but derive (almost verbatim) from North's translation, the argument simply got turned on its head.[12] Richard Farmer's *Essay on the Learning of Shakespeare* (1767) prints Volumnia's speech "Should we be silent and not speak . . ." (V.3.94) beside its source in North, and observes that "our author hath done little more than throw the very words of North into blank verse." This turns out to be all to the good: Farmer duly credits Shakespeare with "the felicity of freedom from the bondage of classical superstition," and says the playwright owed this freedom "to the want of what is called the advantage of a learned education."[13] The need to plagiarize thus becomes, by a piece of remarkable logic, an index to Shakespeare's originality.

The question of the morality of literary imitation, then, starts to appear significantly in England only after the Renaissance, and on the whole in reaction to it. There are a few counter-examples that I shall return to, and we are still very far from the moment when a writer's originality was the measure of his value; but though Jonson's borrowings were in his own time well known, none of his contemporaries—not even those who found him pedantic, egotistical, or (in his last years) inept—ever attacked him for plagiarism. He himself, in the *Discoveries*, recommended the practice as a prerequisite for the poet, not as an educational device, but as a prime source of invention: "to be able to convert the substance or riches of another poet to his own use"; to grow so like his model "as the copy may be mistaken for the principal."[14] In this recommendation Jonson was emphatically following his own precept, because the passage is translated verbatim from a treatise by Joannes Buchler on the reformation of poetry published in 1633. Of course Jonson goes on at once to condemn servile imitation (now copying his precept from Horace), but it is clear that the creation of poetry in his mind is essentially a closed system, involving not merely copies, but copies of copies. "Observe," he says, "how the best writers have imitated, and follow them."[15] One wonders whether he would even have understood a criticism like Dryden's, that there was scarcely a new idea in his work. That quality he might well have regarded as one of his virtues.

2

The visual arts imitate much more directly than poetry does. Poems are statements; they have, in themselves, structure and meaning; but a picture, unless it is entirely abstract, has no such autonomy: an image is an image *of* something. And indeed, we should declare the analogy between poetry and painting far-fetched if it were not so insistently proclaimed throughout the period. Horace's phrase "*ut pictura poesis*" was misapplied with amazing consistency, and Simonides' ubiquitous dictum that poetry was a speaking picture became one of the standard definitions of the art. Both were said to imitate nature, but were in fact throughout the age primarily concerned with imitating models. Scaliger summed it up neatly by observing that we can best imitate nature by imitating Virgil.[16]

But even in the visual arts in this period we find a significant change in attitudes toward copying. Here is a very practical example: all the portraits by Robert Peake, Marcus Gheeraerts, and John de Critz, the "standard" early seventeenth-century English portraitists, are workshop productions. The master did the initial sketches and oversaw the progress of the painting, but to distinguish his hand from that of his assistants is impossible, and nobody at the time would have thought of trying to do so. If the portrait was of an important person, it was usually produced in multiple versions; and in such cases no distinction was made between the original and the copies—all versions would be equally "original," or equally "copies." It is not until the next generation of painters, with Mytens, van Dyck, and most of all Rubens, that we start to find commissions stipulating that a painting be entirely in the master's own hand, thus distinguishing the original from any copies. Rubens' studio had three price ranges, for paintings entirely by Rubens, for those done in the studio but touched up by the master, and for pure workshop productions. Thus the contract for the ceiling of the Roman church of San Carlo Borromeo in 1620 provided that the models be painted by Rubens, but that the actual ceiling panels be full-size copies by his pupils. In such cases a large part of the fee was due on delivery of the models; and in this particular instance Rubens' patrons got more than their money's worth, since the pupil who executed the final paintings was the young van Dyck. How new all this was to English patrons is illustrated by the negotiations between Rubens and Sir Dudley Carleton, the English ambassador to The Hague, over a hunt scene that Carleton had commissioned. When the painting was delivered Carleton complained that it looked as if it was not in Rubens' hand, but had only been retouched by him. Rubens replied admitting the charge, but pointed out that Carleton's commission had been unclear on precisely this point: "I am very sorry that there should have been any dissatisfaction . . . , but he never let me understand clearly, although I asked him to state whether this picture was to be a true and entire original or merely retouched by my hand"; and he explained that "if I had done the entire work with my own hand it would be well worth twice as much."[17] Carleton knew what he ought to want, but his inexperience in this sort of negotiation is evident. Rubens, as a gesture of good faith, agreed to redo the painting himself.

British connoisseurs were latecomers to the art markets, and the tastes that we see Carleton, Arundel, Buckingham, and Charles I acquiring in the early seventeenth century were already well established on the continent. The emphasis on originals, however, the exclusive passion for works in the master's own hand, was not, in fact, even as late as this, universal among collectors and patrons. The congregation of San Carlo Borromeo was satisfied with copies of Rubens' models on the ceiling; but Rubens himself worked on the huge panels for King Charles's Banqueting House. Though severely strapped for funds, the English king would settle for nothing that was not original.

In Erwin Panofsky's view, such an attitude was predominantly a northern phenomenon, related to "the specifically Germanic preference for the particular as against the universal, for the curious as against the exemplary, and for the personal as against the objective." There is clearly a certain amount of question-begging going on here, but whether or not we are prepared to accept Panofsky's explanation, the illustrative incident that accompanies the remark is, for our purposes, extraordinarily enlightening.

> In 1515 Raphael had sent him [Dürer] a stately sanguine drawing showing two splendidly posed and modeled nudes. Dürer first

noted on it the date of receipt, and after Raphael's death in 1520 he characteristically added the following *in memoriam*: "Raphael of Urbino, who was so highly esteemed by the Pope, has made these nudes and has sent them to Nuremberg, to Albrecht Dürer, in order to show him his hand." Now, modern critics have come to realize that this drawing was never made by Raphael himself. They have rightly ascribed it to a member of his workshop ... and have hence concluded that the inscription was a forgery. This conclusion, however, is erroneous. The inscription is unquestionably written by Dürer. He himself was mistaken, and this mistake shows more than anything the irreconcilability of his point of view with that of his Italian fellow painter. For Raphael it was a matter of course to present his German colleague with the best available specimen of a style for which he felt responsible, no matter whether the manual execution was his or a pupil's. Dürer, on the contrary, took it for granted that an Italian master, whom he respected and loved, could only have wanted to "show him his hand." [18]

What Dürer prized so highly—not the work of art, but the hand of the master—began to appeal to English collectors only in the seventeenth century. Carleton said he was especially disappointed to find that his hunt scene was not a true original because there was only one true original Rubens in England at the time. Holbein's English patrons would never have justified their commissions in this way. Henry VIII and his court admired Holbein because they believed that he drew the most accurate likenesses: they conceived themselves to be buying not emanations of the artist but aspects of themselves.

The emphasis on the originality of the visual artist, and the attendant feeling that the copy was less real, or less valid than the work in the master's own hand, reflects a significant change in the status of the visual arts. In 1563 the painters, sculptors, and architects of Florence petitioned to be allowed to form an *academy*, and to be exempted from membership in the craftsmen's guilds. The academy obtained full legal recognition in 1571, and painting, sculpture, and architecture in Florence became thereby not crafts but liberal arts, as (according to Pliny) painting had been in ancient Rome. The Florentine academy's first major public act was a magnificent memorial service for its most famous member, an account of which was published under the title *Obsequies of the Divine Michelangelo Buonarotti*—the adjective says it all. When Titian dropped his brush, the king of Spain stooped to pick it up for him. Rubens became Charles I's ambassador extraordinary, and was knighted, as, after him, was van Dyck. No English artist was treated in this way until Lely; in Charles I's time the artists' union was still the Painters' and Stainers' Guild, which had banded together in 1502, and was active primarily in attempting to prevent lucrative commissions from going to foreign workmen. Inigo Jones was a craftsman, trained, we are told, as a joiner, first referred to not as an artist or even as a painter, but as a "picture-maker." There is more than irony in the fact that his collaborator and adversary Ben Jonson's detractors were fond of reminding him that he had been apprenticed to a bricklayer. The arts in England were still very much crafts.

They were, however, useful and necessary crafts. Richard Haydocke's *Tracte Containing the Artes of Curious Paintinge, Carvinge, Buildinge* (1598) explains the benefits of displaying beautiful portraits of rulers by saying that they "will appear most evidently in things appertaining to *Civile discipline*. For it is strange to consider, what effects of piety, reverence and religion are stirred up in mens mindes by meanes of this sutable comelinesse of apte proportion."[19] Portraits were often claimed to be, quite literally, surrogate persons. The Bishop of Winchester, Thomas Bilson, said that the honor given to princes' portraits "is accepted as rendred to their owne persons when they can not otherwise be present in the place to receive it,"[20] and there were many attempts to harm Queen Elizabeth by attacking her picture. For example, one of the models for Nicholas Hilliard's Great Seal was discovered imbedded in poison, and this was at once understood to be an attempt on the queen's life.

Portraits are copies in the most obvious sense—though at this point the modern critic may wish to balk: have we not stopped comparing equals? Surely no one in his right mind would describe an artist copying the features of a sitter as plagiarizing the sitter's face. But portraitists do not merely reproduce their subjects' physiognomies. As Sir Ernst Gombrich has so often reminded us, the question of whether a painting is recognized to be a true representation or not has much more to do with how we want to see ourselves and what we want to model ourselves on than with how we actually look to others. In the period we are considering, the situation in the visual arts is in fact far more closely analogous to that in literature than we can easily perceive from where we stand. But if we recall Scaliger's precept that the best way to imitate nature is to imitate Virgil, the importance of models to all the arts in the Renaissance will be easier to bear in mind.

But what exactly do portraits imitate—aside, that is, from other portraits? The external appearance obviously; but, in Renaissance portraits, more particularly the public self—the badges of office or robes of state, the gown worn when participating in some extraordinary occasion: the official persona. Portraits in Bishop Bilson's formulation *represent* this persona as an ambassador represents a monarch or a lawyer a client; they retain the authority of their originals and exemplify it—in the case of portraits iconographically. Thus in the various versions of portraits of Queen Elizabeth that derive from the relatively small number of prototypes, we may see the queen's physiognomy growing less and less individualized, while her royal trappings—dress, jewelry, symbolic attributes—are correspondingly elaborated.

This public self, indeed, is the technical meaning of a *person*: not the individual physiognomy merely (and sometimes hardly that at all), but the position in society, the status, the role. As Thomas Hobbes observed, the concept of a *person* involves a theatrical metaphor:

> The word Person . . . in latine signifies the *disguise*, or *outward appearance* of a man, counterfeited on the Stage; and sometimes more particularly that part of it, which disguiseth the face, as a Mask or Vizard: And from the Stage, hath been translated to any Representer of speech and action, as well in Tribunalls, as Theaters. So that a *Person*, is the same that an *Actor* is, both on the Stage and in common conversation; and to *Personate*, is to Act, or *Represent* himselfe, or an other. . . .[21]

This, then, is what the portrait copied and thereby preserved: the person, or representation of the sitter; and there were legal limits on the kinds of copies one might cause to be made of oneself. For example, only gentlemen might display their effigies on their tombs. These showed and preserved their roles in the public world; whereas a commoner, explained *The Blazon of Gentrie* in 1586, is one "whose estate and life, the lawes have esteemed so base, that they deeme him not worthie of memoriall, but that his name shall end with his life, and no man shall see the steps of his way, no more then the furrowes of a Shippe, is discerned in the swallowing gulphes of the Ocean."[22] This is why God, and God alone, can afford to be no respecter of *persons*.

All of this helps to explain the tendency toward extreme formality in Renaissance portraits, the almost total absence of intimate or unofficial versions of the Renaissance self. Painters in England before Rubens and van Dyck were in demand chiefly as portraitists, and they were judged almost exclusively on their ability to produce what were described as precisely accurate copies of the external man. Thus Holbein is always praised for the absolute fidelity of his renderings, and even one hundred and fifty years later Lovelace eulogizes Lely in the same terms: "Thou dost the things orientally the same"—you paint things exactly as they are.[23] Modern aestheticians always tell us that the aim of painting has never been mere photographic realism; but in fact this has been the case only since the invention of photography. When Paul Delaroche, Delacroix's teacher and one of the most admired historical painters of his time, saw the first Daguerrotypes, he said "From today paint-ing is dead."[24] The photograph achieved perfectly the aim of painting as this very successful painter understood it. It is, of course, demonstrably untrue that photographs reproduce more accurate images than paintings do (we probably believe this because of the scientific claims of the photographic process), but in any case, for the history of art before Daguerre, there was nothing "mere" about optical realism. And despite the revolution in painting that is apparent to us in every work of Titian or Rembrandt, the critical ter-minology, as Lovelace's remark about Lely reveals, remained essentially unchanged.

All this leads to some basic and very old questions about the nature of artistic imitation, whether visual or literary. Greek and Roman painting does not look notably realistic to us, yet ancient writers are full of stories about artists who painted bowls of fruit so accurately that birds came to peck at them. The stories are obviously nonsense, but the point is that these are the terms critics chose with which to praise art. Plato's famous attack on painting in *The Republic,* indeed, is based on the assumption that art is imitation of a peculiarly mechanical kind: the craftsman imitates the ideal bed in the mind of God, the painter imitates the craftsman's imitation. *Ergo*, painting is a dou-ble lie. Of course, we might object that painters have not, on the whole, spent their time making paintings of beds, but of gods and goddesses, ideal land-scapes, and the like; but even these are always described as imitations (of the best elements in nature, for example), and the artist's virtue is still the depic-tion of something, whether real or imagined, that is perfectly 'lifelike'—a copy. For Aristotle, the mimesis of poetry is a lie, false logic, a paralogism; it imitates actions, but they are actions that never happened. Its lies, neverthe-less, are "like truth"—copies. Ben Jonson was being perfectly Aristotelian when he said that the poet writes not the truth but "things like the truth."[25] Writers of truth, imitators of real actions, were demoted by the Renaissance to the status of historians. Sidney tried to answer Plato's condemnation of poetic lying by claiming that the poet "nothing affirms, and therefore never lieth."[26] This is hardly a solution to the problem, since the basic questions are still why anyone *wants* to create imitations of actions in the first place, and what moral effects they have on their audiences. It is difficult to see how any amount of semantic juggling could get Plato and Sidney to come to terms on those issues. Aristotle argued more boldly, simply and cogently that people imitate because that is their nature; that there are perfectly good reasons for telling lies, and one of them is the creation of poetry.

Ironically, it is the idealist Plato's formulation that is object-oriented and bound by the things of this world (e.g., beds); but even he could not forgo art's ability to imitate the unrealized ideal. Sidney could have found Plato refuting himself in Book V of *The Republic.* Glaucon has objected to Socrates' commonwealth on the grounds that it is so perfect that it could never be put into practice, and Socrates replies, "Suppose a painter had drawn an ideally beautiful figure complete to the last touch, would you think any the worse of him if he could not show that a person as beautiful as that could exist?" "By Zeus, I would not," replies Glaucon, and the argument is over.[27] So the painter *does* create a pattern of the ideal, just as Socrates has delineated his ideal, unrealizable republic.

Still, running counter to this sort of easy assumption of the virtues of imitation, and especially counter to the Aristotelian claim that drama is both natural and beneficial (its effect, after all, is medicinal: it purges through pity and terror) is a very old conviction that imitation is bad for people. Plato contended that theater had evil enough effects on the audience, but infinitely worse ones on the actor: the practice of mimesis weakens his spirit and destroys his integrity. This notion does not stop with Plato. Actors in Rome were slaves, and even those who became rich and famous enough to purchase their freedom could not enjoy full citizenship—the profession itself was considered to be tainted with *infamia*, disgrace. The traditional association of actors with highwaymen and whores persisted long beyond the reach of Platonic philosophy.[28]

Common as this attitude has been, it should nevertheless give the theorist and historian pause, because it assumes that the characters in a drama are more real than the actors. We always say that an actor represents or impersonates a character. In fact, however, we might more reasonably argue that the actor is not representing the character at all: he is *representing* the playwright, exactly as Hobbes says a lawyer represents a client, or an ambassador a monarch. But we would never put it that way. Dramas have more autonomy than any other kind of art, and verbs like act, perform, appear express simultaneously both the real and the feigned, both the action and its imitation. It is this ambivalent autonomy that made dramatic imitation indispensable to the Renaissance monarch, and to the Puritan sensibility made it the only really dangerous form of art.

Imperceptibly but quickly the Idea that Plato had tried to locate only in God's mind moved into the mind of the artist, and to imitate it became a virtue, not a vice. The transition, as Panofsky has shown, was complete by Seneca's time.[29] For the ancient writers, imitation was a process of creation and re-creation; for the Renaissance it was a process of recovery and preservation as well. The structure of the world, temporal, physical, moral, depended on replicas: "Christ's cross and Adam's tree"; "The mind, that ocean where each kind / Does straight its own resemblance find." Light, for Ficino, "imitates God," "God and the sun are exemplar and image"—original and copy—and "the movements of the soul [are] the models of those of the body."[30] And most to the point, we know about the nature of the originals—God, the soul—only through the copies; these are our paths to truth. Analogously, then, the good life was found in the imitation of Christ; the palace of the most Catholic king, the Escurial, was a replica of Solomon's temple; and Europe contained dozens of replicas of the Holy Sepulchre. Now none of these replicas is what we would call an exact copy: the practice of imitation allowed for a good deal of invention. Nevertheless, it was their relation with the prototype that gave the replicas the special force that Bishop Bilson found, too, in portraits of rulers.

Painters were expected to follow their models more closely than architects, and, moreover, not only in portraits. Artists like Rubens, Bernini, Domenichino regularly went to iconographic handbooks for examples of allegorical figures like Wisdom, Truth, Self Control. Some variation in the figure was permissible, but it had to remain a recognizable version of the model. A Victorian painter would have felt perfectly free to invent his own iconography, as the allegorical paintings of Lord Leighton or William Etty frequently do. Such a procedure would have seemed incomprehensible to the Renaissance artist: he copied not from lack of invention, but because imitation gave meaning and historical validity to his work.

3

At what kinds of imitation, then, were charges of plagiarism leveled?[31] It is a rare charge, but not unknown. Sometimes it serves merely as an artful strategy, like Astrophil's claim that he is no pickpurse of another's wit, in a sonnet sequence so heavily and openly indebted to Petrarch. Here the point is that there is no other poet like Astrophil—not Sidney, not anyone in the community of literature. When the charge is intended seriously, it is generally directed against those harbingers of things to come, writers who so prize originality that they are willing to lie to conceal their lack of it. Thus Stefano Guazzo reprehends orators "so impudent that they have not been ashamed to affirme them selves to bee the Authours of some thinges as newe, which . . . neverthelesse are most stale, and founde written a thousande yeeres agoe in other mens workes." This occurs during a discussion of sincerity and plain dealing; the fault, despite some evident ambivalence in the passage, is not in the staleness of the matter, but chiefly in the lie—"for that they appropriate to themselves the honour that is due to others."[32] In far stronger terms Sir Thomas Browne arraigns almost the whole of classical antiquity for plagiarism: "the wittiest piece of Ovid is beholden unto Parthenius Chius; even the magnified Virgil hath borrowed, . . . his *Eclogues* from Theocritus, his *Georgics* from Hesiod and Aratus, his *Aeneids* from Homer, the second book whereof he hath verbatim [!] derived from Pisander," and so forth through Aristotle, who cribbed from Hippocrates without acknowledgment, and Pliny, who did the same to Dioscorides.[33] Here plagiarism exemplifies for Browne those two greatest of human failings, the age-old desire "to plume themselves with others' feathers" and, more especially, the pernicious adherence to authority. It is a vice, as Browne continually laments, that has always been with us: plagiarism is the Original Sin of literature.

Jonson too attacks plagiarists. He cites those writers in whom one "may find whole pages together usurp'd from one Author, their necessities compelling them to read for present use, which could not be in many books." Here the point is not so much the copying as the mental incapacity it reveals— the mind that is limited to a single source rather than to a multitude, that must read for immediate citation, that has no *copia* (supply, storehouse) on which to draw. But Jonson reserves his greatest scorn for those who do *not* plagiarize, but rely, like Swift's spider, exclusively on their own originality. He calls them "the obstinate contemners of all helpes, and Arts; such as presuming on their owne Naturals . . . dare deride all diligence."[34] And the whole argument is again, characteristically, wonderfully, cribbed almost verbatim from Quintilian.

What Jonson recorded in his *Discoveries* was the common property of the world of letters, and it testifies to an enviably easy intercourse between writer and writer, between scholarship and creativity. Jonson was proud of writing with his authorities open about him. The only difference between his use of Tacitus and Shakespeare's of North is that Jonson liked to boast about it. For such writers, the whole body of art provided the material from which their originality created new works of art; and so too for Rubens, van Dyck, Inigo Jones. This is the inexhaustatable *copia* from which the Renaissance artist produced, in the words of Shakespeare's first editors, the true original copies.

8

GENDERING THE CROWN

I AM CONCERNED HERE with the interpretation of Renaissance symbolic imagery in relation to certain issues of gender construction, particularly in the representation of royalty, but I begin with the question of interpretation itself. How do we know how to read a Renaissance image? In the simplest cases, we have Renaissance guides to interpretation, in the form of iconologies and handbooks of symbolism. But such cases immediately become less simple when we observe that reading imagery through them depends on reading texts, and therefore shares in all the interpretive ambiguity of that process: the reading of texts is a dialectical, and sometimes even an adversarial procedure. Interpretation depends, moreover, on what texts we select as relevant, and even on what we are willing to treat as a text.

I begin with the well-known emblem of the pelican (figure 8.1), which Renaissance iconologies declare to be *typus Christi*. Here, in Valeriano's *Hieroglyphica*, she resembles the phoenix, rising in flame from the top of the cross. Most often she is the model of *caritas*, selflessly nourishing her young with her heart's blood. Cesare Ripa's Bontà, Kindness (figure 8.2), holds the pelican feeding her offspring. The image is gendered, but the female is an attribute of the male: the maternal *Caritas* is a type of Christ.

Figure 8.1. The pelican as symbol of Christ,
from G. P. Valeriano Bolzani, *Hieroglyphica*, 1610.

Figure 8.2. *Bontà* (Kindness), from Cesare Ripa, *Iconologia*, 1611.

The image's applicability, however, is more profligate than this. The pelican topos is invoked by Laertes, vowing to avenge his father's death:

> To his good friends thus wide I'll ope my arms,
> And, like the kind life-rend'ring pelican,
> Repast them with my blood. (*Hamlet* 4.5.145–7)

The pelican's gift of life has become a metaphor for killing, and the image of maternal love and familial piety is also an image of vengeance. John of Gaunt, berating Richard II, says

> O, spare me not, my brother Edward's son; . . .
> That blood already, like the pelican,
> Hast thou tapped out and drunkenly caroused. (2.1.124–6)

The attention here has shifted from the altruistic mother pelican to her brood callously accepting her bounty. King Lear uses the topos for a similarly vitriolic indictment of his "pelican daughters" (3.4.77), who have taken the all he gave them. In these cases, even Laertes' family piety is gone; the pelican is a type not of the *caritas* typified in the relation of parent and child, but of its precise opposite, filial ingratitude—reading is an adversarial procedure. The contradiction, however, is both eminently logical and a function of interpretation, and all these readings remain strictly within the terms set by the emblem itself: if the mother pelican is a type of the endlessly self-sacrificing

Christ, the next generation of pelicans are, it follows, a race of cannibals—the only way to have the topos is to have it both ways. The *caritas* emblem in *Lear* is therefore of a piece with the play's invocation of "the barbarous Scythian, / And he that makes his generation messes."

There is to my knowledge no Renaissance handbook in which the pelican is revealed as a type of inhumanity, but this is obviously no impediment to its interpretation as such: the Shakespearean examples are not at all unusual, and the interpretive technique in which anything can also be its opposite (as well as any number of other things) is so common as to constitute a critical topos in the age. Thus the story of Apollo and Daphne was for Bernini about lust, and the laurel tree meant that if we give in to our passion, we will end with only bitter leaves and berries;[1] but for George Sandys the fable was about chastity, and the laurel tree meant that if we adhere to our virtue we will be preserved.[2] The Pygmalion story told Arthur Golding that the man who reserves his love exclusively for virtuous women will be rewarded with an ideal wife,[3] but it told Sandys that there is no woman so chaste that she cannot be brought to yield by sufficient entreaty,[4] and it told William Caxton something entirely different from either: that a servant may, with sufficient effort on the part of her master, be turned into a lady.[5] Even within individual handbooks, the breadth of interpretive possibility often seems both endless and, for modern readers looking for a key to Renaissance symbolism, distressingly arbitrary. Renaissance iconographies and mythographies are in this respect the most postmodern of texts, in which no meaning is conceived to be inherent, all signification is constructed or applied; the fluidity and ambivalence of the image are of the essence.

With the polysemous pelican in mind, let us now turn to an image that looks to modern eyes particularly disconcerting. Figure 8.3 is a transvestite portrait of François I done by the Fontainbleau artist Nicolo Bellin da Modena around 1545. The poem appended to it explains that though the king is a Mars in war, in peace he is a Minerva or Diana—as with the pelican, the feminine has become an attribute of masculinity. To attempt to account for this extraordinary image by claiming that it cannot mean what it appears to mean is, in a sense, to miss the point; the poem is there precisely to redirect the obvious response: therein lies its wit—it is genuinely outrageous. It descends from those moralizations of the story of Hercules and Omphale that invert the charge of effeminacy, and praise the transvestite hero for embodying the virtues of women as well as of men. The topos, in a less extreme form, also served to celebrate François' son Henri II, this time as a specifically military hero (figure 8.4).[6] The imagery by this time has been almost naturalized, and the wit particularly has disappeared. Just as the maternal pelican was an ema-

Figure 8.3. Transvestite portrait of François I, engraving by P. Chenu after Niccolò Bellin da Modena, c. 1545. Bibliothèque Nationale de France.

Figure 8.4. Medal of Henri II. © The British Museum.

nation of Christ the king, so this image says that gender is subordinate to the purposes of royalty. Analogously, the English government was shortly to declare that for legal purposes, Queen Mary Tudor was a man.

The imagery of transvestism is positive, even heroic here. It has quite different implications, however, when applied to François' grandson Henri III.[7] In figure 8.5, the effeminate king is a monstrous harpy; the breasts, says the accompanying commentary, indicate how profoundly he has violated nature—to be a moral hermaphrodite is now no longer a virtue. He holds in his right hand a case that is half reliquary, half looking glass, containing a portrait of the perfidious Machiavelli—effeminacy has become an aspect of unprincipled politics. In figure 8.6, another satiric attack on the king, the noble effeminacy of his father and grandfather is inverted: the royal hermaphrodite is elaborately coiffed, beardless, with a suggestion of breasts, and

Figure 8.5. Anon., Henri III as a harpy. Bibliothèque Nationale de France, Cabinet des Estampes.

Figure 8.6. Henri III as hermaphrodite. Frontispiece to Thomas Artus, Sieur d'Embry, *Les Hermaphrodites* (Paris, 1605).

without a codpiece: beneath his clothes, says this image, the king is really a woman. The accompanying verse says "I am neither male nor female; why should I choose? I enjoy the pleasures of both." The figure in the poem has it both ways, but in fact, in the image, the unstable gender has been stabilized: the king's effeminacy is not a heroic role, but a revelation of his true nature.

Attacks on Henri and his *mignons*, including accusations of sodomy, were part of the repertory of political satire throughout his reign, and even after, providing cautionary emblems of the moral obligations of kingship. The attacks come from conservative Catholic sources, and have to do with Henri's accommodations with the Huguenots—sodomy here is a code word for Protestantism. Representing the effeminate king as a woman in drag, however, was unquestionably less inflammatory than representing him as a womanish man would have been, on the model of his heroic father and grandfather— the iconography of his dangerously subversive sexuality is precisely what is being avoided. The imagery was, nevertheless, no doubt understood: in figure 8.7, a Spanish emblem of 1610, it is inverted once more. The commentary says that this is is a bearded lady, not a transvestite man, but it is offered as a warning against male effeminacy; the accompanying poem presents the "afeminado" as a monster, combining the polymorphism of the verses on Henri the transvestite with the moral outrage of the commentary on Henri the harpy.[8]

Perhaps we can bridge the gap between the image that cannot mean what it says and the image that cannot say what it means with a mythological drawing by Giulio Romano (figure 8.8). Art historians have identified the subject as Apollo, his viol discarded, making love to a youth, Hyacinthus or Cyparissus, as a woman observes the scene.[9] Commentators call the woman a voyeur, and note that such a figure is commonly found in Giulio's licentious images, but this ignores the woman's curious gesture. If the god is really Apollo, the gesture would seem to be the gesture of silence, the index finger on the lips, indicating the requisite discretion at divine indecency. The gesture was origi-

Figure 8.7. The effeminate man as a bearded lady, from Sebastián de Covarrubias Orozco, *Emblemas morales* (Madrid, 1610), II, no. 164.

Figure 8.8. Giulio Romano, Orpheus, a youth and a maenad.
Nationalmuseum, Stockholm.

Figure 8.9. Personifications of Silence, from Vincenzo Cartari,
Les Images des Dieux, Lyons, 1623.

nally that of the god Harpocrates, shown in figure 8.9 on the right, patron of
hermetic, hence silent, knowledge. In the earliest editions of Alciato's
emblems, it becomes the gesture of the wise man, who knows how to keep his
counsel (figure 8.10). By the mid-century, the gesture of wisdom becomes a
topos for the scholar, poring over his book (figure 8.11), indicating now not
only that wisdom keeps its counsel, but also that study requires silence and,
more specifically, that the mark of the scholar is his ability to read silently.
And the quintessentially male emblem of the philosopher and scholar, like the
pelican in reverse, was quickly transferred to women: figure 8.12 is the goddess
Agenoria, so called, according to Charles Estienne, from *agendum*, "what must
be done," hence the goddess of deeds-not-words.[10] Figure 8.13 shows the bot-

Figure 8.10. Emblem of Silence, from Andrea Alciato,
Emblemata, Augsburg, 1531.

Figure 8.11. Silence, from Andrea Alciato, *Emblemata*, Padua, 1621.

Figure 8.12. The silent goddess Agenoria,
from Pierre Cousteau, *Pegma*, Paris, 1555.

Vxoriæ virtutes.
To my Sister, M. D. COLLEY.

THIS reprefentes the vertues of a wife,
Her finger, ftaies her tonge to runne at large.
The modeft lookes, doe fhewe her honeft life.
The keys, declare fhee hathe a care, and chardge,
Of hufbandes goodes: let him goe where he pleafe,
The Tortoyfe warnes, at home to fpend her daies.

M 3

Figure 8.13. Wifely Virtue, from Geoffrey Whitney,
Choice of Emblemes, Leiden, 1586.

tom line, Geoffrey Whitney's virtuous wife: "Her finger stays her tongue to run at large."[11] Like Giulio Romano's discreet voyeur, the good woman is the silent woman.

This is as far as art history will take us; but as a reading of the mythological drawing, the account fails to satisfy me. Giulio Romano's woman looks more distressed than discreet; moreover, her finger appears to be in her mouth, not on her lips. In any case, considering the notorious profligacy of Renaissance symbolism, it is usually a mistake to stop with a single interpretation. Let us return to the figure of Silence: Pierio Valeriano describes the personification, with finger to mouth; but he also includes the image in figure 8.14, whose gesture appears the same but is in fact intended to be *biting* his finger, and represents, Valeriano says, *Meditatio vel Ultio*—meditation or revenge. If these seem odd alternatives, they are certainly no more so than the pelican's eminently logical combination of charity and cannibalism. Giulio used the gesture again for an angry Mars with an armed Venus (figure 8.15), a sketch for a painting in which they are expelling a fury from a garden of putti. Giulio's voyeur certainly looks more vengeful than meditative, and if the figure is indeed a vengeful woman rather than a salacious observer or a silent accomplice, then the pederastic musician is surely not Apollo but Orpheus, who turned to boys after the death of Eurydice and was credited with the introduction of pederasty into Greece, an insult to womanhood that was ulti-

Digitos cõ
mordens,
quid.

Figure 8.14. Meditation or Revenge, from G. P. Valeriano Bolzani,
Hieroglyphica, 1610.

Figure 8.15. Giulio Romano, Venus and Mars as avenging deities.
Hermitage, St. Petersburg.

mately avenged by the murderous bacchantes, of whom the observer—if this analysis is correct—is now clearly one.

This brings us to a larger issue: how far is this (or any) image limited, or defined, by such an explanation? Naturally I believe that my interpretation of this drawing is right and all the art historians have been wrong; but the drawing was not, therefore, up to this moment meaningless, or even misinterpreted. Images are not limited by their inventors' intentions; moreover, they always say more than they mean—like Hamlet's players, they cannot keep counsel. The controlling, limiting, explanatory word represents only the secrets the wise man or the good woman keep to themselves, the secrets of meaning, which are, paradoxically, public knowledge; but the image represents far more—beyond the silent woman lies the vengeful fury, beyond *Caritas* lies inhumanity, behind all of these lies the unspoken. The image, unlike the word, that is, also represents what does not signify, the unexplained, the unspeakable—all those meanings we reject because we believe nobody in the Renaissance could have conceived them. With this by way of introduction, let me turn now to the royal impresa that is the real subject of my essay.

Figure 8.16 is the frontispiece to Saxton's *Atlas of England and Wales*, published in 1579, the first national atlas ever undertaken, patronized and largely paid for by the crown. It is unsigned, but has been ascribed to Remigius Hogenberg on stylistic grounds. I begin with a quick survey of the iconography. In a large central niche, Queen Elizabeth is enthroned between two heroic male figures, Astronomy, left, holding a celestial sphere, Geography, right, with a terrestrial globe and compass. On the plinths below them are the female figures of Fortitude with her column on the left, Prudence with a serpent and looking glass on the right. Tudor roses adorn the outer sides of the molding. On the throne itself, lions sit at the front bearing shields with the initials E/R, and atop the chair-back two male figures in classical armor stand guard. On the frieze are two small classical heads, that on the right clearly male, and crowned, that on the left ambiguous, but possibly female, and two grotesque masks. In a cartouche in the middle Peace, naked, with an olive branch, embraces Justice, clothed, with a breastplate and carrying a sword; behind Justice, Cupid or a putto carries a set of scales. Above these, two putti carry wreaths, and the royal arms appear in the center, supported by a crowned lion and a griffin. Below the whole composition, within a double cartouche, is a Latin poem in praise of Elizabeth, and on either side of this are two more personifications of geography and astronomy: on the left, a cartographer draws a map of England; on the right, an astronomer observes the heavens with a cruciform sighting instrument, and beyond them, observes the queen.

My concern here is with the central impresa (figure 8.17), certainly the most intriguing part of the iconography. Above the queen, in an oval at the center of the frieze, is a group of three figures. A naked woman bearing an olive branch and an armed woman bearing a sword embrace; behind the armed woman, a putto holds a set of scales. The loving union of Justice and Peace is predicted by Psalm 85, "iustitia et pax deosculatae sunt," and Roy Strong therefore calls the impresa an allusion to that biblical verse.[12] Now it is certainly true that the iconography of peace and justice were to become, in the 1580s, an essential element in the re-creation of the royal image: Strong calls attention to the proliferation of such imagery, epitomized in a portrait of 1585

Figure 8.16. Christopher Saxton, *Atlas of England and Wales*, 1579,
title page. By permission of the Folger Shakespeare Library.

Figure 8.17. Peace and Justice embracing (detail of figure 8.16).
By permission of the Folger Shakespeare Library.

attributed to Marcus Gheeraerts in which Elizabeth holds an olive branch while the sword of justice lies at her feet.[13] The problem, however, with viewing the embracing women as an allusion to the psalm is that Justice and Peace kiss only in the Vulgate.[14] The Geneva Bible and the Bishops' Bible—that is, the Elizabethan Protestant bible—says that "*righteousnes* and peace shall kisse one another," a reading followed by the Authorized Version, which is in fact a more accurate rendering of the Hebrew than the Vulgate's "justice." Is Elizabeth's impresa, then, really alluding to the Catholic scripture?

The question (as is usual with such questions) begs a number of others and conceals a set of very complex relationships. The simple answer is yes, in the sense that the emblem does not originate with Elizabeth, and in its original form it certainly depends on the Vulgate text. It was an impresa devised for Pope Julius III, much commented upon, and appears on a stucco relief in the Villa Giulia. This is too badly eroded to be clearly photographed, but the image by the end of the century was widely circulated, and is visible, for example, on one of the title pages to another atlas, Georg Braun and Franz Hogenberg's compendious and magnificent *Civitates Orbis Terrarum* (figure 8.18). For Elizabeth's iconography to retain an allusion to the Vulgate is probably not surprising; Milton, even in his most radically Protestant years, always uses the Vulgate form of biblical names. But the source of the emblem is certainly ironic: Julius III was vilified in England as a persecutor of Protestants, and was even called antichrist.[15]

In one sense, all this reveals is, once again, the notorious profligacy of Renaissance symbolic imagery, its endless adaptability to conflicting, and often diametrically opposed, ideologies. But at the same time, the adaptation of Roman Catholic imperial iconography was an increasingly visible element in the creation of a British royal self. In Crispin van de Passe's 1596 engraving

Figure 8.18. Peace and Justice embracing. Detail of the title page of G. Braun and F. Hogenberg, *Civitates Orbis Terrarum*, Part 5, Cologne, 1586.

Figure 8.19. Crispin van de Passe, Queen Elizabeth between columns, 1596. Mansell Collection/TimePix.

of the queen (figure 8.19), Elizabeth stands between the pillars of Hercules, originally devised as an impresa of the emperor Charles V (figure 8.20), and signifying his determination to sail "Plus Ultra," to retake the Holy Land and expand his empire beyond the boundaries of Europe; it subsequently became the impresa of his son Philip II of Spain, the husband of Elizabeth's Catholic half-sister Mary Tudor, and the first of her suitors after she herself became queen. The queen's image, with its naval background, not only celebrates the

Figure 8.20. Impresa of the Emperor Charles V.

maritime victory over her brother-in-law in 1588, and the more recent naval triumph at Cadiz, but, at a time when the exploration and colonization of the New World were starting to be a critical element in English political life, asserts Elizabeth's own imperial claims, to Wales, to Ireland, and to the lands beyond the sea. The Herculean columns of the Most Catholic King are hung with trophies of her triumph, the arms of England on the left, of the Tudors on the right. Atop the columns are, on the left, the pelican feeding her young with her own blood, the emblem of Caritas applied here to Elizabeth's care for her people; on the right, a phoenix rises in flame, asserting at once the queen's uniqueness, her virginity, and, so many years after the scandal of her mother, the immaculateness of her birth.[16] An open book beside her, alluding (once again in the Latin rendering) to the 88th Psalm, declares that she has made God her help. The imagery here was public and familiar; its deployment, however, was political and intensely personal.

There may, therefore, have been something quite self-conscious about the appropriation of a papal emblem for Saxton's frontispiece. But there is a significant difference between the papal and the Elizabethan impresas. The pope's version consists only of the two women, both clothed; to create the queen's emblem, Peace has been undressed, and the putto bearing scales has been added. The revision both simplifies and complicates the image. To begin with, it serves to clarify the identity of the armed goddess: she is not the warlike Bellona or the militant Pallas, but Justice, a figure who may logically unite with Peace. In fact, though the sword was a more common attribute identifying Justice than the scales familiar to us (Othello fears lest Desdemona's balmy breath "persuade / Justice to break her sword," not to drop her scales), its warlike implications were sometimes felt to be troublesome. Thus Crispin de Passe's memorial engraving of the queen (figure 8.21) takes no chances, clearly labeling not only the sword but the word of God that supports it; and God's word, once again for this English Protestant, is Latin.

Figure 8.21. Crispin van de Passe, Memorial portrait of Queen Elizabeth, 1603.
By permission of the Folger Shakespeare Library.

Figure 8.22. Attributed to Cornelius Kettel, *Queen Elizabeth I,*
the Sieve Portrait, 1580. Pinacoteca di Siena.

But the scales could easily have been introduced without the putto. The cherub in company with a naked Peace brings into the emblem a set of implications that are quite different from those of Pope Julius's impresa. If the erotic force of the original image is subsumed in the psalmist's allegory, with the women clothed and their identity controlled by their attributes of olive branch and sword, the English version makes the issue of female sexuality insistently manifest. A naked woman accompanied by a putto inescapably suggests Venus and Cupid; and indeed, one's first impression of the impresa is that it represents the more commonplace coupling of Venus and Mars—in the topos, the armed woman, Pallas or Bellona, has replaced the god of war. Nor is the association of Venus with Elizabeth necessarily unintended: Saxton's Atlas was published in 1579, in the midst of the negotiations over the Alençon match, the last time the queen was to represent herself as a marriageable woman. The allusion to Venus, moreover, makes a genealogical claim: Elizabeth is descended from Venus, the mother of Aeneas and the great-grandmother of Brutus, legendary founder of Britain and Elizabeth's ancestor. The goddess of love is the source of the British royal line.

The erotic is clearly the main issue in the iconography of the series of Sieve portraits from the same period. In figure 8.22, the most elaborate of the paintings, Elizabeth stands beside a column, a type of Fortitude. The queen holds a sieve, emblem of her chastity, an allusion to the story of the Roman vestal

Tuccia, who, when accused of unchastity, proved her virginity by carrying water from the Tiber to the Temple of Vesta in a sieve. But what is represented in the ovals on the column are scenes from the story of Dido and Aeneas. Dido often served as a type of Elizabeth; the analogy was an easy one, since the Carthaginian queen's given name was Elissa—by the end of the century, the name is being recorded in mythological and historical dictionaries as Eliza. The multiple allusion sets two traditions about Dido against each other, one, considered historical, in which Dido, the chaste widow of Sychaeus, commits suicide to prevent her enforced marriage to a neighboring king, and Virgil's poetic one, considered fictitious, in which she succumbs to the charms of Aeneas and is destroyed by her passion. The double allusion ingeniously provides Elizabeth with both genealogical and typological ancestors, Aeneas and Dido; the sieve assures us that she will be an embodiment of the chaste Dido, not the fallen one. When the monarch was a woman, such assurances were always necessary. Mantegna depicted the chaste Dido (figure 8.23), standing before her own funeral pyre holding the urn containing her husband's ashes. Elizabeth is invoked as both Venus and Vesta by John Lyly in *Euphues and his England*:

Figure 8.23. Andrea Mantegna, *Dido*, c. 1500-05. The Montreal Museum of Fine Arts, Purchase, John W. Tempest Fund. Photo: The Montreal Museum of Fine Arts.

> having the beauty that might allure all . . . , she hath the chastity
> to refuse all, accounting it no less praise to be called a virgin, than
> to be esteemed a Venus;

and he goes on to compare her to the notable vestals Aemilia and Tuccia.[17]

The vestal here is obviously privileged over the goddess of love. But the scene in Saxton's impresa is unquestionably erotic, and it shows Venus, moreover, paired with another woman—the biblical reference, indeed, has had to be toned down: "deosculari" is a good deal stronger than embracing, a demotic word for a deep kiss, the word for the kind of kissing people do in the comedies of Terence. Lesbian sexuality is all but invisible in surviving sixteenth-century English sources (in contrast, for example, to French texts of the period, both literary and legal) and it is tempting to assume that for the Renaissance, whatever English women might do with each other, it did not constitute sex. This is very largely the case with sex between men: despite the legal and theological fulminations against sodomy, with very few exceptions, it was a vice conceived to be practiced only by foreigners. It is also true that in much (though by no means all) of the standard gynecological literature, female sexuality exists primarily to evoke, and satisfy, male sexuality; and in this context, the notion of two women making love would be literally inconceivable.

This is the version of Renaissance gynecology that modern commentators have tended to concentrate on. Nevertheless, I do not think it settles the matter; the nature of women is no more stable than the nature of images, and the Renaissance is full of alternative gynecologies. By the 1590s, Thomas Nashe could write an obscene poem, *A Choice of Valentines*, in which a dildo figures significantly; it is evidently not a novelty, but a familiar instrument, and though it is used in the context of sex with a man, it constitutes a powerful testimony to the English Renaissance's conviction that, whatever gynecology says, women do indeed have an independent sexuality, which needs to be satisfied. By the 1590s, a word for lesbian sex has entered the language: tribadry. It is deployed, in the earliest example I have found, in a way that is neither uncomprehending nor hostile. John Donne's correspondent T. W. writes in a verse letter,

> Have mercy on me and my sinful muse,
> Which, rubbed and tickled with thine, could not choose
> But spend some of her pith, and yield to be
> One in that chaste and mystic tribadry.[18]

In Ben Jonson's usage a decade later (the earliest citation in the *OED*—not a good guide in this sort of investigation), the word becomes a term of contempt for women who have declared their independence of men. Pallas Athena, the "mankind [mannish] maid," is sent off to join the muses, "thy tribade trine," a lesbian trio, to

> invent new sports;
> Thou nor thy looseness with my making sorts[19]

—the "making" being, I would think, both his poetry and his own kind of sex, that "doing" which, he says, following Petronius, "a filthy pleasure is, and short / And done, we straight repent us of the sport."[20]

These two examples suffice to show that sex between women was both conceivable and conceived, and to suggest the breadth of the English Renaissance response to it. "Chaste and mystic tribadry" therefore may well be an element in the impresa that hangs above Elizabeth's head, and its point would be, like the substitution of Pallas/Bellona for Mars, to preserve at once Elizabeth's sexuality and her virginity. The same strategy is evident in the extraordinary passage in Sir Philip Sidney's *Arcadia* describing Pamela and Philocleia in bed together:

> They impoverished their clothes to enrich their bed, which for
> that night might well scorn the shrine of Venus; and there cherishing one another with dear, though chaste, embracements, with
> sweet, though cold, kisses, it might seem that Love was come to
> play him there without dart, or that weary of his own fires, he was
> there to refresh himself between their sweet-breathing lips.[21]

I do not think it can be argued that such a scene would not have been considered overtly sexual in 1590: Sidney's insistence that the embracements were chaste, the kisses cold, are surely there to contradict the inevitable assumption that they were, respectively, libidinous and hot. The usual way of dealing with this sort of thing is to declare it masculine titillation because the author was a man. But *Arcadia* was written for the Countess of Pembroke and her circle, and the readership of romances was overwhelmingly female. If the relation between texts and their readers means anything, then the passage is feminine titillation as well. Elizabeth's impresa too was, no doubt, devised by a man; but it insists on the absolute authority of the feminine: beauty and love, wisdom and military valor, and justice, are presented as functions of female sexuality, militant chastity and innocence under maternal control (in that order, reading from left to right). The iconography is, so far as I know, unprecedented, but it is characteristically Elizabethan in its determination both to include and disarm the realities of lust and conquest within the concept of imperial power.

The image of Elizabeth as patron of geography makes an imperial claim: the arms of England at the top are crowned specifically with an imperial crown; and virginity was an increasingly critical element in that claim. The essential relation between the imperial and the virginal is clearly implicit, for example, in Ralegh's selection of the name Virginia for his new colony: this was devised as a compliment to Elizabeth, but the name was not, say, Elizia or Tudoria. The epithet acknowledges the extent to which virginity had become, by the last years of Elizabeth's reign, a crucial attribute of royal power.

But virginity is a double-edged sword, and power is constituted, paradoxically, in the ability, and authority, to deflower it. We have only to recall Ralegh's famous passage on Guiana:

> To conclude, Guiana is a country that hath yet her maidenhead, never sacked, turned, nor wrought. . . . It hath never been entered by any army of strength, and never conquered or possessed by any Christian prince.[22]

In the potential of virginity lay not only civilization but the promise of infinite bounty within a hegemonic order. Needless to say, however, in Ralegh's construction it is only Elizabeth's chastity that must be preserved intact; impenetrable herself, she is the Christian prince who is to enter and possess the virgin land. Ralegh's plans for Guiana—which are Elizabeth's plans: he acts in her name and on her authority—are amply indicated by his servant Lawrence Keymis's description of the country as a potential prostitute soliciting trade:

> whole shires of fruitful rich grounds lying now waste for want of people do prostitute themselves unto us, like a fair and beautiful woman in the pride and flower of desired years.[23]

Elizabeth is constructed here as a type of Pallas, a "mankind maid" in Jonson's hostile epithet; it is to her imperial virginity that the new land is being prostituted. Whether the persona implied in such assertions was one that she constructed for herself or one that was constructed for her is beside the point; the foreign policy was hers, and when divine and mystic tribadry becomes a principle of foreign policy, there is no reason to expect it to be less predatory than any other imperial ideology.

I have been, I confess, quite surprised at how far I was able to pursue this reading of Elizabeth's impresa without feeling that I had lost the sense of its historical context. I am always wary of historical claims that begin "nobody in the Renaissance would have thought . . . ," especially when what nobody would have thought is something that we prefer to suppress in our own culture. At the same time, it is obvious that nobody would have described the emblem in the terms I have used, or attempted to account for it in the way I have done: neither the critical language nor the concerns of our era are those of 1579, and however much we may undertake to think ourselves back into the past, no amount of historical perspective can erase the history that has formed our sensibilities. Insofar as Elizabeth would have thought of the project she was pursuing in the New World, and (as we tend to forget) much more significantly, energetically and ruthlessly in Ireland, as imperialistic, she would certainly have conceived it as a good thing, not a predatory and morally dubious one. Nevertheless, to presume to explain away her policies on the grounds of a grand historical naiveté, a necessarily insufficient sense of long-term historical consequences, is to indulge in a degree of condescension that historians can scarcely afford with regard to their subjects. I see no reason not to credit Elizabeth with understanding as much about the implications of her policies as we do about the implications of ours—which is to say, whenever we can say it with hindsight, not very much. History is not something that happened only in the sixteenth century. Renaissance symbolic forms are cultural artifacts, and if they speak to us at all, that is a measure of the extent to which we have been able to re-create the world that made them and find ourselves in it.

9

THE PLAY OF CONSCIENCE

THE OPENING is irresistible:

> I have heard
> That guilty creatures sitting at a play
> Have by the very cunning of the scene
> Been struck so to the soul that presently
> They have proclaimed their malefactions . . .
>   I'll have these players
> Play something like the murder of my father
> Before mine uncle. . . .
>   If he but blench,
> I know my course. . . .
>   The play's the thing
> Wherein I'll catch the conscience of the king.

To talk about the fortunes of catharsis in the Renaissance is to deconstruct this passage.

1

I am concerned here with Renaissance readings of the catharsis clause in Aristotle's *Poetics*, but I have also necessarily to deal with the prior assumption, quite common in the modern critical literature, that we now understand what Aristotle meant when he wrote that 'drama effects through pity and fear the purgation of such emotions,' and that we can therefore see how far the Renaissance was, unlike us, adapting the Aristotelian dictum to its own purposes. The two major commentators on the fortunes of the *Poetics* in sixteenth-century Italy, R. S. Crane and Bernard Weinberg, observe repeatedly—and undoubtedly correctly—that Renaissance critics tend to view Aristotle through Horatian glasses. This affects not only the obvious assumptions about the dramatic unities, but more subtly, determines the nature of claims about the social and political function of drama, its public status as rhetoric and oratory, and thereby its utility within the Renaissance state. Weinberg's and Crane's own assumptions, both about drama and about Aristotle, form no part of the discussion, but they are where I want to begin: both critics, like most commentators on Aristotle throughout the history of criticism, assume that by the term catharsis Aristotle is describing the effect of the drama on the audience, and that it is therefore the spectators who are purged through pity and fear. There has been no such general agreement about what the spectators are purged of.

How exactly the purgation works has been a matter for endless debate; what has had little resistance is the notion that Aristotle is in fact talking about the audience here. That, therefore, is the part I wish to press on first: this has seemed to be the one thing we have thought we could be sure of about Aristotle's intentions. For modern scholarship, the chief opponent of this view has been Gerald Else, who argues that what is being described makes more sense if we understand it as something that takes place entirely within the drama itself, an element of dramatic structure, rather than of dramatic effect. Thus the pitiable and terrible events that precipitate the tragedy—Oedipus's murder of his father, Orestes' of his mother—are purged by the pitiable and terrible sufferings of the hero. The catharsis takes place within the structure of the drama: it is Thebes or Athens, the world of the play, that is purged, not the audience. Such a reading makes good sense within the logic of the *Poetics* because, as Else points out, the context in which the catharsis clause appears is not concerned with the audience: it says that tragedy is an imitation of a serious action, that it uses heightened language, operates through performance rather than narration, and that it ends by bringing about, through pity and fear, the purgation of such emotions. Aristotle then goes on to discuss the characters, and to deduce the six parts of drama. Read in this way, catharsis provides a symmetrical movement for the dramatic action. An elliptical and parenthetical shift to the psychology of audiences at this point would need some explanation.[1]

Few critics have been persuaded by this argument, though to my knowledge there has been no real refutation of it, just a general insistence that it is implausible.[2] This is doubtless true, but will hardly settle the matter: plausibility is the least transhistorical of critical categories, the most particularly time-bound. The principal objection that has been raised to Else's view is that it leaves out of account a passage in the *Politics* about the cathartic effect of music, which is certainly concerned with audiences, and refers the reader for an explanation of catharsis specifically to Aristotle's works on poetry. But this is less than conclusive because the catharsis clause in the *Poetics* can hardly be the explanation intended (it doesn't explain anything), and it is impossible to know how broadly or narrowly defined the presumably lost account of the term would have been. After all, if we are inventing definitions of catharsis that Aristotle might have written in some work that has not survived, we can certainly imagine one that explains the operation of elements of the tragic plot on the characters in terms of the operation of music on its listeners—for example, that the process of revelation and purgation endured by Oedipus is like the curative operation of ritual music on the pathological listener.[3] Needless to say, I am not claiming that this is what Aristotle wrote, but only that a formalistic argument that takes the laconic reference in the *Politics* into account is perfectly plausible. It is clear, however, why no refutation of Else has been found necessary: for all its clarity and elegant simplicity, Else's Aristotle doesn't say what we want Aristotle to say. The great disadvantage of Else's reading for the critic who wants what critics have wanted from Aristotle since the *Poetics* was first rediscovered at the end of the fifteenth century, a compendious guide to dramatic praxis, is precisely that it makes catharsis a purely formal element, and thus leaves the *Poetics* saying nothing whatever about dramatic effect: if Aristotle is anywhere concerned with audiences, this has got to be the place.[4]

As a metaphor for the operation of drama on the audience, however, the notion of purgation has always been found problematic, not least in Aristotle's apparent assumption that ridding ourselves of pity and fear is something desirable. A few critics, starting in the Renaissance, have undertaken to deal with this difficulty by arguing that it is not we who are purged, but the emotions—that is, we end up with our emotions in a purified form—but this raises as many problems as it solves: what is impure about pity and fear? Moreover, most critics have been at least uncomfortable with the medical metaphor itself, observing that its operation is at best obscure. How does the evocation of pity and fear purge these emotions? Students of classical science point out that this is not even an accurate version of Greek medicine, which worked on the whole allopathically, by opposites, not homeopathically, by similarities—that is, to purge melancholy, you made people happy, not sadder. Therefore, if Aristotelian catharsis is really a medical metaphor, drama would purge pity and fear by evoking their opposites, whatever these might be. This has been more a problem for modern commentators than it was for Renaissance exegetes, since much of Renaissance medicine did work homeopathically, and therefore Aristotle, however ahistorically, seemed to be saying something true; but it was a truth that did little to clarify the ambiguities of the passage. One recent critic, Elizabeth Belfiore, has undertaken to resolve the question by insisting on the literalness of the medical metaphor, arguing that if we conceive pity and fear as purging not more pity and fear, but their opposites (she is rather vague about what these might be), the process makes perfect sense.[5] She does not notice that this requires us to believe that when Aristotle says that drama effects through pity and fear the purgation of such emotions, what he must mean is that it effects the purgation of the opposite emotions. Unless 'the same' in Greek can mean 'the opposite,' allopathy will not solve the problem.

Aristotle wrote a compressed, elliptical, and radically ambiguous passage about catharsis that has, historically, simply not been capable of any single firm elucidation and has defied any critical consensus. I take this as the single basic, incontrovertible fact about the passage: like so many biblical and Shakespearean cruxes, its meaning has only developed over time, has changed with the generations, and inheres entirely in the history of its elucidation. Indeed, it was the very indeterminacy of the dictum that made it so extraordinarily enabling a feature of the *Poetics* as a basis for both the theory and practice of Renaissance drama. Nevertheless, we should begin by noting the genuine insignificance of the passage within Aristotle's argument, in contrast with the tremendous emphasis that has been placed on it by the critical tradition generally. This is the only place in the essay where tragic catharsis is mentioned; the clause occupies a total of ten words, and the subject is then dropped. In the one other reference to catharsis in the *Poetics*, the term has nothing to do with dramatic theory but refers to the ritual purification of Orestes when he is recognized by Electra in Sophocles' *Iphigenia in Tauris*.[6] The reference in *Politics* 8 is, as we have seen, equally unhelpful, merely referring the reader for a discussion of the operation of catharsis to Aristotle's work on poetry.[7] Other uses of the term in *The Generation of Animals* and *The History of Animals* seem even less relevant, referring to physiological processes like menstruation, urination, and the ejaculation of semen. To understand the nature of tragic catharsis, those ten words in the *Poetics* are all the help the surviving texts of Aristotle provide.

2

The textual history of the *Poetics* is a meager one.[8] No manuscript of the work was known in western Europe until the end of the fifteenth century; and it was first published not in Greek but in a Latin translation by Giorgio Valla in 1498, ten years before the first publication of the Greek text, the Aldine edition of 1508. Before this time, the essay was known in Europe only in Latin versions of Averroës's incomplete and often confused Arabic text. I begin, therefore, with the earliest translations of the catharsis clause.

Here is how Averroës renders the passage: tragedy 'is an imitation which generates in the soul certain passions which incline people toward pity and fear and toward other similar passions, which it induces and promotes through what it makes the virtuous imagine about honorable behavior and morality.'[9] Obviously a good deal has been added to the clause to attempt to make sense of it, but one indubitably clear thing about it is that pity and fear are conceived to be good things, and far from being purged, are what we are expected to end up with. Now of course it is necessary to remind ourselves that Averroës has none of the context essential for understanding the passage in any historically relevant way. He does not know what drama is, and assumes that tragedy and comedy are simply poetic forms analogous to eulogy and satire. Nor does he understand that Aristotle's categories of character, plot, melody, etc., are all elements of the same single poetic structure, but assumes them to be the names of other sorts of poetry. All these matters are, however, tangential to his real interest in the *Poetics*, which lies in its discussion of figurative language. He takes *mimesis* to mean simply the devising of tropes; he has no real concept of imitation, since he assumes that the function of poetry is merely to tell the truth and make it beautiful. Nevertheless, despite all the confusions and lacunae, Averroës's notion that the *Poetics* promulgates a view of drama as ethical rhetoric is one that persists long after the discovery and analysis of the Greek text. Averroës in many respects continued to be the basis of Renaissance views of the essay, enabling it from the outset to be easily harmonized with Horace's *Art of Poetry*.

I turn now to the earliest Renaissance translations of the clause from the newly discovered Greek; but it is necessary first to pause over two key terms in the passage. First, the word *catharsis* itself is made to carry a good deal of philosophical and spiritual baggage when it is translated 'purgation,' as it generally is in English. But in Greek the word's basic meaning is simply 'cleansing' (one can speak of the *catharsis* of a house); it can imply any sort of purification, from the most elementary and practical to the most profound and complex, and the standard rendering involves an unacknowledged assumption about the context. The second term is Aristotle's *pathemata*, the word that refers back to pity and fear, usually rendered 'emotions'—'tragedy effects through pity and fear the purgation of such emotions.' *Pathemata* too is a term upon the interpretation of which a good deal depends. It means literally 'sufferings'; its root, *pathé*, is translated by Liddell and Scott 'anything that befalls one'—what happens to you, as opposed to what you do. (In contrast, when Plato talks about the emotions, he uses the much more abstract term *thumos*, which is also the word for the soul, or the much more specific word *orgé*, passion in the sense of violent emotion.) *Pathemata* thus include both actions and reactions, both what the hero undergoes and how he feels about it. The word implies, literally, passive action, what is implied etymologically in English by its cognates 'passion' and 'patience,' which together comprise the passive of 'action.'

Now to our Renaissance translators. Giorgio Valla, in 1498, has tragedy 'completing through pity and fear the purgation of such habits'[10]—'completing,' *terminans*, is an etymologically precise translation of the word usually translated 'effecting,' Aristotle's term *perainousa*, literally 'bringing to an end': both words have as their root the word for a boundary or limit. Valla's Latin, however, probably misconstrues the force of the Greek: *perainousa* can also mean simply 'bringing about, accomplishing,' which need not imply an action already in progress. Valla's word for Aristotle's *pathemata*, passions or emotions, is, oddly, *disciplinae*, what we have been trained to do (this is the word I have translated 'habits').

A generation later, Alessandro Pazzi, who in 1536 edited and published the Greek text with a Latin translation that became the standard one, has tragedy 'through pity and fear purging passions of this kind':[11] the passions in this case are *perturbationes*, disorders or violent emotions, something more like the Greek *orgia*, and a more loaded term than *pathemata*. In both these cases, there is obviously some bafflement about what is being described and how it works; both attempt to make the process a more reasonable one, something we would want drama to do—rid us of (implicitly bad) habits, cure disorders. A more subtle problem that neither translator really knows how to address is what Aristotle means by '*such* emotions,' *ton toiouton pathematon*: are they the same emotions, of pity and fear, that are being purged, or others like them, or perhaps the whole range of emotions to which pity and fear belong? Valla's version, 'talium disciplinarum,' implies that the purged emotions are the same as the ones doing the purging, whereas Pazzi's 'perturbationes huiusmodi,' emotions of this kind, leaves the question open.[12]

3

This then is what the Renaissance theorist of the effects of drama had to go on when he wished to invoke Aristotle on catharsis. The first commentary, that of Francesco Robortello, did not appear till 1548, but thereafter elucidation and debate were frequent and energetic—the matter was, indeed, increasingly important in the development of dramatic theory. Needless to say, there was no consensus, but most commentators offered some version of one of three standard views: that tragedy is only concerned with the two passions of pity and fear, and it is therefore only these that are purged (and the argument then centered on trying to explain why this was beneficial); or that, on the contrary, pity and fear are good things and it is the other, antisocial passions that tragedy purges, e.g., envy, anger, hatred, etc.; or (the position enunciated by Guarini in the course of defending his *Pastor Fido*) that tragedy purges us in a much more general way by tempering all our passions through its vision of the pity and fear inherent in the uncertainties of great men's lives, thereby making our own ordinary unhappiness easier to endure. The last of these has obviously added a good deal to the ten words of Aristotle's clause, but it is also the one that makes Aristotle most easily applicable to the uses of the Renaissance playwright.

If all these interpretations seem uncomfortably restrictive, they nevertheless enabled Renaissance theorists to project a surprisingly broad critical and psychological perspective for drama, and one not at all irrelevant to modern views of the passage. For example, Lorenzo Giacomini in 1586 produced a proto-psychoanalytic argument (anticipating the more famous proto-psychoanalytic argument of Freud's uncle Jacob Bernays in 1857),[13] explaining that we purge our passions by expressing them, and that tragedy permits the spirit to vent its emotions and thereby releases us from them.[14] Giraldi Cintio in 1558 preempted Gerald Else's new critical reading by suggesting that through pity and terror, 'the personages introduced in the tragedy are purged of those passions of which they were the victims'[15]—the catharsis, that is, takes place in the characters, not in the audience. And Giason Denores, in a strikingly historicized (not to say New-Historicized) account anticipating Jack Winkler by four centuries, explained Aristotle's focus on pity and fear by observing that Greek drama constituted a vital part of the citizen's training for warfare and the defence of the state, and hence ridding the prospective soldier of these potentially disabling emotions was of primary importance to the playwright.[16]

Of course, there are also commentators who reject all three positions, which sometimes involves rejecting Aristotle entirely—it is important to stress that, for all the age's notorious devotion to the authority of the ancients, this was always an option. J. C. Scaliger, for example, denies that catharsis can be a defining feature of tragedy, observing succinctly that it simply does not describe the effects of many tragic plots.[17] Tasso similarly argues that catharsis will not account for the operation of many kinds of tragedy, citing as examples 'those tragedies which contain the passage of good men from misery to happiness, which confirm the opinion that the people have about God's providence'[18]—catharsis is faulted, in short, for not being applicable to medieval tragedy, and more specifically, in this construction at least, for not being Christian. But the largest issue in the debates over the clause, and the source of the general unwillingness to treat it simply as an abstruse and marginal moment in Aristotle's argument, was its apparent assertion of some sort of real social utility for drama. It is, from late antiquity onward, generally accounted for as an answer to Plato's charge that poetry conduces to immorality, and the consequent exclusion of poets from his ideal republic. On the contrary, the catharsis passage seems to insist that poetry serves an essential function, something more vital than its mere persuasive force as ethical rhetoric, in maintaining the health of the state.

But even here, many commentators observe that such a reading puts Aristotle in the position of contradicting himself. Early in the essay he implies that the purpose of drama is to give pleasure;[19] how then can its function also be to purge us through pity and fear? There are some attempts to reconcile these two claims (e.g., we feel better when we're purged), but the real problem is that for most Renaissance theorists the defining feature of drama has nothing to do with its medicinal character, but lies in its quality as spectacle, and its consequent ability to evoke wonder—this is what makes it different from epic poetry, though critics are fairly equally divided about whether it is therefore better or worse. Woe and wonder constitute the essence of the tragedy Horatio proposes to produce out of the story of Hamlet, and Hamlet says it is 'the very cunning of the scene' that strikes the spectator 'to the soul.' Poetry alone will not have this effect; theater—'the scene'—is of the essence.[20]

As I have indicated, this is not invariably a point in tragedy's favor. Castelvetro, for example, argues that plays are designed to appeal to the ignorant multitude, who are incapable of reading philosophy; drama's sole end, he concludes, is to satisfy the vulgar desire for pleasure.[21] And though this is an extreme position, it is nevertheless the case that the Renaissance is in general so deeply concerned with theater as a way of managing the emotions that the notion of drama as a mode of knowledge (as, for Aristotle, it is a form of logic) hardly plays a significant role in the poetics of the Renaissance stage. Renaissance theorists are interested in everything Aristotle marginalizes in his argument, all the emotive, performative, and spectacular elements of drama, and just for that reason catharsis, which has so momentary and casual a presence in Aristotle, becomes for the Renaissance of correspondingly vital importance.[22] Through the invocation of catharsis, most critics are able to present drama as a genre of considerable social utility. The Belgian scholar Nicaise van Ellebode sums it up when he recommends the patronage of tragedy particularly to rulers, as a way of improving the citizenry, observing that the effect of virtue

> is especially to hold in check the turbulent movements of the soul and to restrain them within the bounds of moderation, and since tragedy, more than that, curbs these emotions, it must surely be granted that tragedy's usefulness to the state is extraordinary. For it causes two troublesome passions, pity and fear—which draw

the soul away from strength and turn it toward a womanish weakness—to be regulated and governed by the soul with precise moderation.[23]

It is only the catharsis clause that makes such a claim at all tenable.

4

The broadly political implications of catharsis for the Renaissance assume that the audience of drama is composed of basically virtuous people who attend the theater for virtuous reasons, to be perfected, refined, or made better citizens. Critics like Castelvetro who deny this, who assume that audiences attend theater primarily to be amused and that the function of drama is to amuse them (though it may thereby succeed in inculcating in them some of that philosophy they are too ignorant and shallow to read), also necessarily deny that Aristotle is correct about catharsis. Catharsis tends to be the basis for any utilitarian claim that is made for theater in the Renaissance.

Except, that is, in England—England is in this, as in its theatrical practices generally, the great exception in the European Renaissance. To begin with, Aristotle does not figure especially significantly in English discussions of tragedy—it is to the point that the first English translation of the *Poetics* appears only in 1705, and was itself a translation of a French version. The major Elizabethan literary theorist, Sidney, is certainly aware of the classic essay, but he bases his claims for drama primarily on the mimetic and idealistic qualities of the art. The one gesture toward catharsis forms a marginal and curiously arbitrary part of the argument, but its claims are characteristically both hyperbolic and ambiguous: tragedy is praised because it 'maketh kings fear to be tyrants, and tyrants manifest their tyrannical humors; that, with stirring the affects of admiration and commiseration, teacheth the uncertainty of this world.'[24] The second 'tyrants,' those who 'manifest their tyrannical humors'—or perhaps, on a second reading, those who *fear to* manifest their tyrannical humors—turn out on a *third* reading, after we get through the next clause, to be only stage tyrants; but syntactically they are identical to the kings, and that extended moment of syntactical ambiguity is surely to the point, a reflection of the profoundly ambiguous theatricality of the Renaissance monarchy. Tragedy is claimed here to guarantee that the only tyrants will be stage tyrants in a world where the audience is composed of kings, but it takes us three readings to assure ourselves that Sidney has moved from monarch to player, spectator to actor, and the distinction between real kings and theatrical tyrants is perceptible only through repeated and very close reading. Is Sidney's use of the gendered 'kings,' in preference to 'monarchs,' or 'rulers,' or even 'princes' (the term Queen Elizabeth used to refer to herself), a reflection of just how close to home such an observation might have hit in Elizabethan England?

George Puttenham's account of drama in *The Arte of English Poesie* does not mention catharsis at all, which, however, appears instead in its most literal medical sense to explain the operation of elegies or 'poetical lamentations':

> Therefore of death and burials ... are the only sorrows that the noble poets sought by their art to remove or appease, not with any medicament of a contrary temper, as the Galenists use to cure [i.e., not allopathically] but as the Paracelsians, who cure making one dolor to expell another [i.e., homeopathically], and in this case, one short sorrowing the remedy of a long and grievous sorrow.[25]

It was, ironically, the enemies of theater who found in the concept of catharsis a potent argument through its acknowledgment that drama's function is in fact to elicit the emotions—though in these accounts, instead of freeing us from passion, theater only enslaves us to it. Such arguments are, of course, intended as refutations of the claims to social utility made in Aristotle's name, but insofar as catharsis is interpreted throughout the Renaissance as a kind of physical mimesis, an extension of dramatic mimesis into the audience, the anti-theatrical polemics, for all their obvious Platonic bias, might be said to be perfectly Aristotelian. Needless to say, however, the *Poetics* remains a tacit source, never directly cited in such arguments. Aristotle appears as an authority on drama instead, ubiquitously, in a passage from the *Politics* where he recommends against young men attending theater 'till they be settled in mind and immoveable in affection.'[26] Where Italian theorists had used Aristotle to answer Plato, Gosson, Stubbes, and Prynne use Plato to refute Aristotle.

One would expect Ben Jonson, the most thoroughgoing dramatic classicist in Renaissance England, and thoroughly familiar with both Aristotle and the continental commentaries, at least to take some notice of the catharsis clause. But the long account of the *Poetics* in his *Timber, or Discoveries* is only concerned to harmonize Aristotle and Horace, and catharsis again is not mentioned. The theory here is the mirror of Jonson's dramatic practice, which was, in its primary emphasis on the unities, more Horatian than Aristotelian. Only Milton in England saw in classic catharsis a genuine theoretical basis for tragedy, once again through the mediation of homeopathic medicine:

> Tragedy ... hath ever been held the gravest, moralest, and most profitable of all other poems: therefore said by Aristotle to be of

power by raising pity and fear, or terror, to purge the mind of those and such-like passions, that is, to temper and reduce them to just measure with a kind of delight . . . for so in physic things of melancholic hue and quality are used against melancholy, sour against sour, salt to remove salt humours.[27]

So Samson, his followers, the audience, all conclude the drama with what the Renaissance understood to be an impeccably Aristotelian purgation, 'calm of mind, all passion spent.'[28] This is surely the purest example the English Renaissance affords of the explicit utility of catharsis to the practice of drama. We may perhaps wish to find some notion of the Aristotelian doctrine at work in plays like *King Lear*, *Macbeth*, and *Hamlet*, but if we think of their endings, it is clear that Shakespeare is far less convinced than Milton and the theorists that the experience of catharsis leaves us in any way reconciled, calm or happy.

5

Let us now return to Hamlet on the therapeutic drama he plans to present before the king. The play within the play is itself part of a much larger purgative drama, as Hamlet's *pathemata* work to effect the catharsis of his father's spirit in Purgatory: in this sense, which is the sense described by Gerald Else, catharsis may be said to be the subject of the whole play. But Hamlet's more pragmatic notion that tragic catharsis is designed not for the satisfactory resolution of the plot, nor for the refining and purification of virtuous citizen-spectators, but for the exposure and punishment of criminals is, to say the least, a very special application of the Aristotelian doctrine, an *expansio ad absurdum* of the dramatic theory, so to speak. Behind Hamlet's *Mousetrap*, however, lies not only Aristotle's catharsis clause but a moral topos that reappears in a number of forms throughout Shakespeare's age. Thomas Heywood recounts two versions of it in his *Apology for Actors*, one of the very few defences of the stage in Renaissance England; the topos is invoked as a telling argument in favor of theater. It concerns a woman who has murdered her husband, and years later attends a play on the same theme, and when the murder is represented on the stage, suddenly cries out in a paroxysm of repentant guilt, confesses, and is duly punished.[29] This is, in its way, a genuine instance of the Renaissance notion of Aristotelian catharsis at work, the pity and terror of the action eliciting a particularly pointed reaction of pity and terror in the spectator. Such a story is an obvious model for the projected revelation of Claudius's crime.

But in Hamlet's play, does the catharsis really work? Claudius sits through the dumb show, a clear mirror of his villainy, apparently quite impassively—

directors have a good deal of trouble with this, and often deal with it by cutting the dumb show entirely (radical surgery is the normal theatrical cure for
the dangerously interesting moments in Shakespeare). Nor is Claudius alone
in failing to rise to *The Mousetrap*'s bait: the Player Queen's implicit criticism
of Gertrude's doubly culpable remarriage, 'In second husband let me be
accursed; / None wed the second but who killed the first,' elicits no acknowledgment of an o'er-hasty and incestuous union, but only a famously cool
response: 'The lady doth protest too much, methinks.' The king, indeed, seems
to feel that what is potentially offensive about the play has to do with its relevance to the queen, not to him. And the point at which he finally rises and
flees is not when the murder is represented, but when Hamlet identifies the
murderer, 'one Lucianus, nephew to the king,' and reveals his intention to
seize the throne—when it becomes clear that the players are presenting a play
about the murder of a king not by his usurping brother but by his usurping
nephew. Claudius is driven from the theater by the revelation of Hamlet's
threat to his throne and his life; and the crucial admission that has been
elicited by the play concerns not Claudius's crime but Hamlet's intentions.
Still, Hamlet is partly correct about the ultimate effects of tragic catharsis,
which does elicit a confessional soliloquy from Claudius in the next scene,
without, however, any corresponding gesture of repentance. In effect,
Claudius refuses the catharsis.

A more striking instance of theatrical dubiety about the effects of catharsis is found in Massinger's play *The Roman Actor*. I assume this is unfamiliar,
so I summarize the plot: Parthenius, the toadying factotum of the tyrant
Domitian, has an avaricious father. Paris, the Roman actor of the title, proposes curing him through the operation of dramatic catharsis: he will present
a play about a miser in which the father will recognize his own vice, and will
reform. The effectiveness of the treatment is guaranteed by reference to the
usual story about the murderer brought to confess by witnessing a play on the
subject. Domitian approves of the project, and orders the father to attend on
pain of death. The miser in Paris's play acknowledges the error of his ways and
is duly cured of his avarice, but Parthenius's father in the audience is unim-
pressed, and declares him a fool. Domitian warns the father that he is in mortal peril if he fails to take the play's lesson to heart, but he remains adamant
and is led off to be hanged.

In a second performance, the empress Domitia, already dangerously infat-
uated with Paris, commands him to play a tragedy of unrequited love. This so
moves her that at the point when the rejected hero is about to kill himself she
cries out to stop him (like the famous spectator at the murder of Desdemona), and the emperor calls a halt to the play. The love scene has, in fact,
evoked a violent passion in her, and she determines to have Paris as her lover.

She sends the emperor away, summons the actor, and orders him to make love to her; a spy informs the emperor, who watches Domitia woo Paris, interrupts them, has her imprisoned, and devises a theatrical punishment for the actor. He commands Paris to perform a play about a master who, as a test of his wife's fidelity, pretends to go on a journey, leaving her in the care of a trusted servant. Paris is to play the servant; Domitian announces his intention of playing the role of the husband himself. The play begins: the wife declares her passion for the servant. He initially refuses her, but finally yields when she threatens to claim to her husband that in his absence the servant had raped her. They embrace, Domitian enters as the husband, draws his sword, kills Paris in earnest, and pronounces a self-satisfied eulogy.

The final act abandons the metatheatrical for the dubiously moral: all the principal characters who remain alive, including the lustful empress and the toadying factotum, join together and assassinate Domitian. There is a certain Tom Thumbish quality to the dénouement, as the conspirators shout 'This for my father's death'; 'This for thy incest'; 'This for thy abuse'; and the empress— whose seduction of Paris was, after all, directly responsible for his death— stabs her husband crying 'This for my Paris!' But the play aborts any Bakhtinian tendency to an anarchically celebratory finale with the rather lame promise that the assassins will be duly punished by the tyrant's successor.

6

If one wanted a text to demonstrate the genuine relevance of the wildest antitheatrical polemics to actual theatrical practice in Renaissance England, *The Roman Actor* would do nicely. It acts out the charge that mimesis can only be pernicious, since we inevitably imitate the bad and ignore the good; it shows drama confirming us in our passions, not purging them, and far from providing moral exempla, turning us into monsters of lust. Massinger represents theater just as Gosson, Stubbes, and Prynne do, as the appropriate art for a pagan tyrant.

This is no doubt an extreme example, but it is also a very English one. A much more positive version of the same sort of directly theatrical catharsis is presented in Corneille's *L'Illusion Comique*, in which a disapproving father, confronted with a spectacle revealing the implications of his demands regarding his son's career, relents, and the two are reconciled: across the Channel, the didactic purgation of the play within the play works just as it is supposed to do. One of the most striking characteristics of the Elizabethan and Stuart stage is the degree to which its playwrights seem to share, and even to make dramatic capital out of, the prejudicial assumptions of their most hostile critics. Marlowe's damnable Faustus is a theatrical illusionist; the dangerously, seductively theatrical Cleopatra herself condemns the quick comedians who stage her and the squeaking actor who boys her greatness; Jonsonian drama constitutes a positive anatomy of anti-theatrical attitudes—*Epicoene,* with its transvestite con-artist heroine, *The Alchemist* and *Volpone,* those handbooks of charlatanry, greed, whoredom. Hamlet himself, attending the play within the play, offers to lie in Ophelia's lap, and thereby confirms the essential interdependence of theater and lechery. But perhaps even these examples are cathartic, miming the moralists to disarm and expell them.

I O

SHAKESPEARE AND THE KINDS OF DRAMA

WHEN SAMUEL JOHNSON, citing the authority of Thomas Rymer, asserted that Shakespeare's natural disposition was for comedy, not tragedy, he was assuming that there were only two genres of drama: comedy and tragedy. The assumption was made apparently without strain and without any sense that its categories imposed undue limitations on the practice of either drama or criticism. Shakespeare was allowed to violate the rules, exculpated by his ignorance of them, and was praised for his fidelity to nature. "Shakespeare's plays are not, in the rigorous or critical sense, either tragedies or comedies, but compositions of a distinct kind; exhibiting the real state of sublunary nature, which partakes of good and evil, joy and sorrow . . . in which, at the same time, the reveller is hasting to his wine, and the mourner burying his friend."[1] If we look closely at Johnson's "distinct kind," we shall see that it is not a new genre but a mixture of the two old ones: the kinds remain comedy and tragedy.

For Diderot, however, writing at the same time (though for a culture that admittedly had always taken its categories more seriously than the British), there was more to life, even to dramatic and critical life, than comedy and tragedy. Diderot therefore proposed a third genre, a serious bourgeois drama of a sort that could not be described within the limits of either of the traditional kinds.[2] In doing this, Diderot assumed that he was doing something new and that the old forms could not express certain types of experience that were growing increasingly important for the arts.

To both critics, as to multitudes before and since, comedy and tragedy constituted a dichotomy, a pair of alternatives, that together, whether fortunately or not, comprised the whole that was drama. My essay may be described as a walk round this dichotomy. The text from which Johnson was working, the Shakespeare folio, did in fact contain a third genre: the history. But "History," wrote Johnson, "was a series of actions, with no other than chronological succession, independent of each other, and without any tendency to introduce or regulate the conclusion. . . . As it had no plan, it had no limits."[3] Now this claim is, of course, nonsense, as anyone who has compared the history plays with their sources will be aware; but the important point for my purposes is the assumption that if a play is not comedy or tragedy, it is merely chronology and possesses no structure at all.

The implications of such a view are worth pausing over, for the notion that drama is a whole dichotomized into comedy and tragedy, eccentric or limited as it may appear when stated as a thesis, in fact underlies a good deal of our own thinking about theatrical forms. We can perceive this notion whenever we assume that comedy is an alternative to tragedy as we do, for example, when we ask a question like "Is Beckett's world view essentially comic or tragic?" The fact that this seems a perfectly sensible question (as it does, at least, to me) tells a good deal about our view of drama. We can see much more clearly the limitations imposed by a critic who asks whether Pope's impulse in the *Iliad* was essentially epic or lyric. Why are these categories being presented as alternatives? Why should we assume that one excludes the other? Pope was, in his own time, attacked with just this dichotomy—"A pretty poem, Mr. Pope, but you must not call it Homer"—but the criticism now strikes us as narrow and misguided.

Firm as the dramatic dichotomy was for the eighteenth-century critic, it proved to be of little value in analyzing Shakespearean drama. Most of the plays, as Johnson says, partake of both comedy and tragedy, and some could as easily be called one as the other: neoclassicism had to forget about the rules when dealing with Shakespeare. And in fact, though the genres had initially been invoked to categorize Shakespeare's "natural disposition" for comedy, generic questions do not figure significantly in Johnson's subsequent discussion. Nevertheless, the categories, however one chose to define them, had always been crucial to the critic's sense of Shakespeare, and it is probably a measure of Johnson's independence that he was willing finally to set the question aside; for it had descended to him not only from commentators like Rymer but from the first folio itself.

Hemminge and Condell's decision to organize the plays according to genre was a more radical one than we may be able to appreciate from this distance, though most critics have at some point observed that it was a decision with which the plays themselves are not entirely comfortable. Thus *Troilus and Cressida* is a tragedy in the folio, although the quarto declares it as witty "as the best comedy in Terence or Plautus," and *Cymbeline,* despite its concluding reconciliations and happy marriage, appears among the tragedies as well. Mere convenience no doubt had much to do with the folio's arrangement: but why was this arrangement deemed especially convenient? Our filing systems tell a good deal about our minds; Ben Jonson, for comparison, compiling his plays for the 1616 volume of his *Works* (the only English precedent for Shakespeare's editors), identified them by genre on their half-title pages but arranged them according to chronology. Jonson sees his plays, moreover, as belonging to all three of the ancient genres: there are tragedies, like *Sejanus*, comedies, like *Volpone*, and "comicall satyres," like *The Poetaster*. Generic arrangement seemed appropriate to Jonson only for his poetry, where "the ripest of my studies," the *Epigrams*, appear alone as a separate group.

Some of the Shakespearean chronology would doubtless have been forgotten by 1623, so a Jonsonian arrangement for the plays would probably have been impracticable; and associating all the plays according to their subject matter, which was the system employed for those concerned with English history, might well have proved excessively arbitrary. But just as grouping his epigrams together under the rubric of the classical genre seemed to Jonson to confer a special dignity on his favorite poems, so the genres themselves, at any rate those of comedy and tragedy, must also have had the attraction of classical forms for Shakespeare's first editors, conferring the dignity of ancient drama on the work of their fellow actor.

The assumption that genres themselves have value and confer dignity implies that genres possess a reality independent of particular examples and are not simply classifications but carry with them measures of value. I shall return to the question of drama as a dichotomy, but I now wish to consider the notion of genres as value judgments. I begin with two famous critical examples, written a century apart. Sir Philip Sidney complained that the English dramatists of his age failed to observe the rules of generic composition. Despite an exception made for *Gorboduc*, he found even that play "very defectious in the circumstances. . . . For it is faulty both in place and time, the two necessary companions of all corporall actions." Other modern tragedies offended even more blatantly against the decorum of the genre, "where you shal haue *Asia* of the one side, and *Affrick* of the other, and so many other vnder-kingdoms, that the Player, when he commeth in, must euer begin with telling where he is, or els the tale wil not be conceiued."[4] The passage then proceeds to parody the excesses of the tragic stage in Sidney's time. What I find noteworthy in all this is that for Sidney, however grotesque the dramas become, the genre remains capacious enough to contain them. The deficiencies of *Gorboduc* only make the play deficient; they do not banish it from the category of tragedy. The form itself is a good thing, but the classification is essentially descriptive: it is good to have tragedies, but bad tragedies are still tragedies.

For Thomas Rymer, a century later, the genre had no such breadth. *Othello*, he says, is held to be the model of tragedy in his time: "From all the Tragedies acted on our English Stage, *Othello is* said to bear the Bell away."

> The Moral, sure, is very instructive. First, This may be a caution to all Maidens of Quality how, without their Parents consent, they run away with Blackamoors. . . . Secondly, This may be a warning to all good Wives, that they look well to their Linnen. Thirdly, This may be a lesson to Husbands, that before their Jealousie be Tragical, the proofs may be Mathematical.[5]

After an exhaustive discussion of the play, Rymer concludes by asking, "What can remain with the Audience to carry home with them from this sort of Poetry, for their use and edification? how can it work, unless (instead of settling the mind, and purging our passions) to delude our senses? . . . the tragical part is, plainly none other, than a Bloody Farce, without salt or savour." And finally the play is indicted for contributing to the general decay of the arts: "when some senceless trifling tale, as that of *Othello* . . . impiously assumes the sacred name of Tragedy, it is no wonder if the Theatre grow corrupt and scandalous, and Poetry from its Ancient Reputation and Dignity, is sunk to the utmost Contempt and Derision."[6]

The argument here is not that the ambiguous moral and the triviality of the plot render *Othello* a bad tragedy. The play "impiously assumes the sacred name," but it is really not a tragedy at all: it is a farce. For Rymer—just as for Hemminge and Condell—the genre itself conferred a value; and it was a value that Rymer was unwilling to see conferred upon *Othello*; or, as he puts it, to see *Othello* confer upon itself.

It was clear to Johnson that Rymer's effort was misguided, at least insofar as the effort was directed at Shakespeare; but Rymer's assumptions still commonly inform modern notions of dramatic genre. Comedies for us may be high or low and remain comedies, but those that are either not funny enough or too serious we remove from the category: hence *Measure for Measure* becomes a problem play, *The Winter's Tale* a romance. On the other hand, comedies may be demoted for not being serious enough: what Feydeau wrote was not comedy but farce. *The London Merchant* and *Arden of Feversham* are domestic tragedies: here the term is a backhanded compliment since tragedy really ought not to be domestic. When T. S. Eliot in 1919 addressed himself to the question of whether or not *Catiline* and *Sejanus* were tragedies, he was replying to critics who assumed that by denying the plays a place in the genre, they had thereby demonstrated Ben Jonson's inadequacy as a playwright. Eliot adopts a stance that is shared by both Sidney and Johnson:

> To say that he failed because his genius was unsuited to tragedy is to tell us nothing at all. Jonson did not write a good tragedy, but we can see no reason why he should not have written one. If two

plays so different as *The Tempest* and *The Silent Woman* are both
comedies, surely the category of tragedy could be made wide
enough to include something possible for Jonson to have done.
But the classification of tragedy and comedy, while it may be
sufficient to mark the distinction in a dramatic literature of more
rigid form and treatment—it may distinguish Aristophanes from
Euripides—is not adequate to a drama of such variations as the
Elizabethans. Tragedy is a crude classification for plays so different in their tone as *Macbeth,* *The Jew of Malta,* and *The Witch of
Edmonton*; and it does not help us much to say that *The Merchant
of Venice* and *The Alchemist* are comedies. Jonson had his own
scale, his own instrument.[7]

This admittedly begs some large questions—Jonson's "own scale, his own
instrument" was, after all, one that took the categories very seriously. But
Eliot's solution, characteristically double-edged, simultaneously enlarges the
problematic genre and declares it irrelevant.

When Theodore Dreiser chose to call a novel *An American Tragedy,* he was
assuming, like Hemminge and Condell, like Rymer, that the generic term
itself conferred a value on the work: the title at once dignifies the form
(tragedy is a more noble enterprise than the novel), the story, and America as
well—it asserts that we too are capable of so grand a thing as tragedy. An
impressive young critic, reviewing the book when it appeared in 1925, attacked
Dreiser on precisely these grounds:

> *An American Tragedy* is not a tragedy. Aristotle was right (as,
> indeed, why should he not have been in so simple a matter?)
> when he observed that effective tragedies have noble men for
> their heroes. Now, Clyde Griffiths is, not to mince words, a
> moron. This certainly does not preclude him from the boon of
> your pity, but your pity is of a sort that a limed bird evokes. "Pity
> and terror," said the Stagirite, but there is pity and pity, and one
> variety of the emotion is a little unclean, certainly not ennobling.
> As for terror, there is no height here, there can be no fall; when
> this pitiful sharpy prepares his doom there can be no ominous
> sound of the beating on hollow mountains to presage the event.
> There can be no piling up of fateful thunderheads, no sense of
> heavy calamity to come. What you get . . . is a sense of worry—
> nagging, querulous worry as the ignorant Clyde seeks some con-
> traceptive or abortive device, as eventually he carries out, with the
> courage legendarily ascribed to the cornered rat, the brutal and

atrocious murder. The book . . . is immensely, overwhelmingly pathetic; it is not a tragedy.[8]

This is Lionel Trilling at the age of twenty, quite as self-confident as Sidney at twenty-five, and deriving a good deal of his self-confidence from a firm faith in the realities of genre. That wonderfully condescending parenthesis at the beginning, indeed, employs an authentically Sidneian gambit: compare the Elizabethan critic's argument that the amount of time encompassed by a drama "should be, both by Aristotle's precept and common reason, but one day." The rules, such critics maintain, are plain common sense. But the generic argument in both cases is in fact an argument from authority; and for all the accuracy of its observation, the real critical effort of Trilling's review is in finding the right category for *An American Tragedy*, in determining that it is not tragic but something less artistically respectable, pathetic. The effort, finally, is more Rymer's than Sidney's.

Similar arguments were advanced against the claims of *Death of a Salesman* to have achieved the status of tragedy. The grounds of the attack were that Willy Loman was the wrong kind of protagonist ("Hero! Why he isn't even a good salesman," Mark van Doren indignantly told me when I admitted that I had been to the play and liked it); and analogous examples appear constantly in movie and theater reviews. As a concluding modern instance, we might cite a now classic critical text, Northrop Frye's *Anatomy of Criticism*, that epic attempt to rescue generic criticism from value judgments, which fifty years later appears only a brilliant and infinitely subtle monument to the proliferation of categories.

2

It is obvious that with the difference between Sidney and Rymer we have the record of a transformation in cultural attitudes that had important effects on the practice of both criticism and dramaturgy. We can point, for example, to a number of related developments in the period: the institutionalization of the genres in the rule-making authority of quasi-judicial bodies like the Académie Française; the increasing importance in England of dramatic censorship on the one hand but, on the other, the increasingly powerful sponsorship of the stage by the court and the growing protection of royal authority; and, throughout Europe, the rapid centralization of the arts under the crown, where they became significant aspects of royal power and magnificence. But to view the question merely as a historical progression (and, as I have presented it, as one moving downward) is to consider it too narrowly. Criticism is, in its broadest sense, any response to a work of art; and generic criticism is not limited to professional critics. The genres had real vitality for the drama, a vitality which has not been historically delimited. For a critic like Rymer the genres were no doubt a dead hand; but surely we should look further—for example, to Davenant and Dryden, Purcell and Hogarth—before we decide that the notions of comedy and tragedy had become limitary for the critics of even Rymer's era.

I have chosen for my first example a perverse one: the most notorious of Renaissance categorizers, Julius Caesar Scaliger. By beginning with some passages from Scaliger's *Poetics*—in its own time both famous and infamous, since then largely scorned or ignored—I can indicate the breadth and usefulness of the categories for the Renaissance critic.

Scaliger begins, naturally, with Aristotle on tragedy. He says he has no wish to impugn the classic definition but will merely add his own: "Tragedy is the imitation through action [i.e., not through narration] of an important man's fortunes, with an unhappy outcome, and expressed in serious poetic language. Although Aristotle includes melody and song, they are not, as philosophers would say, of the essence of tragedy. . . . Moreover, the term catharsis does not at all describe the effect of every plot."[9] Scaliger, that is, finds Aristotle too limiting, and he expands the boundaries of the definition on pragmatic grounds. Melody and song are considered inessential because the printed version of a tragedy does not cease to be a tragedy. This observation, like the remark about catharsis, to which I shall return, exhibits Scaliger in one of his most characteristic modes: he is exceedingly literalistic, and the critical doctrine that means most to him is his own common sense.

Later in his *Poetics*, Scaliger proceeds to give his own account of the dramatic genres:

> Though tragedy is similar to epic, it differs in that it rarely admits the lower classes, such as messengers, merchants, sailors, and the like. On the other hand, in comedies there are never kings, except in a few cases, such as the *Amphitruo* of Plautus. I am really speaking now of plays with Greek characters [i.e., such as those of Plautus and Terence], for the later Latin playwrights included Roman characters dignified by togas and royal robes. The lively characters of satyr plays are drunken, witty, cheerful, sarcastic. Mimes include cloth workers, shoemakers, butchers, chicken farmers, fishmongers, vegetable growers—figures whom, indeed, Old Comedy did not exclude. . . . Tragedy and comedy have the same mode of representation but are different in subject matter and organization. The subjects of tragedy are great, terrible things—royal commands, slaughter, despair, suicide, exile,

bereavement, parricide, incest, fires, battles, blindings, weeping, moaning, funerals, eulogies, dirges. In comedy there are games, revels, weddings, carousing, slaves' tricks, drunkenness, old men deceived and swindled of their money. (366–67)

Scaliger continues, describing satyr plays and mimes in the same way, and then turns to the nature of dramatic action:

Now a tragedy, if it is really a proper tragedy, is entirely serious. . . . However, many comedies have unhappy endings for some of the characters; this is true of Plautus's *Miles Gloriosus, Asinaria, Persa*, and others. In the same way, there are a number of happy tragedies: in Euripides' *Electra*, except for the death of Aegisthus, there is joy for many; *Ion* has a happy ending as does *Helen*. Then too, although Aeschylus's *Eumenides* contains tragic elements (such as murders and the furies), its structure is more like that of a comedy: the beginning [in *Agamemnon*] is joyful for the guard, though troubling for Clytemnestra because of her husband's arrival; then comes the murder [of Clytemnestra], and Electra and Orestes are happy; the ending is happy for everyone— Apollo, Orestes, the populace, Pallas, the Eumenides. Thus it is by no means true, as we have always been taught, that tragedy must have an unhappy ending: it need only include terrible things. (367)

Scaliger himself had stipulated earlier that tragedy have an unhappy ending, but the requirement is withdrawn here on empirical grounds.

The question of the unities is related for Scaliger both to the problem of verisimilitude and to the function of drama generally:

The events themselves should be so organized that they approach as nearly as possible to the truth, for the play must not be performed merely so that the spectators may either admire or be overwhelmed (as the critics say used to be true of Aeschylus's drama), but to teach, move and delight. We are pleased with joking, as in comedy, or with serious things, if they are properly treated. Most men, however, detest lies. Therefore those battles at Thebes, and those sieges that are concluded in two hours, do not please me, nor is any poet wise who undertakes to complete the journey from Delphi to Athens or Athens to Thebes in a moment of time. Thus in Aeschylus, Agamemnon is killed and immediately buried, so quickly that the actor scarcely has time to catch his breath. Nor can the scene where Hercules throws Lichas into the sea be condoned, for there is no way of representing it without disgracing the truth. (368)

A good deal of Scaliger's discussion is obviously relevant to Sidney. The genres for such Renaissance critics were not sets of rules but classifications, ways of organizing our knowledge of the past so that we may understand our relation to it and locate its virtues in ourselves. The ancient world, says Scaliger's *Poetics*, is not a world of monuments. It is real and recoverable, and the process of creation is also a process of re-creation. (Such an assertion comes appropriately from a man who apparently invented his family history and christened himself Julius Caesar.) Very little of Scaliger's immense treatise is devoted to theory as such; his sense of his categories derives from an exhaustive consideration of particular examples. Critical theories, indeed, are constantly being faulted or dismissed because they fail to account for the realities of dramatic texts: the only authorities Scaliger takes seriously are the works themselves, and he has a great variety of ways of associating and comparing them—by kinds of subject matter, kinds of structure, kinds of denouement; but also by poetic and stylistic devices, the various uses of the chorus, even the relation of the title to the action.

Clearly for a critic like Scaliger, the process of classification constitutes the essence of criticism. On the other hand, his actual responses to the dramas he is classifying tend to be relentlessly superficial: both Scaliger and Sidney are eloquent on the wonders of poetry, but neither is capable of the minimally imaginative effort required by plays which ignore the unities of place or time. Sidney calls such plays preposterous, Scaliger calls them lies. Behind these judgments, obviously, are assumptions about the nature of representation and imitation so limited that they ought to prove crippling for any practical critic. But here the categories become crucial for the Renaissance mind: if we keep our eye on the genres, we shall see that they do not exclude even preposterous or mendacious examples—particular defects are, in fact, of very little significance. There are better plays and worse ones, but the genres constitute a complete system and have room for all. Scaliger's sense of individual works is often exceedingly narrow; but his sense of his categories is, in comparison with ours, generous and capacious.

Scaliger is an important figure for my purposes because his attitude toward genre is so dependent on the particular. His categories constitute basically a filing system, and the system reveals primarily relationships between works, and only incidentally judgments about them. Not that Scaliger is innocent of judgment: he has strong ideas about how drama should be written and does not hesitate to express them. But the judgments derive from the categories only in the sense that comparisons of similar works enable us to see which ones are best and what is best about them. The genres allow us to compare; it is the comparisons and the models they provide that are important. (Indeed, Book 5 of the *Poetics*, entitled *Criticism*, consists of nothing but comparisons—of Greek with Latin writers, of Homer with Virgil, of Virgil with other Greeks, of Latin writers with each other, of descriptions of epic and tragic subjects such as tempests, plagues, and assorted disasters, of accounts of animals, mythological figures, natural wonders, of more disasters, of Lucan with Nicander, and finally of a variety of other poetical passages which seem not to fit into any of the earlier categories and are presumably being filed under miscellaneous.)

It is apparent from even the brief selections I have cited that for all Scaliger's sense of detail, he has very little interest in *how* drama works. The best plays teach, move, and delight, he says, but this quality is felt to be simply a function of their verisimilitude. And the doctrine of catharsis, the mainstay of most Renaissance theories of tragedy, he rejects out of hand. In part, of course, Scaliger is exhibiting here merely the defects of his virtues; and the rejection of catharsis (as I have suggested in "The Play of Conscience") may also spring from an apprehension of the genuine difficulties in the Aristotelian passage. But no alternative theory is proposed, and Scaliger's genres, despite their breadth, leave little room for a critic who wishes to understand the *effects* of drama.

And yet, on the whole, the most serious kind of drama was defined for most Renaissance critics precisely by its effect as described by Aristotle, or at least by Aristotle as the Renaissance understood him. It was generally assumed that drama was a form of rhetoric; imitation was its means, but its function was to persuade. (The principal sixteenth-century exceptions to this are found in Scaliger and Guarini, for whom imitation was not the means but the end of drama. This is a more strictly Aristotelian line, since for Aristotle poetry was a form of logic, not rhetoric.) Tragedy achieved its end by purging the passions of its audience through pity and terror—catharsis was the particular kind of utility produced by tragedy. Now the passage in Aristotle from which this notion derives is brief and notoriously puzzling; I have discussed its ramifications for Renaissance theories of drama in "The Play of Conscience," where the issue is considered in detail. I shall give here, therefore, only a short summary of the relevant points. Tragic catharsis is mentioned only once in the *Poetics*, in a passage that says, literally, that drama "effects through pity and terror purgation of similar feelings"—that pitiable and terrible events (strictly speaking, not the emotions of pity and terror but the things in the play that arouse these emotions) purge similar events and feelings. From the time of the first Renaissance commentators, it has been almost invariably assumed that the purgation takes place in the audience, that it is the spectators who are purged by means of their response to the terrible events of the drama. But it is not clear from the syntax that Aristotle is referring to the audience at this point at all, and Gerald Else, in the most persuasive statement of the argument against the standard reading, maintains that the effect Aristotle is describing takes place entirely within the play's action. The pitiable and terrible events that precipitate the tragedy—the parricide of Oedipus, the matricide of Orestes—are purged by the pitiable and terrible sufferings of the hero. It is Thebes or Athens that is purified, not the audience.[10]

The notion of tragedy as a genre defined by its effect is a Renaissance one. Modern accounts, on the other hand, are far more concerned with *hamartia*, the "tragic flaw," and with the hero. Indeed, we even locate the flaw *in* the hero, whereas Aristotle says that it is to be found in the action. The clearest and most enthusiastic developments of the cathartic thesis in the Renaissance are Italian; they are characteristically broad and inclusive, and often cite the purifying properties of drama as evidence of the utility of theater to the health of the state. English claims tend to be both scarcer and more modest, though Thomas Heywood's *Apology for Actors* invokes a quite sensational instance of the purgative topos in action, citing a story about a woman who had murdered her husband and, seeing a play about a similar crime, was driven to confess in a paroxysm of repentance. Aristotelian catharsis here literally takes place in the audience; and this must be the sort of example Hamlet has in mind when he projects the operation of his play *The Mousetrap* upon the conscience of the guilty king. Such stories were common enough in the period, and so powerful were the effects of tragedy on audiences generally claimed to be that many critics recommended that the emotional impact be mitigated, lest the spectators be utterly overwhelmed. In fact, tragedies were regularly performed in Italy with comic or grotesque *intermezzi* between the acts. Doubtless this was primarily designed to satisfy a taste for variety; but there was also good critical doctrine to justify the practice.

Tragic catharsis, moreover, was quickly accommodated to comedy as well. Francesco Robortello, the first major commentator on the *Poetics* (1548), effortlessly derived an "Aristotelian" theory of comedy from his own translation of the essay, for the most part by simply substituting the word comedy for tragedy. And fifty years later Guarini declared that "comedy, through laughter, releases the soul from melancholy, renders its operation light and quick. Tragedy in a contrary way, calls the flighty soul back to seriousness and reason, making it fear to a proper degree those things which it should fear."[11] Socrates at the end of the *Symposium* had been able to convince Agathon and Aristophanes, tragic and comic dramatists, that their two arts were the same.

I know of no Renaissance theorist who cites the passage as a precedent, but it is clear that by Guarini's time, Socrates had made his case.

Returning now to the notion of drama as a dichotomy, a split between comedy and tragedy, we can see that comedy, in the accounts just cited, is not merely an alternative to tragedy, since their operations are fully complementary. Comedy is as necessary as tragedy to the psychological health of the state; more than this, comedy is necessary *to* tragedy for the proper effects of drama to be achieved in the audience. Our own notions of what is appropriate to tragedy tend to conceive of a drama that is much more unmixed, and when we think about Renaissance tragedies we usually forget about the *intermezzi*. When we consider the effects of *King Lear* or *Hamlet* or *Antony and Cleopatra* on seventeenth-century audiences, we are quick to observe that Shakespeare's comic scenes do not relieve but rather heighten the tragic movement. But do we ever remind ourselves that tragedies on the English stage invariably concluded with jigs? The deaths of Cordelia and Lear, Hamlet, and Cleopatra were followed by dances, comic songs, plays of wit, even clowning. This was not merely considered acceptable; it was an invariable practice, catering no doubt to a popular taste for variety but also serving to mitigate the tragic catastrophe.

Sebastiano Serlio, designing the prototype stage settings for the three Aristotelian dramatic genres, summed up the Renaissance attitude toward the dramatic categories in a concise visual statement. The comic and tragic scenes are both cityscapes, two versions of the same society, two views of the same world. But the satiric scene is wooded and wild; it takes place somewhere altogether different. Palladio and Scamozzi institutionalized the dichotomy in the Teatro Olimpico at Vicenza: the permanent setting, five perspective street scenes, can accommodate either comedy or tragedy. But the theater has no way of presenting the third kind, the satiric or pastoral.

3

The dramatic dichotomy in the Renaissance, then, expressed not a sense of limitation but a real and fruitful interrelationship between the genres. By the same token, mixed forms were felt to be good because, as Sidney put it, "if seuered they be good, the conjunction cannot be hurtfull."[12] There was a comedy of wonder and delight, fully appropriate to the decorum of tragedy.[13] What this argues, I think, is not that the Renaissance took its tragedies less seriously than we do, but rather more so. We can see the descent of the *intermezzi* and jigs in Nahum Tate's revision of *King Lear*, which Johnson himself condoned precisely because he found the play so overwhelming, or in Davenant's *Macbeth*, which provided flying machines and a sinking cave and expanded the witches' scenes into a full set of musical and ballet entries.

Pepys gives a curious testimony to the dramatic force of the latter production. He first went to see *Macbeth*, his diary records, on November 5, 1664 at Davenant's Duke of York's Theater and thought it only "a pretty good play, but admirably acted."[14] Two years later, on December 28, 1666, he went again, this time with his wife, and was much more enthusiastic: "to the Duke's House, and there saw Macbeth most excellently acted, and a most excellent play for variety" (p. 451). Ten days later, on January 7, 1667, he was back, and this time he undertook to account for his growing interest in the production: "To the Duke's house and saw *Macbeth*, which, though I saw it lately, yet appears a most excellent play in all respects, but especially in divertisement, though it be a deep tragedy; which is a strange perfection in a tragedy, it being most proper here and suitable" (p. 453). Pepys knows what he is supposed to think about "divertisement" in tragedy; but the critical principle is contradicted by the aesthetic facts, and he accedes to the facts. On April 19 he returned once more "to the playhouse, where saw *Macbeth*, which, though I have seen it often, yet is it one of the best plays for a stage, and a variety of dancing and music, that ever I saw." On this occasion, however, his wife tells him that the servants "do observe my minding my pleasures more than usual, which I confess, and am ashamed," and he determines to "leave it till Whitsunday" (p. 486)—no small self-denial, for in that year Whitsunday fell on May 26, more than a month away. He saw the play again on October 16, but this time he "was vexed to see Young, who is but a bad actor at best, act Macbeth in the room of Betterton, who, poor man! is sick, but Lord! what a prejudice it wrought in me against the whole play" (p. 569). Nevertheless, three weeks later, on November 6, he was back with his wife at "*Macbeth*, which we still like mightily, though mighty short of the content we used to have when Betterton acted, who is still sick" (p. 579). On the next August 12 he and his wife again "saw *Macbeth*, to our great content" (p. 670); and they went yet again on December 21, 1668. This time, however, the performance had to compete for Pepys's attention with both a bearded lady in the afternoon ("bushy and thick . . . a strange sight to me, I confess, and what pleased me mightily") and the presence in the theater of the king and court (p. 702). Three weeks later, on January 15, 1669, he was engaged with the lords of the Treasury, but he sent his wife and a friend to see the play once more by themselves (p. 707).

Pepys here is a true heir of the Renaissance spectator, endlessly enthusiastic about tragedy and finding that the inclusion of "divertisement" only adds to its effectiveness. In fact, as I have indicated in "Macbeth and the Antic Round," what is probably most notable about Davenant's version of *Macbeth* is not its inclusion of *intermezzi*, which had, in one form or another, been a feature of popular tragedy both on the Continent and in England for over a century, but the decision to incorporate them directly into the structure of the play and thus to make *Macbeth* itself a dramatic dichotomy.

In the examples I have been discussing, comedy had its place as an adjunct to tragedy, necessary but nevertheless dependent. There is a generic truth in this: the tragic purgation of the state and the spirit and the reassertion of norms that is the end of tragedy leave us in the world of comedy. Tragedy is what makes comedy possible—or, putting it another way, comedy is the end of tragedy—and the Renaissance liked to emphasize this aspect of tragedy by concluding its tragedies with jigs. But of course comedy is also an independent genre, and its nature has always proved far more elusive to critics than that of tragedy. Aristotle could not learn its history; and though Robortello and Guarini undertook to infer theories of comedy from the theory of tragedy, their accounts fail to persuade precisely because they fail to distinguish sufficiently the two genres from each other. Comedy cannot simply be tragedy with the name changed. We may be unclear about tragic catharsis, but at least we know it is there, convincing us that tragedy *works*—even if we do not know how or on whom. We have had, historically, no such conviction about comedy, not even a general agreement about what constitutes its "working." Discussions of comedy have traditionally tended to be concerned primarily with its subject matter, its structure, or its personnel.

Comedy has usually been described as inhering in the general, tragedy in the particular: comedy is a world of types and eccentrics, tragedy of individuals and unique occurrences. There has never been a *tragedia dell'arte*, but the *commedia dell'arte*, a set of stock characters with a variable scenario, has provided a norm for comedy since Greek and Roman times. This is, of course, only a norm, and will not account for all examples, nor is it by any means the only comic norm. Still, even considering the broadest range of comedy, we tend to find the really individualized comic characters not in plays but in novels, in figures like Don Quixote and Mr. Micawber. If we turn to drama for counter-examples, the most obvious is Falstaff, and he is certainly a comic character—no one more so. Is it entirely a quibble to remark that he was created not for a comedy but for a history, and one which, moreover, the contemporary observer Francis Meres classified as a tragedy? When Falstaff subsequently became the center of his own comedy, *The Merry Wives of Windsor*, he was far less individualized, much more of a type. There are, in any case, very few Falstaffs in comedy. The greatest comic characters of drama have tended to be either stock characters (Harlequin and Scaramouche) or actors—W. C. Fields, Chaplin, the Marx Brothers, Zero Mostel (or Will Kempe, or Robert Armin)—who always play essentially the same role. The most highly individualized comic characters in Shakespeare are figures like Rosalind, Berowne, Beatrice, Benedick who are unique by virtue of being critics. But even these characters, even when they are as central as Rosalind is to the action of her drama, we do not treat in the way we treat tragic protagonists; criticism does not feel a need to investigate and explain their psychologies as it does with Hamlet, Lear, and Coriolanus; we do not think of them as individuals, that is to say, as existing outside of their dramatic contexts, apart from their plays. And individualized as are Jonson's or Molière's great comic creations—say Sir Epicure Mammon or Alceste the Misanthrope—they are individual by virtue of being eccentric: their eccentricity posits a norm; and if they cannot ultimately be accommodated to that norm, they will ultimately be expelled by it. When Coriolanus is banished, his play moves with him: there is, dramatically speaking, a world elsewhere. But Alceste stalks offstage, we hear no more of Malvolio or Don John, and all that is left of Shylock in the final act of his play is an admonitory precept about the man who hath no music in himself. I am not, of course, denying that tragedy also uses eccentrics and stock characters—the orphaned child, the widowed mother, the moustache-twirling villain, the lecherous landlord, the heartless plutocrat. Comedy, however, *normally* works in this way; and the less tragedy does so, the more seriously we are willing to take it.

The generalizing and normative nature of comedy may be seen too in an important linguistic phenomenon. In most European languages in the Renaissance the generic term for drama was comedy. The Swiss traveler Thomas Platter in 1599 reported that when he was in London he "saw the tragedy of the first Emperor Julius [Caesar] with at least fifteen characters very well acted. At the end of the comedy," he continues, "they danced according to their custom. . . ."[15] Comedy, for Platter, *includes* tragedy. Platter's word for actor is "comedian"; *comedien* is still a generic term for actor in French, as is *commediante* in Italian. Although the *OED* does not note this usage in English, Johnson gives as a definition of comedian "a player in general, a stage-player."

If we think about comedy in terms of stock characters, Shakespeare provides some interesting examples. Here, for instance, are two hypothetical casts: (1) A jealous husband, a chaste wife, an irascible father, a clever malicious servant, a gullible friend, a bawdy witty maid; (2) A pair of lovers, their irascible fathers, a bawdy serving woman, a witty friend, a malicious friend, a kindly foolish priest. Both of these groups represent recognizable comic configurations, though in fact they are also the casts of *Othello* and *Romeo and Juliet*. Being able to see them in this light, I think, reveals something important about how both these tragedies work. Much of their dramatic force derives from the way they continually tempt us with comic possibilities. We are told in a prologue that Romeo and Juliet are star-crossed, but if inevitability is a requisite of tragedy, neither play will qualify for the genre: they are the most iffy dramas in the Shakespeare canon. At innumerable points in both plays, had anything happened differently, the tragic catastrophe would have been averted. *Othello* particularly teases audiences in this way—as the famous story about the man who lept from his seat, furious at the impending murder of Desdemona, and shouted "You fool, can't you see she's innocent?" reveals. The story is no doubt apocryphal (I have even heard it told about Verdi's opera), but the point is that it is unique to this play: there are no similar tales of spectators leaping up to rescue Cordelia, to save Gloucester from blinding, to dash the asp from Cleopatra's hand. Thomas Rymer's analysis of *Othello* is perverse and insensitive; but his rage at the play constitutes an absolutely authentic response.

Conversely, I think that *Measure for Measure* tempts us with tragic possibilities. For the Jacobean spectator (or editor), the play's conclusion was sufficient to define it as a comedy. Modern critics, however, want a term that accounts for the whole of the play's tone and action; hence we call it a dark comedy, or a problem play, as if it could not start out one way and end another. What would a Renaissance audience have expected of a drama called *Measure for Measure*? The title says we get what we deserve: it is surely not the title of a comedy. Comedy gives us *more* than we deserve; treat everyone according to their deserts, and the results are very serious indeed. All the expectations that are raised in the first three acts are consistent with the title and promise a tragic conclusion. The play then changes its course not by suddenly imposing a happy ending but by adopting in the final two acts a radically new tone toward its central questions of morality and license, law and justice, chastity and lust. Indeed, its transformed attitude toward sexuality is even realized in that classic device of low comedy, the bed trick. Obviously this sort of thing will be successful only with an audience willing to follow changes of tone and not expecting consistency from its genres. But if one takes tragedy seriously, one will also take seriously being rescued from it.

Shakespeare could make such a play effective and the spectators could respond to it because they believed in the living reality of the dramatic genres. The categories were not only what related the culture to its past but also what related the playwright and his audience to one another. Like Scaliger, Shakespeare thought of genres not as sets of rules but as sets of expectations and possibilities. Comedy and tragedy were not forms: they were shared assumptions.

MACBETH AND THE ANTIC ROUND

I BEGIN MY CONSIDERATION of *Macbeth* some years before the folio, for what seem to me good historical reasons: while it is certainly true, as historians of the book from Stanley Morison to D. F. McKenzie and Randall McLeod have insisted, that works of literature do not exist independent of their material embodiment in texts, the printing of Shakespeare's plays is, nevertheless, really incidental. In their inception, in their conception, they are not books but scripts, designed to be realized in performance; and in this form they are not at all fixed by their material embodiment, whether quarto or folio (to say nothing of Riverside, Oxford, or Pelican), but fluid and open-ended. To realize them requires an infinite number of collaborative, often non-authorial, decisions, both textual and interpretive, which in turn eventuate in continual, increasingly non-authorial, revisions, excisions, additions. In this respect, Shakespeare plays have always been the free-floating signifiers of postmodern theory, standing for an infinitely variable range of signifieds. As I have argued in "What Is a Text," the play, even in print, is always a process.

In the case of *Macbeth*, we are well into the process from the outset, since the earliest surviving version of the play, that included in the folio, is demonstrably a revision. It includes songs for the witches, given in the text only as incipits ('Come away, come away, etc.'; 'Black spirits, etc.'). These are songs from Middleton's play *The Witch*. In performance they would have been accompanied by dances, which means that in the theater these scenes took a good deal longer than they do on the page. The manuscript of Davenant's version of the play, prepared around 1664, includes the whole text of the witches' songs from Middleton—these are really musical dialogues, short scenes. The fact that Davenant did not supply his own witches' material at these points, as he did elsewhere, suggests that the Middleton material was already a standard feature of the play.[1]

The elaboration of the witches' roles could have taken place anywhere up to about fifteen years after the play was first performed, but the presence of the Middleton songs suggests that Shakespeare was no longer around to do the revising, which presumes a date after 1614. Why, only a decade after the play was written, would augmenting the witches' roles have seemed a good idea? To begin with, by 1610 or so witchcraft, magic, and the diabolical were good theater business—Barnabe Barnes's *The Devil's Charter* was at the Globe in the same season as *Macbeth*, and Marston's *The Wonder of Women*, with its sorcery scenes, was at the Blackfriars. Jonson's *Masque of Queens*, performed at court in 1609, inaugurated a decade of sorcery plays and masques, including *The Tempest*, *The Alchemist*, *The Witch*, *The Witch of Edmonton*, *The Devil Is an Ass*, and the revived and rewritten *Doctor Faustus*.

The ubiquitousness of theatrical magic is perhaps sufficient reason for the elaboration of the witches in *Macbeth*, but for me, it does not account for everything. When Macbeth, after the murder of Banquo, goes to consult the witches, and they show him a terrifying vision of Banquo's heirs, Hecate proposes a little entertainment to cheer him up:

> I'll charm the air to give a sound
> While you perform your antic round,
> That this great king may kindly say
> Our duties did his welcome pay. (4.1.151–4)[2]

The tone of the scene here changes significantly: the witches are not professional and peremptory any more, they are lighthearted, gracious, and deferential. We may choose to treat this as a moment of heavy irony, though Macbeth does not seem to respond to it as such; but if it is not ironic, the change of tone suggests that the 'great king' addressed in this passage is not the king on stage, but instead a real king in the audience, Banquo's descendant and the king of both Scotland and England.

The editors of both the recent Oxford and Cambridge editions have resisted the suggestion that this moment in *Macbeth* reflects the local conditions of a court performance, observing that nothing in the scene positively requires such an assumption. This is true enough, but I also see nothing implausible about it, and though there is no record of a court performance, King James surely must have wanted to see a play that included both witches and his ancestors. What are the implications if we assume that the text we have is a revision to take into account the presence of the king, and that his interest in witchcraft also accounts for the augmentation of the witches' scenes, so that the 'filthy,' 'black and midnight hags' become graciously entertaining after they have finished being ominously informative? Such a play would be significantly less author-centered than our familiar text: first because it is reviser-centered—and the presence of the Middleton scenes implies that Shakespeare was not the reviser—and second, because it is patron-centered, taking a particular audience into account. To this extent Shakespeare's *Macbeth* is already, in the folio version, a significantly collaborative enterprise. But if this is correct, it also means that this version of *Macbeth* is a special case, devised for a single occasion, a performance at court, not the play in repertory, the play for the public.

This leads us to another question: how did this text become the 'standard' version—why was it the right version to include in the folio? It needs to be emphasized that this is a question whether we assume that a performance before the king is involved or not: there is no denying that this is a revised text with non-Shakespearean material. Most attempts to deal with this issue beg the question, assuming that what we have is indeed the wrong text, and that Shakespeare's first editors would never have included it if they had had any alternative. The right text, the text we want (the promptbook, or even better, Shakespeare's holograph) must have been unavailable, lost—burned, perhaps, in the destruction of the Globe in 1613, as if only a conflagration could explain the refusal of Hemminge and Condell (who promise, after all, 'the true original copies') to give us what we want. But perhaps it was included precisely because it was the right text—whether because by 1620 this, quite simply, was the play, or, more interestingly, because the best version of the play was the one that included the king.

This would make it an anomaly in the folio, a version of the play prepared for a single, special occasion, rather than the standard public theater version. In fact, the play as it stands in the folio is anomalous in a number of respects. It is a very unusual play textually: it is very short, the shortest of the tragedies (half the length of *Hamlet*, a third shorter than the average), shorter, too than all the comedies except *The Comedy of Errors*. It looks, moreover, as if the version we have has not only been augmented with witches' business, but has also been cut and rearranged, producing some real muddles in the narrative: for example, the scene between Lennox and the Lord, 3.6, reporting action that has not happened yet, or the notorious syntactic puzzles of the account of the battle in the opening scenes, or the confusion of the final battle, in which Macbeth is slain onstage, and twenty lines later Macduff re-enters with his head. Revision and cutting were, of course, standard and necessary procedures in a theatre where the normal playing time was two hours; but if theatrical cuts are to explain the peculiarities of this text, why was it cut so peculiarly, not to say ineptly? Arguments that make the muddles not the result of cutting but an experiment in surreal and expressionistic dramaturgy only produce more questions, rendering the play a total anomaly, both in Shakespeare's work and in the drama of the period.

The very presence of the witches is unusual. Shakespeare makes use of the supernatural from time to time—ghosts in *Richard III*, *Julius Caesar*, and most notably in *Hamlet*, fairies and their magic in *A Midsummer Night's Dream*, Prospero's sorcery in *The Tempest*, Joan of Arc's and Marjory Jourdain's in the *Henry VI* plays, and Rosalind's claim to be a magician at the end of *As You Like It*—but there is no other play in which witches and witchcraft are such an integral element of the plot. Indeed, whether or not King James was in the audience, the fact that it is the witches who provide the royal entertainment can hardly be accidental. The king was intensely interested in witchcraft; his dialogue on the subject, *Dæmonology*, first published in Edinburgh in 1597, was reissued upon his accession to the English throne in 1603—there were three editions in that year alone. This and the *Basilicon Doron*, his philosophy of kingship, were the two works that he chose to introduce himself to his English subjects, and as I have argued elsewhere, witchcraft and kingship have an intimate relationship in the Jacobean royal ideology.[3] This is a culture in which the supernatural and witchcraft, even for sceptics, are as much part of reality as religious truth is. Like the ghost in *Hamlet*, the reality of the witches in *Macbeth* is not in question; the question, as in *Hamlet*, is why they are present and how far to believe them.

Like the ghost, too, the witches are quintessential theatrical devices: they dance and sing, perform wonders, appear and disappear, fly, produce visions—do, in short, all the things that, historically, we have gone to the theater to see. They open the play and set the tone for it. On Shakespeare's stage they would simply have materialized through a trap door, but Shakespeare's audience believed in magic already. Our rationalistic theater requires something more theatrically elaborate—not necessarily machinery, but some serious mystification. For Shakespeare's audience, the mystification is built into their physical appearance, which defies the categories: they look like men and are women. The indeterminacy of their gender is the first thing Banquo calls attention to. This is a defining element of their nature, a paradox that identifies them as witches: a specifically female propensity to evil—being a witch—is defined by its apparent masculinity. This also is, of course, one of the central charges leveled at Shakespeare's theater itself, the ambiguity of its gender roles—the fact that on Shakespeare's stage the women are really male. But the gender ambiguity relates as well to roles within the play—Lady Macbeth unsexes herself, and accuses her husband of being afraid to act like a man. What constitutes acting like a man in this play? Killing, obviously, but anything else? Lady Macbeth unsexing herself, after all, renders herself, unexpectedly, not a man but a child, and thus incapable of murder: 'Had he not resembled / My father as he slept, I had done't (2.2.12–13). Indeed, the definitive relation between murder and manhood applies to heroes as well as villains. When Macduff is told of the murder of his wife and children and is urged to 'Dispute it like a man,' he replies that he must first 'feel it as a man'

(4.3.220–2). Whatever this says about his sensitivity and family feeling, it also says that murder is what makes you feel like a man.

The unsettling quality of the witches goes beyond gender. Their language is paradoxical; fair is foul and foul is fair; when the battle's lost and won. One way of looking at this is to say that it constitutes no paradox at all: any battle that is lost has also been won, but by somebody else. The person who describes a battle as lost and won is either on both sides or on neither; what is fair for one side is bound to be foul for the other. In a brilliantly subversive essay, Harry Berger, Jr., suggested that the witches are in fact right, and are telling the truth about the world of the play—that there really are no ethical standards in it, no right and wrong sides.[4] Duncan certainly starts out sounding like a good king: the rhetoric of his monarchy is full of claims about its sacredness, about the deference that is due to it, how it is part of a natural hierarchy descending from God, how the king is divinely anointed, and so forth. But in fact none of this is borne out by the play: Duncan's rule is utterly chaotic, and maintaining it depends on constant warfare—the battle that opens the play, after all, is not an invasion, but a rebellion. Duncan's rule has never commanded the deference it claims for itself—deference is not natural to it. In upsetting that sense of the deference Macbeth feels he owes to Duncan, maybe the witches are releasing into the play something the play both overtly denies and implicitly articulates: that there is no basis whatever for the values asserted on Duncan's behalf; that the primary characteristic of his rule, perhaps of any rule in the world of the play, is not order but rebellion.

Whether or not this is correct, it must be to the point that women are the ones who prompt this dangerous realization in Macbeth. The witches live outside the social order, but they embody its contradictions: beneath the woman's exterior is also a man; beneath the man's exterior is also a woman; nature is full of competing claims, not ordered and hierarchical but deeply anarchic; and to acknowledge that is to acknowledge the reality and force and validity of the individual will—to acknowledge that all of us have claims that conflict with the claims about deference and hierarchy. This is the same recognition that Edmund brings into *King Lear* when he invokes Nature as his goddess. It is a Nature that is not the image of divine order, but one in which the strongest and craftiest survive—and when they survive, they then go on to devise claims about Nature that justify their success, claims about hierarchies, natural law and order, the divine right of kings. Edmund is a villain, but if he were ultimately successful he would be indistinguishable from the Duncans and Malcolms (and James I's) of Shakespeare's world.

Here is a little history: the real Macbeth was, like Richard III, the victim of a gigantic and very effective publicity campaign. Historically, Duncan was the usurper—that is what the rebellion at the beginning of the play is about,

though there is no way of knowing it from Shakespeare. Macbeth had a claim
to the throne (Shakespeare does know this: Duncan at one point in the play
refers to him as 'cousin' (1.4.14)—they were first cousins, both grandsons of
King Malcolm II). Macbeth's murder of Duncan was a political assassination,
and Macbeth was a popular hero because of it. The legitimate heir to the
throne, whose rights have been displaced by the usurping Duncan, was Lady
Macbeth. When Macbeth ascended the throne, he was ruling as Protector or
Regent until Lady Macbeth's son came of age (she did have children—it is
Shakespeare who deprives her and Macbeth of those heirs). Macbeth's defeat
at the end of the play, by Malcolm and Macduff, constituted essentially an
English invasion—the long-term fight was between native Scottish Celts and
Anglo-Norman invaders, with continental allies (such as the Norwegian king)
on both sides. One way of looking at the action is to say that it is about the
enforced anglicization of Scotland, which Macbeth is resisting.

Shakespeare knows some of this. In Holinshed, Macbeth not only has a
claim to the throne, he also has a legitimate grievance against Duncan. Moreover, in Shakespeare's source, Banquo is fully Macbeth's accomplice, and the
murder of Duncan has a good deal of political justification. All this would be
very touchy for Shakespeare, because Banquo is King James's ancestor, and if
Duncan is a saint, then Banquo is a real problem, the ancestor one wants to
forget. Shakespeare's way of handling Banquo fudges a lot of issues. Should he
not, as a loyal thane, be pressing the claim of Malcolm, the designated heir,
after the murder? Should he remain loyal to Macbeth as long as he does? In
fact, this is precisely the sort of question that shows how close the play is to
Hamlet: in both plays, the issue of legitimacy remains crucially ambiguous.
Nobody in *Macbeth* presses the claim of Malcolm until Malcolm reappears
with an army to support him, anymore than anyone in *Hamlet* presses the
claim of Hamlet. In both plays, there is deep uncertainty about the relation
between power and legitimacy—about whether legitimacy constitutes anything more than the rhetoric of power backed by the size of its army.

The issue of legitimacy provides, in fact, a powerful tragic impetus in the
play. Duncan tries to legitimize his son Malcolm's succession by creating him
Prince of Cumberland, thus declaring him heir to the throne. Macbeth is surprised at this, for good reasons: Prince of Cumberland is a title designed on
the analogy of the Prince of Wales; but this is not the way the succession
works in Scotland. Cumberland is an *English* county, which was briefly ceded
to the Scottish crown, and Malcolm's new title is the thin edge of the English
invasion—a Jacobean audience would have had deeply divided loyalties at
this point in the play. James I himself became king of England not because he
was the legitimate heir (he was one of a number of people with a distant claim
to the throne), but because he was *designated* the successor by Queen Eliza-

beth; or at least several attendants at her death claimed that he was, and the people in control supported him. This is much closer to the situation in *Hamlet* and *Macbeth* than it is to any system of hereditary succession. And Macbeth is, even in the play, a fully legitimate king, as legitimate as Duncan: like Hamlet's Denmark, Scotland is not a hereditary monarchy; Macbeth is *elected* king by the thanes, and duly anointed. The fact that he turns out to be a bad king does not make him any less the king, anymore than the rebellion that opens the play casts doubt on Duncan's right to the throne.

Let us return to the witches' royal entertainment, with its songs and dances from Middleton. *The Witch* was written between 1610 and 1615; so by that time there was felt to be a need for more variety in the play, of a specifically theatrical kind, singing and dancing. I have suggested that witchcraft was good theatrical capital, but this does not really account for the revisions. Witchcraft was good theater no matter what the witches did—spells, incantations, visions, appearances and disappearances, diabolical music were their stock in trade. It would not have been at all necessary to transform them into the vaudevillians they become for Macbeth's entertainment. If variety was required, Duncan's hosts could have entertained him at dinner as the King of Navarre in *Love's Labor's Lost* entertains the Princess of France, with dances and a disguising; or Banquo's ghost, like Puck in *A Midsummer Night's Dream*, or Hamlet, could have interrupted a play within the play; or like Prospero in *The Tempest*, Duncan could have presented a royal masque to celebrate his son's investiture as Prince of Cumberland. Why bring the witches into it? But, to judge from the play's stage history, the vaudevillian witches constituted a stroke of theatrical genius.

Or did they? Consider the play's stage history. How successful, in fact, was *Macbeth* in its own time? Though it seems inconceivable that King James would not have been interested in the play, there is, as I have said, no record of a court performance—nor is there, indeed, any record of *any* pre-Restoration performance other than the one Simon Forman saw at the Globe in 1611, and reported in his diary. The *Shakespeare Allusion Book* records only seven other references to the play before 1649; of these, only three, all before 1611, seem to me allusions to performances. A fourth, from 1642, is quoting it as a classic text. The remaining examples merely refer to the historical figure of Macbeth.[5] This, it must be emphasized, is a very small number of allusions: for comparison, there are fifty-eight to *Hamlet*, thirty-six to *Romeo and Juliet*, twenty-nine to the *Henry IV* plays, twenty-three to *Richard III*, nineteen to *Othello*.

This is all we know of the stage history of the play up to the Restoration. So perhaps reinventing the witches was not a stroke of theatrical genius after all; perhaps all it did was undertake, with uncertain success, to liven up an unpopular play. When Davenant revised *Macbeth* for the new stage, he inserted the whole of the singing and dancing scenes from Middleton—this, as I have indicated, was at least arguably how the play had been performed on the public stage for two decades or more before the closing of the theaters in 1642, and it would thus have been this version of the play that Davenant saw throughout his youth. (Davenant was born in 1606, so he was going to theater in the 1620s and '30s). Indeed, since *The Witch* remained unpublished until 1778, it is likely that Davenant took his text not from Middleton at all, but directly from the King's Men's performing text of *Macbeth*. Pepys provides a good testimony to the success of these and Davenant's other additions (Pepys's response is discussed in more detail in "Shakespeare and the Kinds of Drama"). Between 1664 and 1669 he went to the play nine times. The first time he found it only 'a pretty good play, but admirably acted'—the admirable Macbeth was Betterton, soon to be the most famous actor of the age, at the outset of his career. What Pepys saw on this occasion was certainly the folio text, with its Middleton additions. Thereafter he saw the play as Davenant refurbished it, and his response changed dramatically. It was, at various times, 'a most excellent play for variety'; 'a most excellent play in all respects, but especially in divertisement, though it be a deep tragedy; which is a strange perfection in a tragedy, it being most proper here and suitable'; and finally, 'one of the best plays for a stage, and a variety of dancing and music, that I ever saw.'

The interesting point here is the relation between 'deep tragedy' and 'divertisement,' which clearly for Pepys is a critical one. It is what he likes best about the play—indeed, it is what makes him revise his opinion of the play from 'pretty good' to 'most excellent.' And what Davenant added to the play—songs, dances, spectacle—is not simply something to appeal to Restoration taste. He expanded and elaborated elements that were already being added even before the folio text was published in 1623. So that is something to pause over: the really striking theatricality of the tragedy, its emphasis not just on visions and hallucinations, but on spectacle of all kinds, and even overtly—in scenes like the witches' dances—on entertainment, and its move toward the court masque. We see *Macbeth* as the most intensely inward of Shakespeare's plays, in which much of the action seems to take place within Macbeth's head, or as a projection of his fears and fantasies. But if we look again at the text we have, and fill in the blanks, we see that, as far back as our evidence goes, a great deal of the play's character was always determined by what Pepys called 'variety' and 'divertisement.' Perhaps for early audiences, then, these elements were not antithetical to psychological depth after all. In this respect *Macbeth* resembles *The Tempest* more than it does the other tragedies.

The play's 'divertisement' is a quality that is largely lost to us, partly because it is only hinted at in the folio text, which merely indicates that the songs are to be sung, but does not print them, and partly because it is so difficult to imagine doing the full-scale grotesque ballet they imply in a modern production. Pepys thought divertisement should have seemed radically indecorous too; but, to his surprise, he did not find it so. What is the relation between tragedy and the antic quality of the witches? Why does that antic quality keep increasing in size and importance in the stage history of the play from the seventeenth through the nineteenth century? Addison, for example, recalls his attention being distracted at a Betterton performance by a woman loudly asking 'When will the dear witches enter?';[6] Garrick, despite his claim to have returned to the text as originally written by Shakespeare, kept all Davenant's witch scenes; and in 1793, when Mrs Siddons was the Lady Macbeth, Hecate and her spirits descended and ascended on clouds, and the cauldron scene constituted a long interpolated pantomime.[7] Clearly Mrs Siddons did not think she was being upstaged. Can we imagine similar elements playing a similarly crucial role in the stage history of *Lear* or *Hamlet*? In fact, we can: in *Lear*, if it is the antic quality we are concerned with, there are Lear's mad scenes and the fool's zany speeches, which we find so hard to understand and pare down to a minimum, but which must have been popular in Shakespeare's time because new ones were added between the 1608 quarto and the 1623 folio. As for *Hamlet*, perhaps the witches externalize that anarchic quality that makes the prince so dangerous an adversary to the guilty king.

Suppose we try to imagine a *Hamlet* written from Claudius's point of view, in the way *Macbeth* is written from Macbeth's. Look at it this way: the murder Claudius commits is the perfect crime; but the hero-villain quickly finds that his actions have unimagined implications, and that the world of politics is not all he has to contend with. Even as it stands, *Hamlet* is a very political play, and does not really need the ghost at all: Hamlet has his suspicions already; Claudius tries to buy him off by promising him the succession, but this is not good enough. It turns out that the problem is not really conscience or revenge, it is Hamlet's own ambitions—he wanted to succeed his father on the throne; Claudius, Hamlet says, 'Lept in between the election and my hopes.' The ghost is really, literally, a deus ex machina. But in a *Hamlet* that did not center on Hamlet, Claudius's guilty conscience, which is not much in evidence in the play, would have a great deal more work to do. So would the ghost—who should, after all, logically be haunting Claudius, not Hamlet. This play would be not about politics but about how the dead do not disappear, they return to embody our crimes, so that we have to keep repeating them—just like *Macbeth*. In this version of *Hamlet*, Hamlet is hardly necessary, any more than in *Macbeth*, Malcolm and Macduff are necessary—the drama of Macbeth is really a matter between Macbeth and his ambition, Macbeth and the witches and his wife and his hallucinations and his own tortured soul, the drama of prophecies and riddles, and how he understands them, and what he decides to do about them, and how they, in themselves, constitute retribution.

What, then, about the riddles, those verbal incarnations of the imperfect speakers the witches? Macbeth is told that he will never be conquered till Birnam Wood comes to Dunsinane; and that no man of woman born will harm him. Are these paradoxical impossibilities realized? Not at all, really: the Birnam Wood prophecy does not come true, it just appears to Macbeth that it does—the wood is not moving, it merely looks as if it is. Or alternatively, we could say that 'Birnam Wood' is a quibble: Macbeth assumes it means the forest, but it could mean merely wood from the forest, the branches the soldiers are using for camouflage—it comes true merely as a stage device. As for 'no man of woman born,' maybe the problem is that Macbeth is not a close enough reader: he takes the operative word to be 'woman,'—'No man of *woman* born shall harm Macbeth'—but the key word turns out to be 'born'— 'No man of woman *born* shall harm Macbeth.' If this is right, we must go on to consider the implications of the assumption that a Caesarian section does not constitute birth. This is really, historically, quite significant: a vaginal birth would have been handled by women, the midwife, maids, attendants, with no men present. But surgery was a male prerogative—the surgeon was always a man; midwives were not allowed to use surgical instruments—and the surgical birth thus means, in Renaissance terms, that Macduff was brought to life by men, not women: carried by a woman, but made viable only through masculine intervention. Such a birth, all but invariably, involved the mother's death.

Macbeth himself sees it this way, when he defies Macduff and says,

> Though Birnam Wood be come to Dunsinane,
> And thou opposed, being of no woman born . . . , (5.8.30–1)

where logically it should be 'being not of woman born': the key concept is not 'no woman,' but 'not born.' But Shakespeare seems to be conceiving of a masculine equivalent to the immaculate conception, a birth uncontaminated by women, as the Virgin's was uncontaminated by man.

So this riddle bears on the whole issue of the place of women in the play's world, how very disruptive they seem to be, even when, like Lady Macduff, they are loving and nurturing. Why is it so important, for example, at the end of the play, that Malcolm is a virgin? Malcolm insists to Macduff that he is utterly pure, 'yet / Unknown to woman' (4.3.125–6), uncontaminated by heterosexuality—this is offered as the first of his qualifications for displacing and succeeding Macbeth. Perhaps this bears too on the really big unanswered question about Macduff: why he left his family unprotected when he went to seek Malcolm in England—this is what makes Malcolm mistrust him so deeply. Why would you leave your wife and children unprotected, to face the tyrant's rage, unless you knew they were really in no danger?

But somehow the question goes unanswered, does not need to be answered, perhaps because Lady Macduff in some unspoken way is the problem, just as, more obviously, Lady Macbeth and the witches are. Those claims on Macduff that tie him to his wife and children, that would keep him at home, that purport to be higher than the claims of masculine solidarity, are in fact rejected quite decisively by the play. In Holinshed, Macduff flees only *after* his wife and children have been murdered, and therefore for the best of reasons. Macduff's desertion of his family is Shakespeare's addition to the story. Maybe, the play keeps saying, if it weren't for all those women . . . ? It really is an astonishingly male-oriented and misogynistic play, especially at the end, when there are simply no women left, not even the witches, and the restored commonwealth is a world of heroic soldiers. Is the answer to Malcolm's question about why Macduff left his family, 'Because it's *you* I really love'?

So, to return to the increasingly elaborate witches' scenes, the first thing they do for this claustrophobic play is to open up a space for women—a subversive and paradoxical space. This is a play in which paradoxes abound, and for Shakespeare's audience, Lady Macbeth would have embodied those paradoxes as powerfully as the witches do: in her proclaimed ability to 'unsex' herself, in her willingness to dash her own infant's brains out, but most of all, in the kind of control she exercises over her husband. The marriage at the center of the play is one of the scariest things about it, but it is worth observing that, as Shakespearean marriages go, this is a good one: intense, intimate, loving. The notion that your wife is your friend and your comfort is not a Shakespearean one. The relaxed, easygoing, happy time men and women have together in Shakespeare all takes place before marriage, as part of the wooing process—this is the subject of comedy. What happens after marriage is the subject of tragedy—Goneril and Regan are only extreme versions of perfectly normative Shakespearean wives. The only Shakespearean marriage of any duration that is represented as specifically sexually happy is the marriage of Claudius and Gertrude, a murderer and an adulteress; and it is probably to the point that even they stop sleeping together after only four months—not, to be sure, by choice.

In this context, Macbeth and Lady Macbeth are really quite well matched. They care for each other and understand each other deeply, exhibiting a genuine intimacy and trust of a sort one does not find, for example, in the marriage of the Capulets, or in Iago and Emilia (to say nothing of Othello and

Desdemona), or in Coriolanus and Virgilia, or in Cymbeline and his villainous queen (who is not even provided with a name), or in Leontes and Hermione. As I have suggested in "Prospero's Wife," the prospects for life after marriage in Shakespeare really are pretty grim. And in this respect, probably the most frightening thing in the play is the genuine power of Lady Macbeth's mind—not just her powers of analysis and persuasion, but her intimate apprehension of her husband's deepest desires, her perfect understanding of what combination of arguments will prove irresistible to the masculine ego: 'Be a man,' and 'If you really loved me you'd do it.'

But can the play's action really be accounted for simply by the addition of yet another witch? Macbeth's marriage is a version of the Adam and Eve story, the woman persuading the man to commit the primal sin against the father. But the case is loaded: surely Lady Macbeth is not the culprit, anymore than Eve is—or than the witches are. What she does is give voice to Macbeth's inner life, release in him the same forbidden desire that the witches have called forth. To act on this desire is what it means in the play to be a man. But having evoked her husband's murderous ambition, having dared him to stop being a child, she suddenly finds that when he *is* a man she is powerless. Her own power was only her power over the child, the child she was willing to destroy to gain the power of a man.

Davenant, redoing the play, does some really interesting thinking about such issues. His version has had a bad press from critics since the nineteenth century, but like all his adaptations, it starts from a shrewd sense not merely of theatrical realities, but of genuine critical problems with the play—problems of the sort that editors and commentators lavish minute attention on, but directors and performers simply gloss over or cut. Many of his changes have to do with elucidation, clarifying obscurities in Shakespeare's text, especially in the opening scenes. There is also a move toward theatrical efficiency in casting. In the opening, for example, Macduff becomes Lennox, Seyton becomes the Captain—it is difficult to see why these are not improvements. Davenant also worries a lot, to our minds unnecessarily, about the location of scenes and the topography of the action, matters Shakespeare is resolutely vague about. Thus when Lady Macduff fears that she is lost, her servant is able to reassure her that 'this is the entrance o' the heath' (2.5.3)[8]—do heaths even have entrances? Such moments are the price of adapting the play to a stage where topography is realized and location materialized in scenery.

The most interesting aspects of the revision involve the women. It has often been observed that since the Restoration theater employed actresses, it made sense to increase the women's parts; but this is hardly adequate to account for Davenant's additions: for one thing, the witches continued to be played by men. It is the moral dimension of the woman's role that Davenant rethinks. Thus in a domestic scene that has no parallel in the folio, Lady Macduff sharply questions Macduff's motives, accusing him of ambition: 'I am afraid you have some other end / Than meerely ScottLand's freedom to defend' (3.2.18–9)—doesn't he really want the throne himself? Lady Macduff here articulates the same critique of her husband that, in Shakespeare, Hecate does of Macbeth: that he is out for himself alone. Her fear articulates that perennial problem in the play, Malcolm's question about Macduff that never gets answered—where are your real loyalties; why is coming to England to join my army more important than the lives of your wife and children? The problem remains in Davenant, but is mitigated by the fact that Lady Macduff encourages Macduff to flee after the murder of Banquo. If it was a mistake, it was her mistake as well as his. Davenant's Lady Macduff also expresses a conservative royalist line, insisting that the only thing that can justify Macduff's rebellion will be for him to place the true heir, Malcolm, on the throne, rather than claiming it himself—the women, for Davenant, consistently articulate the moral position. Even Lady Macbeth, in a scene of love and recrimination inserted before the sleepwalking scene, accuses Macbeth of being like Adam, following her when he should have led her. But just as Davenant's women are more important, they are also less dangerous: the Restoration Malcolm does not claim to be a virgin.

Revisers and performers have never been happy with the way Lady Macbeth simply fades out, and Macbeth is perfunctorily killed. The play does not even provide its hero with a final speech, let alone a eulogy for Shakespeare's most complex and brilliant studies in villainy. Malcolm dismisses the pair succinctly as 'this dead butcher and his fiend-like queen.' Davenant added a rather awkward dying line for Macbeth ('Farewell vain world, and what's most vain in it, ambition,' 5.7.83), and tastefully resolved the problem of Macbeth's double death by leaving the body on stage and having Macduff re-enter with Macbeth's sword, instead of his head. By the mid-eighteenth century, Garrick—who was claiming to be performing the play 'as written by Shakespeare'—had inserted an extended death speech for the hero:

> 'Tis done! The scene of life will quickly close.
> Ambition's vain, delusive dreams are fled,
> And now I wake to darkness, guilt and horror;
> I cannot bear it! Let me shake it off—
> 'Twill not be; my soul is clogged with blood—
> I cannot rise! I dare not ask for mercy—

>It is too late, hell drags me down; I sink,
>I sink—Oh!—my soul is lost forever!
>Oh!

This Faustian peroration went on being used until well into the nineteenth century.

The editors of Bell's Shakespeare in 1774 declared themselves pleased with the play's ending, observing, with characteristic condescension, that Shakespeare, 'contrary to his common practice, . . . has wound up the plot, punished the guilty, and established the innocent, in such a regular progression of important events, that nothing was wanting but very slight alterations. . . .'[9] But there is a puzzling element in Shakespeare's conclusion, which is less symmetrical and more open-ended than this suggests. Why, in a play so clearly organized around ideas of good and evil, is it not Malcolm who defeats Macbeth—the incarnation of virtue, the man who has never told a lie or slept with a woman, overcoming the monster of vice? In fact, historically, this is what happened: Macbeth was killed in battle by Malcolm, not Macduff. Shakespeare is following Holinshed here, but why, especially in a play that revises so much else in its source material? Davenant recognizes this as a problem, and, followed by Garrick, gives Macduff a few lines of justification as he kills Macbeth: 'This for thy Royall Master Duncan / This for my Dearest freind my wife, / This for those pledges of our Loves; my Children / . . . Ile as a Trophy bear away his sword / To wittness my revenge' (5.7.76–82). The addition is significant, and revealing: in Shakespeare, Macduff, fulfilling the prophecy, is simply acting as Malcolm's agent, the man not born of woman acting for the king uncontaminated by women. But why does virtue need an agent, while vice can act for itself? And what about the agent: does the unanswered question about Macduff abandoning his family not linger in the back of our minds? Does his willingness to condone the vices Malcolm invents for himself not say something disturbing about the quality of Macduff as a hero? Is he not, in fact, the pragmatic soldier who does what needs to be done so that the saintly king can stay clear of the complexities and paradoxes of politics and war? Davenant does not quite succeed in disarming the ambiguities of the ending. What happens next, with a saintly king of Scotland, and an ambitious soldier as his right hand man, and those threatening offspring the heirs of Banquo still waiting in the wings?

I 2

----◆----

PROSPERO'S WIFE

THIS ESSAY is not a reading of *The Tempest*. It is a consideration of five related moments and issues. I have called it "Prospero's Wife" because some of it centers on her, but in a larger sense because she is a figure conspicuous by her absence from the play, and my largest subject is the absent, the unspoken, that seems to me the most powerful and problematic presence in *The Tempest*. In its outlines, the play seems a story of privatives: withdrawal, usurpation, banishment, the loss of one's way, shipwreck. As an antithesis, a principle of control, preservation, re-creation, the play offers only magic, embodied in a single figure, the extraordinary powers of Prospero.

Prospero's wife is alluded to only once in the play, in Prospero's reply to Miranda's question, "Sir, are you not my father?"

> Thy mother was a piece of virtue, and
> She said thou wast my daughter; and thy father
> Was Duke of Milan; and his only heir
> And princess: no worse issued. (I.2.55–59)[1]

Prospero's wife is identified as Miranda's mother, in a context implying that though she was virtuous, women as a class are not, and that were it not for her word, Miranda's legitimacy would be in doubt. The legitimacy of Prospero's heir, that is, derives from her mother's word. But that word is all that is required of her in the play. Once he is assured of it, Prospero turns his attention to himself and his succession, and he characterizes Miranda in a clause that grows increasingly ambivalent—"his only heir / And princess: no worse issued."

Except for this moment, Prospero's wife is absent from his memory. She is wholly absent from her daughter's memory: Miranda can recall several women who attended her in childhood, but no mother. The implicit attitudes toward wives and mothers here are confirmed shortly afterward when Prospero, recounting his brother Antonio's crimes, demands that Miranda "tell me / If this might be a brother," and Miranda takes the question to be a charge of adultery against Prospero's mother:

> I should sin
> To think but nobly of my grandmother:
> Good wombs have borne bad sons. (I.2.118–20)

She immediately translates Prospero's attack on his brother into an attack on his mother (the best she can produce in her grandmother's defence is a "not proved"), and whether or not she has correctly divined her father's intentions, Prospero makes no objection.

The absent presence of the wife and mother in the play constitutes a space that is filled by Prospero's creation of surrogates and a ghostly family: the witch Sycorax and her monster child, Caliban (himself, as becomes apparent, a surrogate for the other wicked child, the usurping younger brother Antonio), the good child/wife Miranda, the obedient Ariel, the violently libidinized adolescent Ferdinand. The space is filled, too, by a whole structure of wifely allusion and reference: widow Dido, model at once of heroic fidelity to a murdered husband and the destructive potential of erotic passion; the witch Medea, murderess and filicide; three exemplary goddesses, the bereft Ceres, nurturing Juno and licentious Venus; and Alonso's daughter, Claribel, unwillingly married off to the ruler of the modern Carthage, and thereby lost to her father forever. Described in this way, the play has an obvious psychoanalytic shape. I have learned a great deal from Freudian treatments of it, especially from essays by David Sundelson, Coppélia Kahn, and Joel Fineman in the volume *Representing Shakespeare*.[2] It is almost irresistible to look at the play as a case history. *Whose* case history is a more problematic question, and one that criticism has not, on the whole, dealt with satisfactorily. It is not, obviously, the case history of the characters. I want to pause first over what it means to consider the play as a case history.

In older psychoanalytic paradigms (say Ernest Jones's) the critic is the analyst, Shakespeare is the patient, the plays his fantasies. The trouble with this paradigm is that it misrepresents the analytic situation in a fundamental way. The interpretation of analytic material is done in conjunction with, and in large measure by, the patient, not the analyst; what the analyst does is *enable* the patient, free the patient to interpret. An analysis done without the patient, like Freud's of Leonardo, will be revealing only about the analyst. A more recent paradigm, in which the audience's response is the principal analytic material, also seems to me based on fundamental misconceptions, first because it treats an audience as an entity, a unit, and in addition a constant one, and more problematically, because it conceives of the play as an objective event, so that the critical question becomes, "this is what happened: how do we respond to it?"

To take the psychoanalytic paradigm seriously, however, and treat the plays as case histories, is surely to treat them not as objective events but as collaborative fantasies, and to acknowledge thereby that we, as analysts, are implicated in the fantasy. It is not only the patient who creates the shape of his history, and when Bruno Bettelheim observes that Freud's case histories "read as well as the best novels,"[3] he is probably telling more of the truth than he intends. Moreover, the crucial recent advances in our understanding of Freud and psychoanalysis have been precisely critical acts of close and inventive reading—there are, in this respect, no limits to the collaboration. But if we accept this as our paradigm, and think of ourselves as Freud's or Shakespeare's collaborators, we must also acknowledge that our reading of the case will be revealing, again, chiefly about ourselves. This is why every generation, and perhaps every reading, produces a different analysis of its Shakespearean texts. In the same way, recent psychoanalytic theory has replaced Freud's central Oedipal myth with a drama in which the loss of the seducing mother is the crucial infant trauma. We used to want assurance that we would successfully compete with or replace or supersede our fathers; now we want to know that our lost mothers will return. Both of these no doubt involve real perceptions, but they also undeniably serve particular cultural needs.

Shakespeare plays, like case histories, derive from the observation of human behavior, and both plays and case histories are imaginative constructs. Whether either is taken to be an objective report of behavior or not has more to do with the reader than the reporter, but it has to be said that Shakespearean critics have more often than not treated the plays as objective accounts. Without such an assumption, a book with the title *The Girlhood of Shakespeare's Heroines* would be incomprehensible. We feel very far from this famous and popular Victorian work now, but we still worry about consistency and motivation in Shakespearean texts, and much of the commentary in an edition like the Arden Shakespeare is designed to explain why the characters say what they say—that is, to reconcile what they say with what, on the basis of their previous behavior, we feel they ought to be saying. The critic who worries about this kind of consistency in a Shakespeare text is thinking of it as an objective report.

But all readings of Shakespeare, from the earliest seventeenth-century adaptations, through eighteenth-century attempts to produce "authentic" or "accurate" texts, to the liberal fantasy of the old Variorum Shakespeare, have been aware of deep ambiguities and ambivalences in the texts. The eighteenth century described these as Shakespeare's errors, and generally revised them through plausible emendation or outright rewriting. The argument was that Shakespeare wrote in haste, and would have written more perfect plays had he taken time to revise; the corollary to this was, of course, that what we want are the perfect plays Shakespeare did not write, rather than the imperfect ones that he did. A little later the errors became not Shakespeare's but those of the printing house, the scribe, the memory of the reporter, or the defective hearing of the transcriber. But the assumption has always been that it is possible to produce a "perfect" text: that beyond or behind the ambiguous, puzzling, inconsistent text is a clear and consistent one.

Plays, moreover, are not only—and one might argue, not primarily—texts. They are performances too, originally designed to be read only in order to be acted, and the gap between the text and its performance has always been, and remains, a radical one. There always has been an imagination intervening between the texts and their audiences, initially the imagination of producer, director, actor (roles that Shakespeare played himself), and since that time the imagination of editors and commentators as well. These are texts that have always had to be realized. Initially unstable, they have remained so despite all our attempts to fix them. All our attempts to produce an authentic, correct, and most of all, stable text have resulted only in an extraordinary variety of versions. Their differences can be described as minor only if one believes that the real play is a platonic idea, never realized but only approached and approximately represented by its text.

This is our myth: the myth of a stable, accurate, authentic, *legitimate* text, a text that we can think of as Shakespeare's legitimate heir. It is, in its way, a genealogical myth, and it operates with peculiar force in our readings of *The Tempest*, a play that has been, for the last two hundred years, taken as a representation of Shakespeare himself bidding farewell to his art—as Shakespeare's legacy.

THE MISSING WIFE

She is missing as a character, but Prospero, several times explicitly, presents himself as incorporating her, acting as both father and mother to Miranda, and in one extraordinary passage describes the voyage to the island as a birth fantasy:

> When I have decked the sea with drops full salt,
> Under my burden groaned, which raised in me
> An undergoing stomach, to bear up
> Against what should ensue. (I.2.155–58)

To come to the island is to start life over again—both his own and Miranda's —with himself as sole parent, but also with himself as favorite child. He has been banished by his wicked, usurping, possibly illegitimate younger brother Antonio. This too has the shape of a Freudian fantasy: the younger child *is* the usurper in the family, and the kingdom he usurps is the mother. On the island, Prospero undoes the usurpation, recreating kingdom and family with himself in sole command.

But not quite, because the island is not his alone. Or if it is, then he has repeopled it with all parts of his fantasy, the distressing as well as the gratifying. When he arrives he finds Caliban, child of the witch Sycorax, herself a victim of banishment. The island provided a new life for her too, as it did literally for her son, with whom she was pregnant when she arrived. Sycorax died some time before Prospero came to the island; Prospero never saw her, and everything he knows about her he has learned from Ariel. Nevertheless, she is insistently present in his memory—far more present than his own wife—and she embodies to an extreme degree all the negative assumptions about women that he and Miranda have exchanged.

It is important, therefore, that Caliban derives his claim to the island from his mother: "This island's mine by Sycorax my mother" (I.2.331). This has interesting implications to which I shall return, but here I want to point out that he need not make the claim this way. He could derive it from the mere fact of prior possession: he was there first. This, after all, would have been the sole basis of Sycorax's claim to the island, but it is an argument that Caliban never makes. And in deriving his authority from his mother, he delivers himself into Prospero's hands. Prospero declares him a bastard, "got by the devil himself / Upon thy wicked dam" (I.2.319–20), thereby both disallowing any claim from inheritance and justifying his loathing for Caliban.

But is it true that Caliban is Sycorax's bastard by Satan? How does Prospero know this? Not from Sycorax: Prospero never saw her. Not from Caliban: Sycorax died before she could even teach her son to speak. Everything Prospero knows about the witch he knows from Ariel—her appearance, the story of her banishment, the fact that her pregnancy saved her from execution. Did Sycorax also tell Ariel that her baby was the bastard son of the devil? Or is this Prospero's contribution to the story, an especially creative piece of invective, and an extreme instance of his characteristic assumptions about women? Nothing in the text will answer this question for us, and it is worth pausing to observe first that Caliban's claim seems to have been designed so that Prospero can disallow it, and second that we have no way of distinguishing the facts about Caliban and Sycorax from Prospero's invective about them.

Can Prospero imagine no good mothers, then? The play, after all, moves toward a wedding, and the most palpable example we see of the magician's powers is a betrothal masque. The masque is presided over by two exemplary mothers, Ceres and Juno, and the libidinous Venus with her destructive son Cupid has been banished from the scene. But the performance is also preceded by the most awful warnings against sexuality—male sexuality this time: all the libido is presumed to be Ferdinand's, while Miranda remains Prospero's innocent child. Ferdinand's reassuring reply, as David Sundelson persuasively argues,[4] includes submerged fantasies of rape, and more than a hint that when the lust of the wedding night cools, so will his marital devotion:

> . . . the murkiest den,
> The most opportune place, the strong'st suggestion
> Our worser genius can, shall never melt
> Mine honor into lust, to take away
> The edge of that day's celebration. . . . (IV.1.25 –29)

This is the other side of the assumption that all women at heart are whores: all men at heart are rapists—Caliban, Ferdinand, and of course that means Prospero too.

THE MARRIAGE CONTRACT

The play moves toward marriage, certainly, yet the relations it postulates between men and women are ignorant at best, characteristically tense, and potentially tragic. There is a familiar Shakespearean paradigm here: relationships between men and women interest Shakespeare intensely, but not, on the whole, as husbands and wives. The wooing process tends to be what it is here: not so much a prelude to marriage and a family as a process of self-definition—an increasingly unsatisfactory process, if we look at the progression of plays from As You Like It, Much Ado about Nothing, Twelfth Night through All's Well That Ends Well, Measure for Measure, Troilus and Cressida to Antony and Cleopatra and Cymbeline. If we want to argue that marriage is the point of the comic wooing process for Shakespeare, then we surely ought to be looking at how he depicts marriages. Here Petruchio and Kate, Capulet and Lady Capulet, Claudius and Gertrude, Othello and Desdemona, Macbeth and Lady Macbeth, Cymbeline and his queen, Leontes and Hermione will not persuade us that comedies ending in marriages have ended happily; or if they have, it is only because they have ended there, stopped at the wedding day.

What happens after marriage? Families in Shakespeare tend to consist not of husbands and wives and their offspring, but of a parent and a child, usually in a chiastic relationship: father and daughter, mother and son. When there are two children, they tend to be represented as alternatives or rivals: the twins of *The Comedy of Errors*, Sebastian and Viola, infinitely substitutable for each other, or the good son-bad son complex of Orlando and Oliver, Edgar and Edmund. We know that Shakespeare himself had a son and two daughters, but that family configuration never appears in the plays. Lear's three daughters are quite exceptional in Shakespeare, and even they are dichotomized into bad and good. We might also recall Titus Andronicus's four sons and a daughter and Tamora's three sons, hardly instances to demonstrate Shakespeare's convictions about the comforts of family life.

The family paradigm that emerges from Shakespeare's imagination is a distinctly unstable one. Here is what we know of Shakespeare's own family: he had three brothers and three sisters who survived beyond infancy, and his parents lived into old age. At eighteen he married a woman of twenty-six by whom he had a daughter within six months, and a twin son and daughter a year and a half later. Within six more years he had moved permanently to London, and for the next twenty years—all but the last three years of his life— he lived apart from his wife and family. Nor should we stop here: we do not in the least know that Susanna, Hamnet, and Judith were his only children. He lived in a society without contraceptives, and unless we want to believe that after the move to London he was either exclusively homosexual or celibate, we must assume a high degree of probability that there were other children. The fact that they are not mentioned in his will may mean that they did not survive, but it also might mean that he made separate, non-testamentary provision for them. Certainly the plays reveal a strong interest in the subject of illegitimacy.

Until quite late in his career, the strongest familial feelings seem to be expressed not toward children or wives but toward parents and siblings. His father dies in 1601, the year of *Hamlet*, his mother in 1608, the year of *Coriolanus*. And if we are thinking about usurping, bastard younger brothers, it cannot be coincidental that the younger brother who followed him into the acting profession was named Edmund. There are no dramatic correlatives comparable to these for the death of his son Hamnet in 1596. If we take the plays to express what Shakespeare thought about himself (I put it that way to indicate that the assumption strikes me as by no means axiomatic) then we will say that he was apparently free to think of himself as a father—to his two surviving daughters—only after the death of both his parents. 1608 is the date of *Pericles* as well as *Coriolanus*.

One final biographical observation: Shakespearean heroines marry very young, in their teens. Miranda is fifteen. We are always told that Juliet's marriage at fourteen is not unusual in the period, but in fact it *is* unusual in all but upper-class families. In Shakespeare's own family, his wife married at twenty-six and his daughters at twenty-four and thirty-one. It was Shakespeare himself who married at eighteen. The women of Shakespeare's plays, of course, are adolescent boys. Perhaps we should see as much of Shakespeare in Miranda and Ariel as in Prospero.

POWER AND AUTHORITY

The psychoanalytic and biographical questions raised by *The Tempest* are irresistible, but they can supply at best partial clues to its nature. I have described the plays as collaborative fantasies, and it is not only critics and readers who are involved in the collaboration. It is performers and audiences too, and I take these terms in their largest senses, to apply not merely to stage productions, but to the theatrical dimension of the society that contains and is mirrored by the theater as well. Cultural concerns, political and social issues, speak through *The Tempest*—sometimes explicitly, as in the open-ended discussion of political economy engaged in by Gonzalo, Antonio, and Sebastian in Act II. But in a broader sense, family structures and sexual relations become political structures in the play, and these are relevant to the political structures of Jacobean England.

What is the nature of Prospero's authority and the source of his power? Why is he Duke of Milan and the legitimate ruler of the island? Power, as Prospero presents it in the play, is not inherited but self-created. It is magic, or "art," an extension of mental power and self-knowledge, and the authority legitimizing it derives from heaven—"Fortune" and "Destiny" are the terms used in the play. It is Caliban who derives his claim to the island from inheritance, from his mother.

In the England of 1610, both these positions represent available, and indeed normative ways of conceiving of royal authority. James I's authority derived, he said, both from his mother and from God. But deriving one's legitimacy from Mary Queen of Scots was an ambiguous claim at best, and James always felt exceedingly insecure about it. Elizabeth had had similar problems with the sources of her own authority, and they centered precisely on the question of her legitimacy. To those who believed that her father's divorce from Katherine of Aragon was invalid (that is, to Roman Catholics), Elizabeth had no hereditary claim; and she had, moreover, been declared legally illegitimate after the execution of her mother for adultery and incest. Henry VIII maintained Elizabeth's bastardy to the end. Her claim to the throne derived exclusively from her designation in the line of succession, next after Edward and Mary, in her father's will. This ambiguous legacy was the sole source of her authority. Prospero at last acknowledging the bastard Caliban as his own is also expressing the double edge of kingship throughout Shakespeare's lifetime (the ambivalence will not surprise us if we consider the way kings are represented in the history plays). Historically speaking, Caliban's claim to the island is a good one.

Royal power, the play seems to say, is good when it is self-created, bad when it is usurped or inherited from an evil mother. But of course the least problematic case of royal descent is one that is not represented in these paradigms at all, one that derives not from the mother but in the male line from the father: the case of Ferdinand and Alonso, in which the wife and mother is totally absent. If we are thinking about the *derivation* of royal authority, then, the absence of a father from Prospero's memory is a great deal more significant than the disappearance of a wife. This has been dealt with in psychoanalytic terms, whereby Antonio becomes a stand-in for the father, the real usurper of the mother's kingdom;[5] but here again the realities of contemporary kingship seem more enlightening, if not inescapable. James in fact had a double claim to the English throne, and the one through his father, the Earl of Darnley, was in the strictly lineal respects somewhat stronger than that of his mother. Both Darnley and Mary were direct descendants of Henry VII, but under Henry VIII's will, which established the line of succession, descendants who were not English-born were specifically excluded. Darnley was born in England, Mary was not. In fact, Darnley's mother went from Scotland to have her baby in England precisely in order to preserve the claim to the throne.

King James rarely mentioned this side of his heritage, for perfectly understandable reasons. His father was even more disreputable than his mother; and given what was at least the public perception of both their characters, it was all too easy to speculate about whether Darnley was even in fact his father.[6] For James, as for Elizabeth, the derivation of authority through paternity was extremely problematic. In practical terms, James's claim to the English throne depended on Elizabeth *naming* him her heir (we recall Miranda's legitimacy depending on her mother's word), and James correctly saw this as a continuation of the protracted negotiations between Elizabeth and his mother. His legitimacy, in both senses, thus derived from two mothers, the chaste Elizabeth and the sensual Mary, whom popular imagery represented respectively as a virgin goddess ("a piece of virtue") and a lustful and diabolical witch. James's sense of his own place in the kingdom is that of Prospero, rigidly paternalistic, but incorporating the maternal as well: the king describes himself in *Basilicon Doron* as "a loving nourish father" providing the commonwealth with "their own nourish-milk."[7] The very etymology of the word "authority" confirms the metaphor: *augeo*, "increase, nourish, cause to grow." At moments in his public utterances, James sounds like a gloss on Prospero: "I am the husband, and the whole island is my lawful wife; I am the head, and it is my body."[8] Here the incorporation of the wife has become literal and explicit. James conceives himself as the head of a single-parent family. In the world of *The Tempest*, there are no two-parent families. All the dangers of promiscuity and bastardy are resolved in such a conception—unless, of course, the parent is a woman.

My point here is not that Shakespeare is representing King James as Prospero and/or Caliban, but that these figures embody the predominant modes of conceiving of royal authority in the period. They are Elizabeth's and James's modes too.

THE RENUNCIATION OF MAGIC

Prospero's magic power is exemplified, on the whole, as power over children: his daughter Miranda, the bad child Caliban, the obedient but impatient Ariel, the adolescent Ferdinand, the wicked younger brother Antonio, and indeed, the shipwreck victims as a whole, who are treated like a group of bad children. Many critics talk about Prospero as a Renaissance scientist, and see alchemical metaphors in the grand design of the play. No doubt there is something in this, but what the play's action presents is not experiments and empiric studies but a fantasy about controlling other people's minds. Does the magic work? We are given a good deal of evidence of it: the masque, the banquet, the harpies, the tempest itself. But the great scheme is not to produce illusions and good weather, it is to bring about reconciliation, and here we would have to say that it works only indifferently well. "They being penitent," says Prospero to Ariel, "The sole drift of my purpose doth extend / Not a frown further" (V.1.28–30). The assertion opens with a conditional clause whose conditions are not met: Alonso is penitent, but the chief villain, the usurping younger brother Antonio, remains obdurate. Nothing, not all Prospero's magic, can redeem Antonio from his essential badness. Since Shakespeare was free to have Antonio repent if that is what he had in mind—half a line would have done for critics craving a reconciliation—we ought to take seriously the possibility that that is not what he had in mind. Perhaps, too, penitence is not what Prospero's magic is designed to elicit from his brother.

Why is Prospero's power conceived as magic? Why, in returning to Milan, does he renounce it? Most commentators say that he gives up his magic when he no longer needs it. This is an obvious answer, but it strikes me as too easy, a comfortable assumption cognate with the view that the play concludes with reconciliation, repentance, and restored harmony. To say that Prospero no longer *needs* his magic is to beg all the most important questions. What does it mean to say that he needs it? Did he ever need it, and if so, why? And does he in fact give it up?

Did he ever need magic? Prospero's devotion to his secret studies is what caused all the trouble in the first place—this is not an interpretation of mine, it is how Prospero presents the matter. If he has now learned to be a good ruler through the exercise of his art, that is also what taught him to be a bad one. So the question of his *need* for magic goes to the heart of how we interpret and judge his character: is the magic a strength or a weakness? If we consider the magic a weakness, as we implicitly do when we say that he no longer needs it, then we believe that his character changes in some way for the better by renouncing his special powers, that he thereby becomes fully human. This is an important claim: let us test it by looking at Prospero's renunciation.

What does it mean for Prospero to give up his power? Letting Miranda marry and leaving the island are the obvious answers, but they can hardly be right. Miranda's marriage is *brought about* by the magic; it is part of Prospero's plan. It pleases Miranda, certainly, but it is designed by Prospero as a way of satisfying himself. Claribel's marriage to the king of Tunis looks less sinister in this light: daughters' marriages, in royal families at least, are designed primarily to please their fathers. And leaving the island, reassuming the dukedom, is part of the plan too. Both of these are presented as acts of renunciation, but they are in fact what the exercise of Prospero's magic is intended to effect, and they represent his triumph.

Prospero renounces his art in the great monologue at the beginning of Act V, "Ye elves of hills, brooks, standing lakes, and groves," and for all its valedictory quality, it is the most powerful assertion of his magic the play gives us. It is also a powerful literary allusion, a close translation of a speech of Medea's in Ovid,[9] and it makes at least one claim for Prospero that is made nowhere else in the play: that he can raise the dead. For Shakespeare to present this as a *renunciation* speech is upping Prospero's ante, to say the least.

In giving up his magic, Prospero speaks as Medea. He has incorporated Ovid's witch, prototype of the wicked mother Sycorax, in the most literal way—verbatim, so to speak—and his "most potent art" is now revealed as translation and impersonation. In this context, the distinction between black and white magic, Sycorax and Prospero, has disappeared. Two hundred lines later, Caliban too is revealed as an aspect of Prospero: "This thing of darkness I acknowledge mine."

But Caliban is an aspect of Antonio, the evil child, the usurping brother. Where is the *real* villain in relation to Prospero now? Initially Antonio had been characterized, like Caliban and Sycorax, as embodying everything that is antithetical to Prospero. But in recounting his history to Miranda, Prospero also presents himself as deeply implicated in the usurpation, with Antonio even seeming at times to be acting as Prospero's agent: "The government I cast upon my brother"; "[I] to him put the manage of my state"; "my trust . . . did beget of him / A falsehood," and so forth. If Prospero is accepting the blame for what happened, there is a degree to which he is also taking the credit.

Antonio is another of the play's identities that Prospero has incorporated into his own, and in that case, what is there to forgive?

Let us look, then, at Prospero forgiving his brother in Act V. The pardon is enunciated ("You, brother mine, that entertain ambition. . . . I do forgive thee" [75–78])[10] and qualified at once ("unnatural though thou art"), reconsidered as more crimes are remembered, some to be held in reserve ("at this time I will tell no tales" [128–29]), all but withdrawn ("most wicked sir, whom to call brother / Would even infect my mouth" [130–31]), and only then confirmed through forcing Antonio to relinquish the dukedom, an act that is presented as something he does unwillingly. The point is not merely that Antonio does not repent here: he is not *allowed* to repent. Even his renunciation of the crown is Prospero's act: "I do . . . require / My dukedom of thee, which perforce, I know, / thou must restore" (131–34). In Prospero's drama, there is no room for Antonio to act of his own free will.

The crime that Prospero holds in reserve for later use against his brother is the attempted assassination of Alonso. Here is what happened. Prospero sends Ariel to put all the shipwreck victims to sleep except Antonio and Sebastian. Antonio then persuades Sebastian to murder his brother Alonso and thereby become king of Naples. Sebastian agrees, on the condition that Antonio also kill Gonzalo. At the moment of the murders, Ariel reappears and wakes Gonzalo:

> My master through his art foresees the danger
> That you his friend are in, and sends me forth—
> For else his project dies—to keep them living. (II.1.295 –97)

This situation has been created by Prospero, and the conspiracy is certainly part of his project—that is why Sebastian and Antonio are not put to sleep. If Antonio is not forced by Prospero to propose the murder, he is certainly acting as Prospero expects him to do, and as Ariel says Prospero "through his art foresees" that he will. What is clearly taking place is Prospero restaging his usurpation and maintaining his control over it this time. Gonzalo is waked rather than Alonso so that the old courtier can replay his role in aborting the assassination.

So at the play's end, Prospero still has usurpation and attempted murder to hold against his brother, things that still disqualify Antonio from his place in the family. Obviously there is more to Prospero's plans than reconciliation and harmony—even, I would think, in the forthcoming happy marriage of Ferdinand and Miranda. If we look at that marriage as a political act (the participants are, after all, the children of monarchs) we will observe that in order to prevent the succession of his brother, Prospero is marrying his daughter to the son of his enemy. This has the effect of excluding Antonio from any future claim on the ducal throne, but it also effectively disposes of the realm as a political entity: if Miranda is the heir to the dukedom, Milan through the marriage becomes part of the kingdom of Naples, not the other way around. Prospero recoups his throne from his brother only to deliver it over, upon his death, to the king of Naples once again. The usurping Antonio stands condemned, but the effects of the usurpation, the link with Alonso and the reduction of Milan to a Neapolitan fiefdom are, through Miranda's wedding, confirmed and legitimized. Prospero has not regained his lost dukedom, he has usurped his brother's. In this context, Prospero's puzzling assertion that "every third thought shall be my grave" can be seen as a final assertion of authority and control: he has now arranged matters so that his death will remove Antonio's last link with the ducal power. His grave is the ultimate triumph over his brother. If we look at the marriage in this way, giving away Miranda is a means of preserving his authority, not of relinquishing it.

A BIBLIOGRAPHICAL CODA

The significant absence of crucial wives from the play is curiously emphasized by a famous textual crux. In Act IV Ferdinand, overwhelmed by the beauty of the masque Prospero is presenting, interrupts the performance to say,

> Let me live here, ever.
> So rare a wondered father and a wise
> Makes this place paradise. (IV.1. 122–24)

Critics since the eighteenth century have expressed a nagging worry about the fact that in celebrating his betrothal, Ferdinand's paradise includes Prospero but not Miranda. In 1978, however, Jeanne Addison Roberts found that in a number of copies of the folio the line reads "So rare a wondered father and a *wife.*"[11] Apparently the crossbar of the *f* broke during the print run, turning it into a long *s* and thereby eliminating Miranda from Ferdinand's thoughts of wonder. The odd thing about this is that Rowe and Malone in their eighteenth-century editions emended "wise" to "wife" on logical grounds, the Cambridge Shakespeare of 1863 lists "wife" as a variant reading of the folio, and Furnivall's 1895 photographic facsimile was made from a copy that reads "wife," and the reading is preserved in Furnivall's parallel text. Nevertheless, after 1895 the wife became invisible: bibliographers lost the variant, and textual critics consistently denied its existence. Even Charlton Hinman with his collating machines claimed that there were no variants whatever in this entire forme of the folio. And yet when Jeanne Roberts examined the Folger

Library's copies of the book, including those that Hinman had collated, she found that two of them have the reading "wife," and two others seem to show the crossbar in the process of breaking. We find only what we are looking for or are willing to see. Obviously in 1978, this was a reading whose time had come.

And whose time, at the beginning of the twenty-first century, may already be past. Peter Blayney, observing that the physical construction of a piece of type surely precludes the crossbar of an f breaking and migrating, examined the "wife" copies under a high powered microscope. What Jeanne Roberts was seeing, he believes, was probably the effects of ink on a piece of lint, caught, for the time it took to print off a few copies, between the s and e of "wise," after which it was dislodged and made its leisurely way out of the text.[12] Once again, we find what we are looking for and are willing to see. Typography, it now appears, will not rescue Shakespeare from patriarchy and male chauvinism after all. Prospero's wife—and Ferdinand's—remain invisible.

13

MARGINAL JONSON

THE FICTIONS OF PLAYWRIGHTS, Stephen Gosson told his readers, were the cups of Circe.[1] The magical power of Renaissance theater, its ability not merely to compel wonder in its audiences but to change them, whether for good or evil, by persuasion or seduction, is assumed by both attackers and defenders of the art, and Gosson's warning fully acknowledges both the danger of the stage and its irresistible attractiveness. When Prospero, near the end of *The Tempest*, renounces his magic with a speech adapted almost verbatim from Ovid's Medea, the evocation of witchcraft through the classic exemplar of a dangerously beautiful woman encapsulates the full range of Renaissance attitudes to the theatrical magician's powers. But the literary allusion goes beyond the anti-theatrical trope; for at this moment the hero ceases to be a character and becomes a text. The script the actor recites is a book, a classic, a passage that every schoolchild in Shakespeare's England could also recite. This is a very Jonsonian moment, the invocation of a classic text to establish the authority of the fiction, to strike the audience with a shock of recognition, to place the drama in the context not of an ephemeral performance, but of the history of poetry.

Jonson debunks the magic of theater in *The Alchemist*, but alchemy in the play is more than the art of charlatans making a quick fortune. It is the stuff of ingenious dramatic plotting and theatrical illusions; it also evokes the magnificent poetry of Sir Epicure Mammon and, indeed, the moral philosophy of Jonson the comic classicist. The play is, in the deepest sense, about Jonson turning the basest materials—charlatanry, greed, whoredom (and perhaps we should include theater)—into gold; and not only the gold of poetry, but his own success as poet and playwright, establishing him as the patriarch to a family of poetic disciples who duly constituted themselves 'the sons of Ben,' a father whose 'best piece of poetry' was his first son Benjamin, the 'child of my right hand,' the hand he wrote with.

Theatrical magic, then, is both a quality of language and a way of establishing oneself, of rising in society; a way for servants (or employees of theatrical companies) to become masters. Like that classic exemplar of theatrical sorcery *Doctor Faustus*, *The Alchemist* is about getting rich and powerful in the world of Renaissance capitalism. The magic of *The Tempest* is less openly concerned with this, but the theme is there: in Stephano's plan to turn his islander-servant into a moneymaking sideshow in London; in Caliban's dream of riches dropping upon him (this is clearly not about life on the island, where riches would have no value: whose dream is this?). It is the servants who have these fantasies; when they become masters, the dreams are dreams of power—but power of a specific kind, the reverse of the servants' dreams: what Prospero's magic enables him to do is precisely to be the head of his household, to control his children and his servants. It is Ariel who, on Prospero's orders, raises the tempest and stages the disappearing banquet; both he and the bad child Caliban serve Prospero, but only under strong compulsion. Magic confers an absolute authority within very narrow bounds: the power to be obeyed by the rest of the family.

It confers, that is, a patriarchal authority, and thereby the authority to arrange marriages. The betrothal of Miranda to Ferdinand is a principal part of Prospero's scheme; in the same way, Face's miraculous larcenies are ultimately validated when he produces a rich widow for his master Lovewit to marry. Magic produces a wife—for Renaissance men the crucially enabling form of property, the key not merely to genetic posterity, but to an income, land, alliances with other powerful men. Faustus, indeed, is all but unique in wanting a wife for sex, 'for I am wanton and lascivious, and cannot live without a wife.'[2] But the magic in this case is suddenly ineffective—as always, Faustus asks for too little. Mephistopheles balks at arranging a marriage (presumably because it is a sacrament), offering instead all the courtesans Faustus can handle. The magician, however, turns to books instead; and when he finally gets the woman he wants, she is neither a wife nor a courtesan, but Helen of Troy, a literary allusion, like Medea or Circe, another text.

The wife as book, compliant, silent, obedient, open only when her husband opens her, the perfect embodiment of male desire, is very much a Jonsonian topos, the topos so decisively and delusively invoked by Morose in *Epicoene*. But the problem with the topos, as Jonsonian wives like the Collegiate Ladies and Lady Politic Would-be demonstrate, is the refusal of women to enact it. The unmanageable wife embodies what Jonson's own theatrical magic could never control, the 'shrew but honest'—chaste enough, but a virago, giving him no satisfaction ('five years he had not bedded with her,' he told Drummond),[3] and by the same token, impossible to satisfy.

What happened, then, when Jonson worked for women, when his success depended on his ability to satisfy them? The persona he and Inigo Jones provided for the queen in their first Twelfth Night masque for the Jacobean court was devised according to her specific stipulations (figure 13.1); Jonson followed orders, and when Sir Dudley Carleton found fault with the result, it was not the poet and designer who were blamed, it was the king's unmanageable wife. If Queen Anne's costume in *The Masque of Blackness* was, as Carleton complained, 'too light and Curtizan-like for such great ones',[4] the queen was clearly wearing what she wanted to wear. The criticism has been taken as the truth about the masque, but it has certainly been generalized too far. If we rely for our understanding of Renaissance events solely on the evidence of the few eyewitness accounts that survive, or take these simply at face value, we become the prisoners of the tastes and prejudices of those witnesses. In this case, it is probably sufficient to observe that fashion descends from above, and it is in the nature of new fashions to displace older ones; part of the function of new styles is to surprise and defeat expectations. Carleton found the costumes transgressive, but the queen and her ladies doubtless saw them as innovative, stylish, and attractive, and they obviously set the style for the next few years. In the masquers' costume for *Love Freed* (figure 13.2) in 1610, the sheer, filmy fabrics that had so offended Carleton have become the stuff of standard masquing dress. Queen Anne's clothes, like those of many women in the upper reaches of society before and since, were characteristically in the forefront of fashion; and were, indeed, what set the fashion.

As for the more basic problem of the queen's blackness, though Carleton could not 'imagine a more ugly sight than a troop of lean-cheeked Moors' and cited the 'danger' that her makeup would soil the lips of a dancing partner who kissed her hand (as the Spanish ambassador, in what Carleton evidently considers an excess of gallantry, did), it is unlikely here again that the queen was undertaking to present herself and her ladies as ugly or even transgressive. The black makeup no doubt did represent a problem for a partner, but hardly a new one: ladies regularly used white makeup on the exposed parts of their bodies—not only faces and bosoms, but hands and forearms as well—and this was just as likely to adulterate the male courtly lip. Kissing a whitened hand is never claimed to be dangerous in any way except morally, though the mercury- and lead-based whiteners were actually quite poisonous. The real key to Carleton's reaction here may lie not simply in the symbolic difference between black and white, but more deeply in the fact that white cosmetics were naturalized because men employed them too.

It is, in any case, unlikely that Carleton's distaste for the performance was widely shared: the Venetian ambassador found it 'very beautiful and sumptuous',[5] and another correspondent, who did not see the performance, reported what he had heard, that it was 'a sumptuous show represented by the queen

Figure 13.1. Inigo Jones, costume design for a nymph in *The Masque of Blackness*, 1605. Devonshire Collection, Chatsworth. Reproduced by permission of the Duke of Devonshire and the Chatsworth Settlement Trustees.

Figure 13.2. Inigo Jones, masquer's costume for *Love Freed from Ignorance and Folly*, 1611. Devonshire Collection, Chatsworth. Reproduced by permission of the Duke of Devonshire and the Chatsworth Settlement Trustees.

and some dozen ladies all painted like blackamores, face and neck bare, and for the rest strangely attired in Barbaresque mantles.'[6] What is cited in these accounts is not ugliness, but richness, innovation, and exoticism. The conceit of the queen in blackface in fact must have been been not offensive but quite pleasing, since it was repeated seven months later when Queen Anne's brother Christian IV came to visit, and the royal party were entertained by Cecil at Theobalds with a masque in which the Queen of Sheba brought gifts to the Solomonic monarchs. Sir John Harington's famous account of the resulting fiasco makes much of the drunkenness of the participants, including the two kings, but includes no complaints about the complexion of the Abyssinian queen, a role performed by an unnamed and unfortunately clumsy court lady; nor did King Christian hesitate to dance with her for fear of being soiled by her blackness—he was in any case already quite soiled by the cream cakes and other sweetmeats she had just spilled on him.

Women's fashion and women's cosmetics, of course, were a continuing source of masculine anxiety. So, if it comes to that, was men's fashion, as all the complaints about the effeminacy of male aristocratic dress in the period make clear. Carleton's dismay at the masquers' dress is part of a larger cultural debate over the decorum and boundaries of gender itself, of what properly constituted the feminine and the manly. The real innovation in the costumes for *Blackness*, indeed, was probably the fact that cosmetics were being allowed to do the work of clothing, the fact that the ladies were not masked and had bare forearms and sheer overmantles that revealed their upper arms. It would most likely have been this, not the dresses, that Carleton registered as 'too light and courtesan-like,' too blatantly feminine, but also, in its aggressive display of sexuality—Queen Anne was visibly pregnant—paradoxically masculine as well.

The king of England, the French ambassador observed, 'was not master in his own house.'[7] The fear that women were adopting the prerogatives of men is so ubiquitous as to constitute a topos in the period, encapsulated in figure 13.3, the emblematic title page to *Hic Mulier*. It is articulated in John Cham-

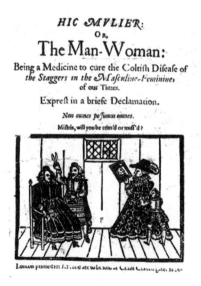

Figure 13.3. *Hic Mulier*, 1620, title page. By permission of the Huntington Library, Calif.

berlain's report to Dudley Carleton of the king's fervent admonition to the London clergy 'to inveigh vehemently and bitterly in their sermons against the insolency of our women, and their wearing of broad-brimmed hats, pointed doublets, their hair cut short or shorn, and some of them stillettos or poniards . . . adding withall that if pulpit admonitions will not reform them he would proceed by another course.'[8] This admonition was directed against what the king saw as a masculine style of dress; but the ministers did not invariably understand the point of the royal injunction. 'The Dean of Westminster,' Chamberlain reported a few weeks later, 'hath been very strict in his church against Ladies and gentlewomen about yellow ruffs, and would not suffer them to be admitted into any pew.' Since yellow ruffs were particularly stylish at the moment, the fashionable parishioners appealed at once to the king, who was obliged to explain that 'his meaning was not for yellow ruffs, but for other man-like and unseemly apparel.'[9]

What constitutes masculinity, however, in apparel as in everything else, is a matter of opinion. Paul van Somer's portrait of the queen (figure 13.4) shows her with broad-brimmed hat, short hair, pointed doublet—and yellow ruffs.[10] The picture, roughly contemporary with the king's expostulation, was painted for her, and shows her own palace of Oatlands in the background; it presents her as she wanted to see herself, as queen and huntress. The implications of the costume are revealed in the contemporaneous French term for a

Figure 13.4. Paul van Somer, Anne of Denmark, c. 1616. (H. M. The Queen)

riding habit, *amazone*. Whether this is seen as transgressive or attractive depends on where one stands; but clearly aristocratic women who dressed in this way were not imitating men, they were imitating the queen. The royal style, moreover, whether 'light and courtesan-like' or 'man-like,' was surely intended to render the queen and her ladies *attractive*: women do not dress to be repellent.

Queen Anne's taste in clothes was individual and innovative. Her taste in poets, designers and entertainments was, too. In "What Is a Text?" I suggested that court masques should properly be viewed as genuine collaborations between the artists and the patrons. I cited an example that has to do precisely with fashion: when I was working on the Inigo Jones drawings, I was initially puzzled by the fact that Jones regularly did his costume designs in monochrome, and indicated the colors with annotations. Why not do the drawings in color, so that the masquers and their dressmakers could see what the costume was actually going to look like? But as the annotations to the drawings make clear, Jones was not the final arbiter. He would do his designs, and submit them, with his suggestions, to the queen. She then chose the colors, and made whatever changes she wished. The inscriptions on the sketch of Queen Henrietta Maria's costume for *Chloridia* (figure 13.5), read, in the margin, 'green, white, white, green,' and below: 'This design I conceive to be fit for the invention, and if it please Her Majesty to add or alter anything I desire to

Figure 13.5. Inigo Jones, sketch for the Queen's costume in *Chloridia*, 1631. Devonshire Collection, Chatsworth. Reproduced by permission of the Duke of Devonshire and the Chatsworth Settlement Trustees.

Figure 13.6. A masquer in *Hymenaei*, 1606. Reproduced by
kind permission of the Berkeley Will Trust.

receive Her Majesty's command and the design again by this bearer. The colors also are in Her Majesty's choice, but my opinion is that several fresh greens mix[ed] with gold and silver will be most proper.'

Hymenaei, performed in 1606, provides an especially striking instance of the independence of the aristocratic performers at these spectacles. The costume as Inigo Jones designed it is described by Jonson:

> the upper part of white cloth of silver wrought with Juno's birds
> and fruits; a loose undergarment, full gathered, of carnation,
> striped with silver and parted with a golden zone; beneath that
> another flowing garment of watchet [light blue] cloth of silver. ...

In the portrait of one of the masquers, in figure 13.6, the double skirt of Jones's design is clearly visible, though the top skirt does not appear to be 'parted,' unless this means simply separated from the upper garment. But the portrait in figure 13.7 shows Lucy Harington, Countess of Bedford dressed for the same masque. Her costume has a single skirt. That is the way this aristocratic dancer preferred to appear; she paid for the costume, and her own dressmaker made it. The other dancers would have felt entitled to make their own alterations in their costumes as well.

When Jonson says that he 'apted' his invention to the commands of Queen Anne in writing *The Masque of Blackness*, he is acknowledging that his poetic

Figure 13.7. Lucy, Countess of Bedford in costume for *Hymenaei*, 1606. By kind
permission of the Marquess of Tavistock and the Trustees of the Bedford Estates.

invention follows, depends upon, and is subject to the authority of the queen;
the conceit of blackness is the queen's. If we took the patronage system seriously, the queen's invention would be as interesting to us as Jonson's. Why did
the queen want to appear black? Inigo Jones's costume emphasizes the richness and exoticism of the conceit; its sources are two figures from Vecellio's
book of national costumes (figure 13.8), a Thessalonian bride for the headdress and an Ethiopian virgin for the striped and embroidered gown. But
though Thessalonica was Turkish at this period, the headdress has a broader
geographical history: it is called a Persian mitre—the daughters of Niger
emanate from the Renaissance imagination of the Orient and of biblical
antiquity. Analogously, Harington opens his account of the festivities provided for the reception of Christian IV by likening them to Mahomet's paradise—figure 13.9, for comparison, shows the costumes for a stylish masca-
rade designed by Boissard in 1595. Harington's analogy is certainly intended
ironically, but the choice of the simile is not accidental, and it reveals a genuine ambivalence, both admiring and disapproving. We inevitably see Blackamoors through the history of black slavery and of modern racism, but in
1605 the English view of blacks was more complex, and the language of racism
was being principally applied to the Irish, where it obviously had nothing to
do with skin color. Interesting recent work on the English response to
Africans sometimes oversimplifies this complexity, but it reveals a much
larger black presence in Elizabethan England than has previously been

Figure 13.8. Cesare Vecellio, Thessalonian bride and Ethiopian virgin,
from *Habiti antichi, et moderni di tutto il Mondo,* Venice, 1598.

Figure 13.9. Robert Boissard, Turkish masquerade, from *Mascarades recueillies,*
Valenciennes, 1597.

acknowledged. Eldred Jones's well-known book *Othello's Countrymen* has
now been supplemented by the work of Ania Loomba, Lynda Boose, Margo
Hendricks, Ruth Cowhig, Gretchen Gerzina, and most fully and lucidly, Peter
Fryer and Kim Hall.[11] In what follows, I am in part indebted to their research.

To begin with, as Carleton's reference to 'lean-cheeked Moors' indicates,
Negroes and Moors were often conflated, as the jet-black Aaron the Moor in
figure 13.10, the *Titus Andronicus* drawing of 1595 shows. The conflation is
almost caricatured in figure 13.11, the plate of a 'Well-to-do Moor' in Vecellio's
1598 Venetian costume book.[12] Moors were more likely to be slave owners and
traders than slaves. Othello's 'thick lips' similarly betoken the conflation; and
Shakespeare makes him both heroic warrior and former slave. Opinion was

divided over whether blackness was an inherent (or as we would say genetic) characteristic, or an acquired one, the result of continual exposure to the equatorial sun. The latter was the line taken about American Indians; it was claimed that if an Indian baby were kept out of the sun, it would grow up white. In contrast, George Best's observations, in 1578, are cited by several critics to indicate the absoluteness of the English attitude toward the skin color of Africans:

> I myself have seen an Ethiopian as black as coal brought into En-
> gland, who taking a fair English woman to wife, begat a son in all

Figure 13.10. Henry Peacham (?), c. 1595, scene from *Titus Andronicus*.
Longleat Portland Papers I f. 159v. By kind permission of the Marquess of Bath,
Longleat House.

Figure 13.11. Cesare Vecellio, Well-to-do Moor, from *Habiti antichi,
et moderni di tutto il Mondo*, Venice, 1598.

respects as black as the father was, although England were his
native country, and an Englishwoman his mother; whereby
it seemeth that blackness proceedeth rather of some natural
infection of that man, that neither the nature of the clime, neither
the good complexion of the mother concurring, could anything
alter. . . .[13]

Against this notion of the black father's 'natural infection,' which inevitably
overwhelms 'the good complexion' of the white mother, however, we might
set the evidence of Aaron the Moor, in *Titus Andronicus*, who, when Tamora
gives birth to his black child, determines to substitute another:

Not far, one Muliteus, my countryman,
His wife but yesternight was brought to bed.
His child is like to her, fair as you are. (4.2.153–5)

This in its way is an even more frightening fantasy, a testimony to the impossibility of determining not only whether one's child is one's own, but even
whether it is 'really' white or black: blackness in this case is not at all a function of skin color. Lynda Boose, in an essay anatomizing the complexity of
English Renaissance attitudes, argues that by Shakespeare's time the genetic
theory—that blacks were racially 'infected' with their skin color, not merely
(like the American Indians) sunburnt—was the predominant and scientifi-
cally correct one,[14] but while this is doubtless true, it overstates the case: both
theories remained current and available; the correctness of either depended
on what one wished to demonstrate.

   When the Prince of Morocco in *The Merchant of Venice* describes his complexion as 'The shadowed livery of the burnished sun, / To whom I am a
neighbor and near bred,' he represents his blackness as acquired, and the
claim serves as a mode of idealization. He comes off a great deal better than
any of Portia's white European suitors, including the English one; and
arguably, indeed, better too than the profligate and mercenary Bassanio. The
fact that Morocco's skin color is the only thing Portia finds to dislike about
him probably says more about xenophobia, something the English understood well, than about racism (a local Italian, after all, is the only suitor Portia likes). Cleopatra, endlessly seductive and desirable, is similarly 'with Phoebus' amorous pinches black,' radically, even erotically, sunburnt. This is an
aspect of what Philo in the first lines of *Antony and Cleopatra* calls her 'gipsy's
lust,' but there is no suggestion anywhere in the play that it renders her ugly.
It makes her, on the contrary, dangerously attractive. The danger here derives
specifically from her designation not as black but as a gipsy, which obviously

has to do with more than its etymological derivation from 'Egyptian.' Buckingham's decision in 1621 to have Jonson represent him and his family as a
band of gipsies evoked from the poet an equally keen sense of both the attractiveness and the danger.

The ambiguous and imponderable issue of blackness was growing increasingly visible because English involvement in the African slave trade, which
was to be considerable by the end of the seventeenth century, was already well
under way. Hakluyt records John Lok's return from a voyage to Guinea in 1555
with five African slaves; by the mid-1560s, the English captain George Fenner
was trading blacks for sugar.[15] Sir John Hawkins maintained a lucrative trade
in Africans in the 1560s and '70s, heavily subsidized by the Earls of Leicester
and Pembroke, and by the queen herself, who not only invested in his voyages
but also supplied him with two ships. As his portrait in figure 13.12 shows,
Hawkins was proud enough of his continuing success in this venture to take

Figure 13.12. Robert Boissard, *Sir John Hawkins, Naval Commander*, c. 1590.
National Gallery of Art, Washington, DC. Photograph © Board of Trustees,
National Gallery of Art, Washington, DC.

as his crest 'a demi-Moor, proper, in chains.' ('Demi' means a half-length figure, 'proper' means in natural coloring, not heraldic colors—the blacks are real, not allegorical.) The slaves were for the most part traded to the Spanish in the West Indies, but blacks were, nevertheless, an exotic presence in London at this period, generally but not invariably as servants—a sufficiently disturbing presence, indeed, for expulsion orders to be issued twice in the decade preceding the performance of *Blackness*. The terms of the expulsion order are instructive:

> Whereas the Queen's majesty, tendering the good and welfare of her own natural subjects greatly distressed in these hard times of dearth, is highly discontented to understand the great number of Negroes and blackamoors which . . . are crept into this realm since the troubles between her highness and the King of Spain; who are fostered and relieved here, to the great annoyance of her own liege people who want the relief which these people consume, as also for that the most of them are infidels having no understanding of Christ or his Gospel: hath given especial commandment that the said kind of people shall be with all speed avoided and discharged out of this Her Majesty's dominions; and to that end and purpose hath appointed Casper van Senden, merchant of Lubeck, for their speedy transportation, a man that hath very well deserved of this realm in respect that by his own labour and charge he hath relieved and brought from Spain divers of our English nation, who otherwise would have perished there. These shall therefore be to will and require you and every of you to aid and assist the said Casper van Senden . . . to take up such Negroes and blackamoors to be transported as aforesaid, as he shall find within the realm of England; and if there shall be any person or persons which are possessed of any such blackamoors that refuse to deliver them in sort as aforesaid, then we require you to call them before you and advise and persuade them. . . .[16]

Van Senden is here apparently being repaid for his assistance in repatriating English nationals marooned in Spain, presumably after unsuccessful marauding ventures, by being granted the right to expropriate and sell blacks resident in England. The order initially describes the blacks as refugees, but subsequently makes it clear that they are, or at least are to be considered, property: 'any person or persons possessed of such blackamoors' are commanded to give them up. The language is once again xenophobic but not racist; the blacks are foreign and heathen, and in a time of spiraling inflation and unemployment are crowding the Elizabethan welfare rolls and threatening English access to work. The fact that the foreigners are infidels relieves the commonwealth of any claim on its Christian charity; the fact that they are property renders them valuable, and a marketable commodity. Blackness is not presented as the primary issue; and in fact the Irish were similarly expelled at this period, though with no suggestion that they were to be sold. Perhaps they were not felt to be marketable; however the first slaves sent to the English plantations in the West Indies in 1623 were Irish. I should add that I can find no evidence that van Senden succeeded in possessing himself of any blacks.

It is doubtful that any of this has any direct connection with the conceit of the queen's masque; but the idea of aristocratic women as blacks, that is, as marketable commodities and rich possessions, is surely not irrelevant to the age's construction of women generally, and specifically of their negotiation in marriage, their status as the property first of their fathers and then of their husbands. Queen Anne in blackface is, in this sense, merely representing herself in the terms set by the culture. Of course, the point of *The Masque of Blackness* is ultimately to render the ladies white and English; but this is something that is only projected to take place, a year later (in the event, the sequel was delayed for three years, until 1608), and outside the confines of the fiction: *Blackness* is, properly speaking, only half the conceit, the antimasque to the transformation scene, which is its sequel *The Masque of Beauty*. What is probably most notable about the resolution, however, is the means by which the ladies are ultimately transformed: they become white by becoming English, by subjecting themselves to the English king, whose 'beams shine night and day, and are of force / To blanche an Ethiope, or revive a corse,' both proverbial examples of the monarch's ability to do the impossible. The option of a royal miracle was not offered to the blacks at whom Elizabeth aimed her expulsion order, but even the rhetoric of that document suggests that their essential defect is not the color of their skin or any racial infection, but simply—like the daughters of Niger before their enlightenment—a failure of comprehension and conversion: 'the most of them are infidels having no understanding of Christ or his Gospel.'

The beneficent magic of whiteness here is the magic of masculine and patriarchal authority, and the final gesture of subjection to it was one that was built into the Jacobean masque as a form, which always acknowledged the king as its center. Three years later when the queen commanded Jonson to present her and her ladies as military heroines, the problem of subjecting her to a pacifist king who, moreover, disapproved of masculine behavior in women must have seemed an especially stringent test of the poet's powers of invention. How he fulfilled it I have discussed in an essay called 'Jonson and the Amazons': the women are disarmed even as they are empowered; their militant presence banishes the malevolent witches of the antimasque, but Jonson's embodiment of Heroic Virtue is not Athena or Bellona, warlike goddesses and prototypes of the armed queen and her ladies, but Perseus, slayer of Medusa, the gorgon, who embodies all the dangerous potential of the feminine.[17] If Jonson's mythography subverts the queen's interests, it fully supports the king's. For James, the defeat and decapitation of the primary sensual and beautiful woman in his life was the crucial act of empowerment.

The attitudes towards women expressed in *The Masque of Queens* are, however, not altogether accounted for by the politics of Jacobean royal patronage. The militant heroines were the queen's idea, but the witches, after all, were the poet's, and they represent an obvious declaration of the community of Jonson's interests with those of the king. The royal treatise on *Demonologie* the fruit of both scholarly research and of continual attendance at witch trials, testified to James's credentials as Britain's principal expert on the subject; but Jonson's elaborate glosses, elucidations, citations of authorities, declare his own expertise to be fully the equal of the king's. The witches are as much a gesture of self-assertion as of compliment, and the fact that they are presented as the alternatives to female heroism says more about Jonson's psychology than about the terms of his employment.

As 'a foil or false masque' to heroic virtue, infernal evil is not an inevitable choice. A year later, devising the antimasque antitheses to the heroic persona of Prince Henry's Oberon, Jonson created a group of rowdy and good-natured satyrs, whose vices were all the lusty and indecorous pleasures that Jonson obviously shared: drinking, sex, practical jokes. Anatomizing his poetic options in *The Forest*, Jonson rejects the classical pantheon en masse, but his strictures specifically against the two female goddesses, Athena and Venus, reveal anxieties that have nothing to do with the composition of poetry, and resonate significantly with the styles of both his royal patrons:

> Pallas, nor thee I call on, mankind maid,
> That at thy birth made the poor smith afraid,
> Who with his axe thy father's midwife played.

> Go, cramp dull Mars, light Venus, when he snorts,
> Or with thy tribade trine invent new sports;
> Thou nor thy looseness with my making sorts. (*Forest* 10, 13–18)

Athena here is both masculine ('mankind,' mannish) and responsible for the feminization of Jove and Vulcan; Venus is not only a wanton who exhausts even Mars, but one who engages in lesbian sex with the Graces—'tribade,' the earliest term in English for a homosexual woman, is first used in print by Jonson. The masculinity of the martial Athena, 'mankind maid,' leads to the much more hostile response to genuinely self-sufficient women, who are both sexually active and erotically independent of men—as on the frontispiece to Saxton's *Atlas* (1579), Athena and Venus, symbolizing Justice and Peace, seem about to be (the image is reproduced as figure 8.17 in "Gendering the Crown," above). I have also observed that the decisive and contemptuous rejection of Venus as Jonson's muse is especially striking since his 'making,' which he declares to be so incompatible with her wantonness, must be not only his poetic craft but his own kind of sex as well, that 'doing' which, he says, following Petronius, 'a filthy pleasure is, and short; / And done, we straight repent us of the sport.' Is the problem with lesbian sex precisely its ability to 'invent new sports,' its revelation of a world of erotic alternatives (and of alternatives to men: the martial goddess on Saxton's frontispiece is replacing Mars)—and its revelation thereby of the insufficiency of his own sexuality, determined as it is by all its good classical masculine precedents?

Clearly women are profoundly destabilizing. Even in explaining 'Why I Write Not of Love,' the love that eludes Jonson's verse is male, not female, Cupid, not Venus. In contrast, for Donne and his libertine correspondents a decade earlier, women were the only subject—the subject, indeed, that binds men together—and tribadry was the very essence of poetry. I again quote "Gendering the Crown": the word is deployed, in the earliest example I have found (not recorded in the *OED*), in a way that is neither uncomprehending nor hostile. Donne's correspondent T. W. writes in a verse letter,

> Have mercy on me and my sinful muse,
> Which, rubbed and tickled with thine, could not choose
> But spend some of her pith, and yield to be
> One in that chaste and mystic tribadry.[18]

Nevertheless, and paradoxically, to praise women for their masculine qualities is often the bottom line of Jonsonian idealization:

> Only a learned and a manly soul
> I purposed her, that should, with even powers,
> The rock, the spindle, and the shears control
> Of destiny, and spin her own free hours.

What is extraordinary here is not that Lucy, Countess of Bedford is being offered control over her fate, and that that is conceived as the work of a 'manly soul'; it is that the control is depicted as involving the most traditional of feminine accomplishments: what the fates do is the domestic work of spinning, and this is the work of the manly soul. What prevents Jonson from imagining a soul so conceived as quintessentially womanly? Women's virtues, as we derive them from the poems in praise of those women whose patronage he courted, are to maintain a well-run and hospitable household, keep a bountiful table, but most of all to stay clear of the world of action and temptation, 'Not to know vice at all, and keep true state', as he puts it in the 'Epode'—to be, in short, fruitful, chaste, and (the unspoken corollary) silent. How difficult Jonson found it to believe in the reality of such an ideal, however, is evident enough simply from the topography of his *Epigrams*, in which a poem in praise of his patron the Countess of Bedford appears immediately after a poem asserting that the words 'woman' and 'whore' are synonyms, or from the chronology of his theater, in which the play composed immediately after *The Masque of Queens* is *Epicoene*.

The three poems written To Elizabeth, Countess of Rutland may serve as an epitome of Jonson's difficulty in negotiating his feelings about the idea of female patronage. Daughter of Sir Philip Sidney, she is praised in the *Epigrams* specifically as a successor to her father. Sidney had no sons 'Save,' as Jonson puts it, 'that most masculine issue of his brain,' his writing, and Nature therefore created, in the Countess, a poet—but a poet who outdoes her father. The praise is evidently heartfelt, since Jonson asserted to Drummond that her poetry was 'nothing inferior' to Sidney's; but embodied in the epigrammatic text, the genial equivalence ('nothing inferior') becomes a hostile confrontation: poetry is male, the woman's excellence is realized only through an invidious comparison with her father, and her success, indeed, does not merely outdo his, but incinerates it: 'if he were living now,'

> He should those rare and absolute numbers view
> As he would burn, or better far, his book. (Epig. 79, 10–12)

Implicit in the articulate woman is the obliteration of the masculine text. In contrast, the much more modest praise of the countess's talent expressed in the epistle to her included in *The Forest* leaves Sidney's reputation intact:

> ... what a sin 'gainst your great father's spirit
> Were it to think that you should not inherit
> His love unto the muses, when his skill
> Almost you have, or may have, when you will? (*Forest* 12, 31–4)

Almost; may have. The final epigram in *The Underwood*, addressed to the countess in her widowhood, praises her hospitality, virtue, and passion not for writing but reading:

> ... you make your books your friends,
> And study them unto the noblest ends,
> Searching for knowledge ... (*Underwood* 50, 27–9)

Her poetry is not mentioned; neither is her father. Both Sidney and Jonson are safe from her at last.

The Jacobean years were good ones for Jonson as a court poet. He maintained both his place and his self-esteem through a finely poised rhetoric of hyperbolic compliment, including as much self-aggrandizement as praise of his patrons. Royal idealization was framed and legitimated by classical authority and historical example. Court masques were not the 'toys' they were for Bacon, the 'punctiloes of dreams' they were for Daniel, the 'vanity of my art' they were for ... well, at least for Prospero; they were instead 'the donatives of great princes,' 'high and hearty inventions ... grounded upon antiquity and solid learnings,' whose 'sense ... should always lay hold on more removed mysteries.' They were, that is, on the one hand, royal utterances, and on the other, scholarship, philosophy, and poetry. As such, they validated both Jonson's social place, his authority to speak for the monarch, and his literary credentials, his authority to speak for the ages. They were, in short, not only texts, but even more powerfully, subtexts.

But perhaps most important in terms of Jonson's ability to assert his continuing control over his masques, and thereby over the world to which they granted him access, they were marginalia (figure 13.13). In a sense the masques of these years pose a far more complex and interesting question than the question of why Queen Anne wanted to appear in blackface: why did she want marginalia? The easy answer would be that she did not want them. Jonson in fact invites this answer in the dedication to the presentation manuscript of the copiously annotated *Masque of Queens*, where Prince Henry is credited with issuing the 'command to have me add this second labour of annotation

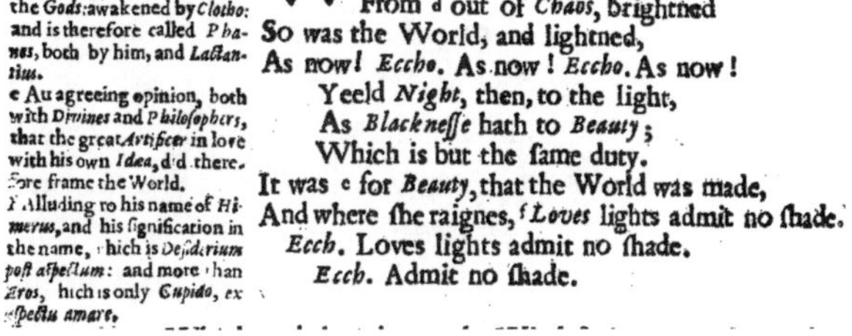

SONG.

d. So is he faind by *Orpheus*, to have appeared firſt of all the Gods: awakened by *Clotho*: and is therefore called *Phanes*, both by him, and *Lactantius*.

e An agreeing opinion, both with *Divines* and *Philoſophers*, that the great *Artificer* in love with his own *Idea*, did there fore frame the World.

f Alluding to his name of *Himerus*, and his ſignification in the name, which is *Deſiderium* poſt aſpectum: and more than *Eros*, which is only *Cupido*, ex aſpectu amare.

W Hen *Love*, at firſt, did move
From d out of *Chaos*, brightned
So was the World, and lightned,
As now! *Eccho*. As now! *Eccho*. As now!
Yeeld *Night*, then, to the light,
As *Blackneſſe* hath to *Beauty*;
Which is but the ſame duty.
It was e for *Beauty*, that the World was made,
And where ſhe raignes, f *Loves* lights admit no ſhade.
Eccho. Loves lights admit no ſhade.
Eccho. Admit no ſhade.

Figure 13.13. *The Masque of Blackness*, song with marginalium, from the 1640 folio.

to my first of invention.'[19] The logical corollary is, then, that the annotations to the prince's masque *Oberon* were similarly done at his command, and that the annotations to the queen's masques of *Blackness* and *Beauty* and to the two wedding masques *Hymenaei* and *The Haddington Masque* were Jonson's own idea.

This is certainly a possible scenario. It is suspect only because it allies Jonson a little too easily and completely with the scholar king on the one hand and his filial disciple on the other, Jonson the royal deputy acting as both servant and master to the young prince, Aristotle to Henry's Alexander. Where is the queen in all this? Was the learning simply thrust upon her? It was she, after all, not the king, who was Jonson's patron for much of the first decade of the reign, though he courted James's favor tirelessly. Why was the queen attracted to this poet? Why did she change her masque writer from the Daniel of 'punctiloes of dreams' to the Jonson of 'antiquity and solid learnings'? Jonson was certainly more sympathetic with James's patriarchalist ideology than was Daniel. It is not clear, however, that this is relevant: it was the queen who established Jonson as court poet. She has traditionally been represented as both flighty and morose, with a particular and somewhat reprehensible interest in masquing; but since Jonson's only court entertainment before *Blackness* was the brief pastoral at Althorp, it can hardly have been his previous successes in the genre that recommended him to her. Perhaps in fact Queen Anne was a patron of taste and discernment—the resistance of modern critics to this idea has been quite striking.[20] Frances Yates, for example, discussing the career of one of the queen's most impressive and original protégés, John Florio, describes her as 'a rather stupid, rather frivolous person,' who, however, 'spoke the Italian language most perfectly.'[21] This is offered as a testimony to Florio's talents as Queen Anne's Italian reader; but surely it may be allowed to redound to the queen's credit as well. In fact, she already knew Italian when Florio came to her attention, having studied it with Giacomo Castelvetro in Edinburgh for five years. Graham Parry is more appreciative, but the condescension is still palpable, with Jonson's genius 'transforming the flimsy, gay devices of the queen into fables of monarchical divinity.'[22]

In fact, Florio provides a good index to the genuine value of the queen's artistic patronage. The first edition of his Montaigne, published in 1603, had six dedicatees, all socially prominent women, four of them notably literary: the Countesses of Bedford and Rutland, Lady Anne Harington, Penelope Lady Rich, Lady Elizabeth Grey, and Lady Mary Neville. For the second edition ten years later, the six ladies were replaced by the queen, who clearly constituted, for a scholar, a much better investment. Florio provided two dedications, the second an Italian poem, a tribute to his patron's linguistic proficiency. The queen subsequently underwrote the revision of Florio's great Italian dictio-

a See the Kings
Majesties book,
(our Severaign)
of Dæmonology,
Bodin Remig.
Delrio. Mal.
Malefi. And a
woild of o-
thers, in the ge-
nerall: But let
us follow par-
ticulars.

..... Jones ..., ... *Scene*, and *Machine*. Only,
Snakes, Bones, Herbs, Ro(
the authority of ancient a1
there be any found; and f
Thefe eleven Witches b
mony at their *Convents*, or
zarded, and mafqu'd) on th(
interrupted the reft, with t

Figure 13.14. *The Masque of Queens*, marginalium from the 1640 folio.

nary, duly re-entitled *Queen Anna's New World of Words*. This surely says as much about the queen's influence on Florio as about his influence on her.

Perhaps, then, the queen was attracted to Jonson precisely for the artistic authority he could bring to her Twelfth Night entertainments—for just what she is claimed to have had no interest in, his seriousness and learning. In that case the marginalia would be as much a validation of her taste as of Jonson's scholarship, her way of justifying and maintaining her control over these extravagant ephemera, just as they were his way of asserting the power and authority of his learning. Patron and poet shared a need for a space in which they could operate independently of the constraints of their situations. Is it irrelevant that both were converts to Roman Catholicism? All Jonson's masques for the queen imagine her transformed, freed, militantly victorious: are these only Queen Anne's fantasies?

But the fantasies are contained, enveloped, by the obsessive marginalia. If they serve the queen's purposes, they serve Jonson's even more. It can hardly be accidental that the witches are far more elaborately authenticated than the queens. Appearing only in the text of the masque, and only after it is no longer a performing text, the glosses are finally all Jonson's; and indeed, the marginalia to *Queens* record a moment of scholarly invention that approaches *lèse majesté* (figure 13.14). Beside an assertion that witches' conventicles commonly begin with dances, Jonson cites an authority: 'See the King's majesty's book (our sovereign) of *Demonology*.' To acknowledge the king's expertise on the subject of witchcraft is doubtless no more than the price of royal patronage; but in fact the note does not acknowledge the king. It is pure ventriloquism: King James does not discuss witches' dances anywhere in *Demonologie*. That Jonson should presume to speak as the king is perhaps not surprising in the playwright who brought Queen Elizabeth onstage to conclude *Every Man Out of His Humour*, treating the monarch as a prop for his

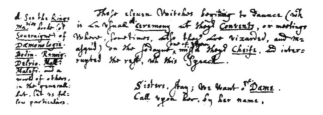

Figure 13.15. *The Masque of Queens*, marginalium in the holograph, 1609.
ROY.18.A.xlv. By permission of the British Library.

drama; but the note records a subtle antagonism along with the obvious, if
meretricious, compliment. Jonson's true source for information about dancing at covens appears to be Reginald Scot's sceptical treatise *The Discoverie of
Witches*, a tract that James attacks in *Demonologie*. Jonson thus marginalizes
the king's scholarship even as he praises it, usurping the royal authority with
a subversive rival expertise.

What particularly interests me here is that parenthetical 'our sovereign.'
This seems designed to preclude any ambiguity about what royal work on
demonology is intended (not, e.g., that of the king of Naples); but in that case,
to whom is the marginal note being addressed? Jonson says the notes were
prepared at the command of Prince Henry; they first appear in the beautiful
holograph dedicated to the prince and presented by Jonson to the queen
(figure 13.15). This is the most personal of copies of the work. Surely the king's
wife and son were in no danger of confusion on the question of which king is
intended. But equally clearly the note is not really addressed to Jonson's royal
patrons, but to all his projected readers; and the parenthesis thereby transforms prince and queen into subjects, not only of the king, which of course
they are, but even more significantly of the sovereign poet. The masque,
indeed, concludes with a realization of the power and permanence, the ultimate authority, of poetry, the House of Fame, an architectural emblem
adopted from Chaucer. It is adorned with statues of Homer, Virgil, and Lucan
on the lower tier, and of Achilles, Aeneas, and Caesar on the upper. The
heroes' fame is supported and preserved by the immortal poets; heroism (and
the heroism now is all male) depends on the ordering and eternizing power of
poetry.

Jonson's claims for himself are royal claims too: poet and king in this text
assert the same authority. Outside the fiction but at the center of the spectacle, James occupies his seat of state, declaring by his presence that in this
masque of queens, heroism may be allowed to be the royal consort, but the

Figure 13.16. Sculpture of King James presenting his works to Oxford on the Tower of the Five Orders. By permission of Bodleian Library, University of Oxford.

highest virtue is that of the Rex Pacificus, scholar and poet: it is finally not the triumphant queen's but the king's peace that Fame's trumpet sounds. James had himself represented on the tower of the Bodleian Library precisely as a scholar, to commemorate his gift to Oxford of the folio of his works, published, like Jonson's, in 1616 (figure 13.16). It is for this that Fame, at his right hand, blows her trumpet. The masque, for all its amazonian heroines, celebrates the sovereign and masculine word. Empowering women was not a Jonsonian ideal, and the queen was not the patron he sought.

14

TOBACCO AND BOYS

How Queer Was Marlowe?

MARLOWE has been a significant figure in the refiguration of the English Renaissance, the working-class/outsider/spy/sodomite who gives the lie to the Elizabethan World Picture and a whole complex of traditional assumptions about the aims of English Renaissance drama. My argument here, however, is that the transgressive Marlowe is largely a posthumous phenomenon. I begin with the portrait that hangs in the hall of Corpus Christi College, Cambridge, (figure 14.1) though with no conviction that it is in fact a portait of Marlowe. It was discovered, badly damaged, in a heap of builders' rubbish during the renovations of the Old Court of Corpus in 1952, and was then thoroughly and conservatively restored. It is inscribed with the date 1585, and the sitter's age, twenty-one, and a motto, to which I shall return. All that could be determined

Figure 14.1. Portrait of a young man said to be Marlowe, 1585. By permission of the Parker Library, Corpus Christi College, Cambridge.

Figure 14.2. Portrait of Edmund Spenser. Eighteenth-century copy
after a lost original. By permission of Pembroke College, Cambridge.

about its previous history was that it had been nailed to a wall in the Master's
Lodge; the Lodge was built in the 1820s, and there is no way of knowing when
after that the picture was installed or where it hung before that, or when it
came into the possession of the college—there is, in short, no record of its
existence before 1952, though it is certainly an Elizabethan painting.[1] The suggestion that it is a portrait of Marlowe was made in 1955, not by anyone con-
nected with the College, which does not claim it represents Marlowe. Nevertheless, it keeps being reproduced as the only extant portrait of the poet. The
problems with this identification are manifold: Marlowe certainly was
twenty-one in 1585, but if this is Marlowe, why would a Cambridge undergraduate, a scholarship boy from an artisan class background, have commissioned such a portrait? If somebody else—some admirer or patron—commissioned it, who was he (or, less likely in Marlowe's case, she), and why did
the painting end up in the possession of the college, rather than of the patron
or the sitter? Charles Nicholl, who is eager for the portrait to be Marlowe, and
uses it on the cover of his book about Marlowe's murder, *The Reckoning*, has
suggested that the college itself commissioned the picture of its famous alum-
nus. This strikes me as inherently implausible, given both the youth and the
presentation of the sitter, and the fact that in 1585 Marlowe was not at all
famous, but utterly obscure. Nicholl cites as corroborative evidence the portrait of Spenser hanging in the hall of Pembroke College, which was certainly
commissioned by the college; but the comparison is surely disingenuous. Fig-

Figure 14.3. After Nicholas Hilliard, Francis Bacon at the age of 18.
Wash drawing by Elena Shvarts. Private collection.

ure 14.2 is the Spenser portrait: it is an eighteenth-century painting, said to be
a copy of an earlier painting of unknown date, now lost. It shows Spenser as a
mature man in the years of his fame, not as an undergraduate; it is, if anything, an argument against the idea that the college would have commissioned a portrait of Marlowe at twenty-one. If the sitter could be shown to be
Marlowe, of course, it would tell us something important about how his erst-
while colleagues wanted to remember him—not, that is, as a distinguished
poet like Spenser. And whoever commissioned the painting, what is the significance of the outfit? The rich velvet jacket is liberally adorned with buttons
that either are or look like gold, and is slashed to show an orange silk lining.
The collar is a simple band, but covered with the finest transparent lawn. Why
the exceedingly rich garment, rather than an academic gown or something a
scholarship boy might reasonably have worn? And—a logical corrolary to all
these questions—if the painting is not Marlowe, why did anyone ever think
it was?

Let us consider a couple of other literary youths in the same period, young
men who are in some way comparable with Marlowe. A Hilliard miniature
now at Belvoir Castle shows Francis Bacon at eighteen. The owner, the Duke
of Rutland, has mysteriously refused permission to reproduce the work, but
the copy in figure 14.3, by the contemporary American artist Elena Shvarts,
gives a good sense of its qualities. The Bacon it shows is a pretty and rather
cheeky youth, in a sober jacket and ruff—the ruff would probably have looked

Figure 14.4. John Donne at the age of 18. Wash drawing by Elena Shvarts
after an anonymous painting. Private collection.

less flamboyant to an Elizabethan viewer than it does to us. The hair is
notable, carefully-carelessly arranged. (A photograph of the original can be
found in Lisa Jardine and Alan Stewart's inflammatory biography of Bacon
Hostage to Fortune [London: Victor Gollancz, 1998], following page 256.) Figure 14.4 is Shvarts's copy of an anonymous painting owned by the Earl of
Lothian, of which the only available photograph was too dark to reproduce
adequately. Donne at eighteen is depicted as a melancholy lover, his collar
casually undone. He positively smoulders under the raffish hat. (There is a
good photograph of the original in Roy Strong, *The English Icon* [London:
Routledge, 1969], fig. 31.) Figure 14.5, the engraved frontispiece of the 1635
poems (after a lost Hilliard miniature), however, shows the eighteen-year-old
Donne as a much more conventionally courtly youth, elegantly dressed, and
grasping the hilt of his sword.

    With these as context, what strikes us as individual about the portrait that
is called Marlowe? The hair seems more unkempt than casual, the gaze is
direct but rather disquieting, even taunting or surly, and the full red lips are
especially unusual—English youths tend to be depicted as a thin-lipped lot.
Donne the melancholy lover is in this respect exceptional; Donne the courtly
youth has lips that are much less romantically inviting. So perhaps the full red
lips of the youth in the Corpus painting do imply an erotic charge—as does
the motto, 'Quod me nutrit me destruit,' what nourishes me destroys me, with

Figure 14.5. John Donne at the age of 18, after a miniature by Hilliard.
Frontispiece to the *Poems*, 1635.

its implication of a consuming passion. The open neck, too, suggesting an easy *déshabillé*, is shared by the melancholy Donne, but there is something altogether more cocky and provocative about this young man than about the youthful poet-lover.

So perhaps that is why we want this to be Marlowe—the cheekiness, the faintly disreputable expression, the suggestion that he is in fancy clothes he doesn't belong in, all summed up in the ominous motto predicting—or recording—an early and unhappy death: the fact that it seems to be a presumptuous picture with the right moral. After all, Bacon and Donne were gentlemen; Marlowe, if this is he, is usurping his place. The splendid jacket even puts him in violation of the sumptuary laws—thirteen years earlier, in 1572, a fellow of King's College was arrested and imprisoned when he was found to be wearing just such a slashed velvet doublet under his academic gown. On the other hand, one way of entering the gentry was precisely via the university, and people did dress up to have their portraits painted, not necessarily in their own clothes. But of course the real connection, the only connection, of the painting with Marlowe is the college and the date: Marlowe *was* twenty-one in 1585, and still at Corpus, in the second year of study toward the M.A. But there were one hundred eleven students in residence at Corpus in 1585—how many of Marlowe's schoolmates would also have been twenty-one? The B.A. and M.A. was a seven-year program; so roughly one-seventh?

Fifteen or twenty? In short, the only reason to identify this as a portrait of Marlowe, rather than one of his classmates, is that it's Marlowe we want a portrait of.

The portrait in a significant sense is modern: even though it is an authentic Elizabethan painting, its identification as Marlowe seems to crystallize modern attitudes toward the playwright—presumably it was hanging on the wall for centuries, but nobody ever claimed the college had a portrait of Marlowe until 1955. The transgressive Marlowe it seems to depict is also largely a posthumous phenomenon, embodied in, if not created by, Richard Baines's and Thomas Kyd's lurid testimony, which formed part of the evidence upon which he was investigated by the Privy Council, and circulated after Marlowe's death. Among Marlowe's opinions, according to Baines, were that Moses was a juggler and that Thomas Hariot, Sir Walter Ralegh's servant, 'can do more than he'—this has always been taken as an invidious comparison between Hariot and Moses, but it may include something even more subversive as well, a claim that Ralegh's servant was a better man than Ralegh too. Marlowe also believed, according to Baines, that 'the first beginning of Religion was only to keep men in awe,' that Christ was a bastard, his mother a whore, his father merely a carpenter, and the crucifixion justified; that Catholicism was a good religion and 'all Protestantes are hypocriticall asses'; that the woman of Samaria and her sister were whores and Christ knew them 'dishonestly'; that Christ was the 'bedfellow' of John the Evangelist and 'used him as the sinners of Sodoma'; that all those who love not tobacco and boys were fools, and that he had as much right to issue currency as the queen of England, and intended 'to coin French crowns, pistolets, and English shillings.'[2] This looks like a jumble, but as Jonathan Goldberg has shown, the charges are entirely consistent, defining a world in which heresy, scurrility, love, sodomy, counterfeiting, and most of all social mobility and the drive toward success are all aspects of the same dangerous set of desires.[3] Henry Peacham's ascending, aspiring, Ganymede, in figure 14.6, might be a figure for Baines's Marlowe:

> Upon a cock here Ganymede doth sit,
> Who erst rode mounted on Jove's eagle's back,
> One hand holds Circe's wand, and joined with it,
> A cup top-filled with poison deadly black;
> The other medals of base metals wrought,
> With sundry moneys, counterfeit and naught.
>
> These be those crimes abhorred of God and man,
> Which justice should correct with laws severe:

Crimina graviſſima. 48.

VPON a Cock, heere *Ganimede* doth ſit,
   Who erſt rode mounted on *I O V E S* Eagles back,
One hand holdes *Circes* wand, and ioind with it,
A cup top-fil'd with poiſon, deadly black:
   The other Meddals, of baſe mettals wrought,
   With ſundry moneyes, counterfeit and nought.

Theſe be thoſe crimes, abhorr'd of God and man,
Which Iuſtice ſhould correct, with lawes ſevere,
In * *Ganimed*, the foule Sodomitan:
Within the Cock, vile inceſt doth appeare:
   Witchcraft, and murder, by that cup and wand,
   And by the reſt, falſe coine you vnderſtand.

Figure 14.6. Ganymede, from Henry Peacham, *Minerva Britanna*, 1612, p. 48.

> In Ganymede, the foul sodomitan,
> Within the cock, vile incest doth appear,
> Witchcraft and murder, by that cup and wand,
> And by the rest, false coin you understand.

The image incorporates sodomy, incest, witchcraft, murder, counterfeiting, all enabled by the beautiful youth's seductive power encapsulated in Circe's wand.

Marlowe, posthumously at least, was a universally dangerous, seductively persuasive radical. Did this result in the proscription of his work? Not, certainly, of his drama: both during his lifetime and long after, his plays were among the most popular in the repertory. It is true that his Ovid translations were called in, banned and burned by episcopal order, six years after his death; but it is not clear in this case that the proscription was aimed at Marlowe: the book was a collection of satirical epigrams by John Davies followed by ten of Marlowe's translations from the *Amores*—'Davyes Epigrams, with Marlowes Elegys' is the way the order puts it. The offensive material may well have been Davies', and the offense thus libel, not incitement to lechery. Still, as the book is constituted, Marlowe is at least guilty by association: all six early editions of the Ovid translations include Davies' epigrams, though those with the complete elegies put Marlowe first, and all are published either abroad, at Middleburgh, in Holland, or surreptiously in Scotland with a false Middleburgh imprint. If Davies was the problem, why not publish Marlowe's Ovid by itself? Or was it the scurrilous Davies that sold the erotic Marlowe? Would a Marlowe untainted by libel not be marketable?

All Ovids Elegies is a strange book. Unpublished during Marlowe's lifetime, the manuscript would have recommended itself to publishers not merely as the work of Marlowe the erotic classicist, cashing in on the success of *Hero and Leander,* also unpublished but circulated in manuscript, but equally as the first translation of the *Amores* not only into English but into any modern language. The *Amores* was the least well known of Ovid's works to the Renaissance, untouched by the allegorizing and moralizing commentaries that had safely contextualized Ovid's other work for Christian readers. It is difficult not to feel, however, that here, as with Marlowe's translation of the first book of Lucan, the publishers were scraping the bottom of the Marlowe barrel. *All Ovids Elegies* reads like a promising first draft, occasionally felicitous but mostly routine, with moments of real brilliance but also moments of striking ineptitude. Time after time the only way to understand Marlowe's English is to use the Latin as a crib. 'So, chaste Minerva, did Cassandra fall / Deflowered except, within thy temple wall' (1.7)[4]—the Latin says that the only chastity left to Cassandra was the fact that she was raped in Minerva's temple; it is difficult to see how one would get this out of the English. 'Hector to arms went from

"Your dog had both motive and opportunity, ma'am: He hated the cat and he's had training in operating heavy machinery. ... Your husband, we feel, was just in the wrong place at the wrong time."

his wife's embraces, / And on Andromache his helmet laces' (1.9)—only the Latin will reveal that it is Andromache who is lacing the helmet on Hector, not the other way round. 'Object thou then what she may well excuse, / To stain in faith all truth, by all crimes use' (2.2)—the Latin says 'accuse her only of what she can explain away; a false charge undermines the credibility of a true one': is there any way of eliciting this from Marlowe? Often the gibberish is undeniably beautiful, the work of a poet with a superb ear working too fast for meaning: 'Wilt thou her fault learn, she may make thee tremble; / Fear to be guilty, then thou mayst dissemble' (2.2)—even the Latin will not help to explain this; 'What day was that which, all sad haps to bring / White birds to lovers did not always sing' (3.11)—Ovid says, this is the day when, as a permanent bad omen, love birds stopped singing, but Marlowe's version is all connotation with no denotation.

Nevertheless, the translation is an impressive achievement, especially if, as appears to be the case, it is the work of Marlowe's undergraduate years; and its completeness is not the least of its virtues. It remained unique in English until an anonymous translation appeared in 1683, followed by Dryden. As for its occasional impenetrability, the Elizabethans had a higher tolerance for obscurity than we have, and though there is evidence that Ben Jonson was involved in the preparation of at least one of the early surreptitious editions, his concern was obviously not with revision or clarification. What Marlowe undertook was the domestication of the erotic Ovid in the wake of the many previous generations' mythographic Ovid. And after Marlowe's sensational death, the combination of Ovid, Marlowe, and English would probably have been sufficient to warrant publication surreptitiously, even if John Davies' scurrilous epigrams hadn't been included. But since the erotic Marlowe looms so large in the modern construction of the poet, it is worth pausing over the sexuality of *All Ovids Elegies*. How erotically transgressive is it?

Transgressive enough, certainly: it is a chronicle not merely of lechery, but of adultery, pandering, promiscuity, faithlessness, irreverence. It is even, on occasion, explicit and smutty where Ovid is merely metonymic: 'The whore stands to be bought for each man's money, / And seeks vile wealth by selling of her coney' (1.10.21–2), where the Latin specifies only 'corpore,' her body. Ovid's urbane cynicism in English, moreover, translates directly into Marlowe's alleged atheism: 'God is a name, no substance, feared in vain, / And doth the world in fond belief detain' (3.3.23–4). Reason enough to publish the book surreptitiously. Still, it is the nature of the eroticism I wish to pause over. Since Marlowe's homosexual interests figure so significantly in both Baines's and Kyd's charges against him, and are certainly manifest in *Edward II*, the opening of *Dido Queen of Carthage* and *Hero and Leander*, and are especially prominent in the construction of the modern Marlowe, it is worth observing that the erotics of *All Ovids Elegies* are exclusively heterosexual—not even Cupid in elegy 1.10 (15–17), a beautiful naked youth selling himself, without so much as a pocket to put his money in, raises Marlowe's rhetorical eyebrow. Ovid himself observes that his sexual interests are primarily in women: he says in the *Ars Amatoria* that the sex he likes is the kind that gives equal pleasure to both partners, and therefore sex with boys doesn't interest him much (2.683–4)—the 'therefore' made sense to Roman readers because the boy, as the passive partner in the buggery, was supposed not to enjoy the sex, a prophylactic fiction designed to licence the practice of pederasty while simultaneously preserving the youth of the realm from any suspicion of real depravity.[5] If Marlowe's erotic imagination was essentially homosexual, and sex was the point, Catullus, Martial, Horace, or even the Virgil of the *Eclogues* would surely have been more likely texts for domestication. Was it then something other than the sex that attracted him to the *Amores*?

Perhaps so: Patrick Cheney makes an intriguing and persuasive case for the young Marlowe's transumption of the *Amores* as part of a grand design, the first step in the creation of a poetic career consciously modeled on Ovid, an anti-Virgilian, and therefore anti-Spenserian model.[6] This may be correct; nevertheless, the sex may well have been a factor after all: perhaps the whole question is anachronistic, the issue construed too narrowly. Perhaps, in short, homosexuality is our problem, not Marlowe's. The first published account of the murder, Thomas Beard's in *The Theatre of Gods Iudgements*, 1597, cites only 'epicurism' and atheism as Marlowe's mortal sins. In the next year, Francis Meres cites Beard, and adds the information, derived from no known source, that Marlowe 'was stabd to death by a bawdy seruing man, a rival of his in his lewde loue'[7]—is this perhaps merely an expansion of the implications of 'epicurism'? Recently Charles Nicholl has elaborated the account still further by suggesting that 'this serving-man was, like Marlowe, a homosexual, and that the cause of the fight, the object of their "lewd love", was another man.'[8] Marlowe's sexual preferences are not really in question, but this surely confuses the issue. To begin with, there is no reason to assume that Meres has a love triangle in mind; 'rival' can mean simply 'partner' (as Bernardo calls Horatio and Marcellus 'the rivals of my watch' at the opening of *Hamlet*), and if we want Marlowe's 'lewd love' to be homosexual, its object may simply be the bawdy serving man. But it is surely to the point that the object is unspecified, the crime 'epicurism,' the pursuit of pleasure. The sin is precisely the subject of the *Amores*, 'lewd love,' illicit sexuality, of whatever kind—if homosexuality had been a worse kind of 'lewd love,' Marlowe would have been guilty of it. A century later Antony à Wood elaborated Meres's account for his age as revealingly as Nicholl has done for ours: 'For so it fell out that he being deeply in love with a certain woman . . . had for his rival a bawdy serving-man, one rather fit to be a pimp than an ingenious amoretto as Marlowe conceived himself to be.'[9]

In fact, homosexuality in the charges against Marlowe is primarily an aspect of his blasphemy and atheism—Baines and Kyd do not assert that Marlowe was a sodomite, but that he said Christ and St. John were: this is apparently worse than being a sodomite oneself. The link between the love of boys and the love of tobacco is one I shall return to, but it is not part of a claim that Marlowe systematically debauched the youth of London, as it might well have been. We can get some perspective on the place of homosexuality in these charges by comparing them with the allegations against two of Marlowe's much more visible contemporaries, Francis and Anthony Bacon. Imputations of sodomy dogged both brothers from the early days of their public life, especially in the 1590s as a result of their intimacy with the Earl of Essex and his circle. As Lisa Jardine and Alan Stewart write, 'the exclusively male, intense and passionate forms of service which surrounded Essex . . . could readily be represented . . . as a world rife with male sexual intrigue and sodomy. Lampoons, letters and intelligence reports from the period contain frequent suggestions that one or other of the rising young men is involved in some homosexual liaison.'[10] Charges of sodomy became almost routine when Francis rose to eminence. John Aubrey, who greatly admired him and had his information from Bacon's secretary Thomas Hobbes, asserts unequivocally that Bacon was a pederast who kept ganymedes and favorites. There were pasquinades circulated on the subject immediately upon Bacon's fall from power—e.g., affixed to the wall of his house, 'Within this sty a hog doth lie / That must be hanged for sodomy' (with 'hog' playing on Bacon). When Bacon's amanuensis and protégé Thomas Bushell appeared in a coat elaborately decorated with gilded buttons, the splendid livery produced the satirical charge that 'his lord's posteriors makes the buttons that he wears'—he was Bacon's lover, and the buttons were both the outward and visible sign of, and the fee for, buggery.[11] Brian Vickers, in a hostile review of the book, indignantly denies that the reference is sexual; he says it only means that Bacon was so frightened that he was shitting buttons.[12] But it can hardly be the case that jokes about Bacon's posterior in the context of charges of sodomy have no sexual component. (In fact, Bushell was a metallurgist, a protégé of Bacon the scientist, and the astonishing buttons may well have been a scientific innovation of his. In any case, the assumptions about them were obviously unexpected: do they have any bearing on the lavishly buttoned outfit of the youth in the Corpus portrait?) Commenting on Bacon's conviction, Sir Simonds d'Ewes remarks, as a matter of common knowledge, 'the practice of his most horrible and secret sin of sodomy, keeping still one Godrick a very effeminate faced youth to be his catamite. After his fall men began to discourse of that his unnatural crime, which he had practised many years; deserting the bed of his lady. . . .' Yet, d'Ewes concludes, 'he never came to any public trial for this crime; nor did ever that I could hear forbear his old custom of making his servants his bedfellows.'[13] His brother Anthony, however, was prosecuted for sodomy in 1586, while he was in France as Burghley's agent. His servants testified to persistent homosexual activity both between the master and his pages and among the servants themselves. Anthony was, moreover, not only charged, but apparently convicted and sentenced. He was extricated by the intervention of King Henri III, for whom the imprisonment of an emissary of Elizabeth's minister was politically embarrassing; and he was, after much legal wrangling, essentially ransomed and ordered home. Both brothers led careers in which charges of buggery played a continuous and significant role.

In Marlowe's case, in contrast, though his own works could easily have been used as evidence against him, the charge appears almost marginal—as it clearly is in the matter of tobacco and boys. Commentators have undertaken to connect tobacco to the charge of atheism, noting its source in the pagan New World, but this seems to me misguided. The point is the same one Jonson makes when, in *Every Man Out of his Humour*, the rustic would-be gentleman Sogliardo is discovered at a London tavern with 'his villainous Ganymede . . . droning a tobacco pipe there ever since yesterday noon' (4.3.83–5). Sogliardo here is certainly assumed to be guilty of the abominable crime against nature, but this is not the issue. Pederasty and smoking are generic vices, not specific ones: Sogliardo practices them because they are the marks of the London sophisticate. His lust is, like Marlowe's, all for upward mobility, for class. The more intriguing conjunction in Baines's document is that of tobacco and Hariot. It leads us to Sir Walter Ralegh, Hariot's patron and employer, the major advocate of tobacco in Elizabethan England, investigated in 1594 on a charge of freethinking; imprisoned, however, not for atheism but for impregnating and secretly marrying, probably in that order, one of Elizabeth's maids of honor—for sexual offenses that were construed as treasonable. Thomas Kyd's charges against Marlowe explicitly associate him with the Ralegh circle, which included not only Hariot, but John Dee and Henry Percy, the 'Wizard Earl' of Northumberland (of whom the *DNB* says he was 'passionately addicted to tobacco smoking'). With Ralegh we are back to atheism and sex, but with Hariot, Dee, and Northumberland we have arrived at conjuring and science.

It is easy to see the ambitions of this group summed up in and refracted through the figure of Doctor Faustus, not least because his drama is one of overreaching ambition combined with relentless failure. What is more difficult to see is how the author of this famous and perennially successful morality could be accused of atheism. The play itself became a powerful argument

for belief. But magic and theater have a complex and contradictory interrelationship in the age. The transition from *Doctor Faustus* to *The Tempest* in only
two decades records something like a paradigm shift: Faustus's magic, after
all, is not the empiricism of Hariot, or the mathematics of Dee, it is theology,
whereas Prospero's magic is art and science. Shakespeare seems to say that if
magic has any validity, any reality, it is because it deals not with metaphysics
and the occult but with the facts of nature—storms, astronomy, human dis-
ease; the body, the mind, and the passions, not the soul. There is nothing
whatever in *The Tempest* about magic leading to damnation; even Sycorax's
putative liaison with the devil eventuates only in Caliban. The worst that can
be said about magic in the play is that it is in the end a retreat from reality and
responsibility: that is why it must be renounced—not because it is damnable,
but because it is finally just as unsatisfactory as it had been for Faustus twenty
years earlier. Ben Jonson offered the audiences of 1610 an alternative way of
looking at Renaissance magic in *The Alchemist*, written within a year of *The
Tempest*, in which the charlatan magicians—a butler, a con-man, and a
whore—and the gullible public that believes in them are all equally culpable.
The only person who is not represented as culpable in this proto-capitalist
system is also the only person who ultimately profits from it, the master, who
is out of town while his servant delivers the goods. Lovewit's acquisition of the
rich widow is the real magic in the play.

What urges are these plays satisfying in a culture in which magic still seems
a real possibility? The question, of course, is moot since the magic in all three
cases is theater, and in that respect, at least, it proved superlatively effective.
Faustus in particular became one of the most famous plays of Renaissance
England, a kind of cultural artifact. As a literary text it survives in two quite
different published versions, both involving collaborators, but these are surely
only indices to a continuous process. The text must have been revised and
augmented constantly, in production after production, thereby becoming
more and more detached from any particular author. Scenes apparently kept
being added to it (the play's structure seems designed to allow for this: a
beginning and an end, and an infinitely expandable and variable middle). It
was produced pretty much continuously, from the early 1590s until the closing of the theaters in 1642, and was played again after the Restoration. In both
published versions, Marlowe's name is as truncated as the play, and grows
increasingly nebulous: it appears first, in 1604, as 'Ch. Marl.' and then, in 1616,
as 'Ch. Mar.'—and in the only surviving copy of the latter, the name has been
expanded with pen and ink to read 'Macklin' or 'Marklin.' The author, the
sense of an author, disappears. In its own time it is less a text than a continuous event.

Something of the nature of that event can be seen in a characteristic group of stories about the play. In one version, during a performance in Exeter, as Faustus was conjuring surrounded by a group of devils, the actors became aware that there was one devil too many, and stopped the play and fled from the town in fear for their lives and souls. In other less stylish versions of the story, Satan himself actually appeared during a performance. These stories are part of the mythology of anti-theatricalism, intended to demonstrate how inherently profane and dangerous an amusement theater is; but they also indicate the extent to which theater was in touch with an aspect of reality that was beyond rational control—they are stories about the power of theater, even of a theater of charlatans, about theater as magic, with *Doctor Faustus* as the paradigmatic instance.

The play as it survives is a strange combination of great poetry and clowning, everything Sidney was describing when he attacked the 'mongrel tragicomedy, mixing clowns and kings.' Faustus himself is both hero and clown. If the play is about unbounded ambition, it is also about insufficient imagination—every reader, every audience has felt that Faustus doesn't make enough of his bargain, doesn't even really know what to ask for. For all its talk of the perils of boundless ambition, there is a continuous sense of disappointment in the play, a sense that Faustus isn't ambitious enough—that he isn't, in fact, as ambitious as any of us would be in the same situation.

The play is in this respect much more a temptation than a warning. In his opening soliloquy, Faustus rejects philosophy, medicine, and law, and comes at last to divinity, and he quotes St. Jerome's Bible: '*Stipendium peccati mors est.* Ha! / . . . The reward of sin is death. That's hard' (A 1.1.40–41).[14] It has often been observed that the unspoken second half of the biblical sentence promises eternal life through Christ; what Faustus omits—or ignores—is the promise of grace through repentance, a promise that will be in the mind of every Elizabethan spectator. Faustus is throughout the play convinced that he won't be *allowed* to repent, but this is because he simply hasn't read far enough; he hasn't read as far as we have. Theological arguments citing strict Calvinist doctrine about the impossibility of repentance for the confirmed sinner are doubtless technically correct, but dramatically irrelevant: the point is surely not that God's mercy isn't infinite, but that, even at the end, Faustus still doesn't believe in it. For an audience, this has a curious double edge: it means that we're always on top of the action, that we understand from the beginning why Faustus is doomed to failure and we fully approve of his damnation; but it also means that we see that we could do it better, make the bargain and get away with it, have the world and have repentance too. This is the sense in which the play is as much a temptation as a warning.

Marlowe starts with a fantasy of unlimited desire and unlimited power to satisfy it. When Faustus summons Mephistophilis, he articulates a megalomaniac dream—to live in all voluptuousness, to be the emperor of the world, to control nature and the supernatural: this is what the diabolical deal promises him. But four scenes later, when his bad angel urges him to think on the wealth he can have, his eager reply is 'The seignory of Emden shall be mine!' (A 2.1.23)—Emden is a rich commercial port; the dream is already a good deal less ambitious than ruling the world, and he hasn't even signed the bond yet. By the end of the same scene his voluptuousness has diminished significantly too: 'Let me have a wife, the fairest maid in Germany, for I am wanton and lascivious, and cannot live without a wife' (143–5). But Mephistophilis will not supply a wife, presumably because marriage is a sacrament. He produces instead a devil dressed as a woman furnished with fireworks, at once an allegory of lust and of theater (the only beautiful women this stage provides are sparkling female impersonators); and a bit of clowning ensues that calls the whole assumption of omnipotence into question. Faustus's indignation in the 1604 text—'A plague on her for a hot whore' (153)—by 1616 includes a revelation of the limits of his bargain: 'Here's a hot whore indeed; no, I'll no wife' (B 2.1.149)—if this is a woman, I don't want any. Mephistophilis then produces an alternative proposal, to bring Faustus the fairest courtesans in the world to sleep with. These will be entirely polymorphous, chaste as Penelope and wise as Sheba, but beautiful as Lucifer: the moral and intellectual ideals are female, but the ideal of beauty is male. This sounds like a much more attractive proposition than marriage for a truly wanton and lascivious voluptuary, especially one with sexual tastes like Marlowe's; but Faustus doesn't even comment on it, and Mephistophilis effortlessly moves him on to what it turns out he really wants, books. The books are books of incantations, astronomy, and natural history: universal power is construed as power over the supernatural, the celestial, the natural, but epitomised in the written word—the power is literacy, the pact with the devil is an allegory of Marlowe's own education, the search for the right books.

What do you do with power in Marlowe's world? Faustus's initial instincts are altruistic. A good deal of the play's appeal is to English anti-Catholic sentiments—deeply felt, obviously; the feelings Burghley must have appealed to when he recruited Marlowe into government service. All the horseplay with the pope is the other side of the ambition to build a wall of brass around Protestant Germany. The real English fear of the danger of Catholic power is disarmed by magic's ability to make fools of its audience. From this aspect, the play can be seen as part of the long history of English Protestant militancy: Faustus's magic is the fantasy of Sidney's aborted political and military career, Leicester's momentary triumph in the Netherlands, Essex's and Nottingham's minuscule Spanish campaigns, Prince Henry's fantasmic Protestant army of European liberation. Faustus is, for a little while, a version of the Protestant hero—the damnable magic is on our side, working for us; the megalomaniac Faustus, the megalomaniac Marlowe, is playing it both defensive and safe.

But where do the real ambitions lie? At the play's center, after all, is a confrontation with Catholic power itself in the person of the Holy Roman Emperor. The visit to Charles V ought to be a triumphant entry: Faustus has humiliated the pope; in the B text he has even freed Bruno the antipope and flown him to the imperial court; he is more powerful than any earthly monarch. Why isn't this a scene of two emperors, either paying homage to each other or threatening each other? But Faustus appears instead as an entertainer, 'The wonder of the world for magic art' (B 4.1.11), and from the sorcery materializes not a promise of infinite power but simply a magic show—he produces, at the emperor's request, 'the royal shapes / Of Alexander and his paramour' (93–4). Only shapes, however, impersonated by spirits; so the emperor's wish to embrace, or even to question, Alexander, is disappointed—there's simply nothing there. All he can do, all he finally wants to do, is look for a mole on the phantom lady's neck. The really satisfying show is what follows: the spectacle of the taunting unbeliever knight Benvolio getting his comeuppance, furnished by Faustus's magic with horns—the greatest triumph isn't ruling the world, it's revenge; the best joke is sexual subversion, cuckolding your enemy. But then it turns out that Faustus *hasn't* cuckolded Benvolio—the horns are a pointless joke: as the emperor immediately points out, Benvolio isn't even married. So Faustus has his joke, but the transgressiveness is harmless: nobody's wife has been debauched, Faustus hasn't committed lechery; there is nothing here that the most moral of Elizabethan audiences can't laugh at with a clear conscience.

What Faustus presents is nothing but what Marlowe's stage presents, the mongrel tragicomedy that Sidney abhorred, the wondrous adulterated with the clownish. Faustus comes to Charles V as Dr. Dee came to the emperor of Hungary, not in triumph but as a petitioner, a supplicant. What he seeks is a job in the emperor's service—the dream of glory and power is finally only an upwardly mobile lower-middle-class Elizabethan dream: Spenser's dream of a good civil service job, Jonson's dream of the Mastership of the Revels; not even Sidney's dream of political influence and independence. Most of all, it is the dream of Marlowe the working-class boy with a high-class university education which somehow didn't get him the kind of life he thought it would, Marlowe trying to find a niche in the bureaucracy, a place in the service of some powerful courtier impressed by his learning and poetry, but also able to see beyond it to his shrewdness, unscrupulousness, willingness. The fantasies of unlimited power are consistently scaled down in the play, until they finally seem to represent something that really ought to be obtainable—do you have to make a pact with the devil just to get a decent job or someone to go to bed with? But the only job Faustus gets turns out to be Marlowe's job, inventing theatrical spectacles for rich audiences.

Here then is the progression of fantasies: imperial power is almost immediately abandoned for money, and not even for what we would call 'real money,' all the gold in the New World or the riches of Asia, but something much more modest and localized, the revenues of the profitable commercial city of Emden. Women get short-circuited as soon as it turns out marriage is impossible—if marriage is impossible, so is sex: Faustus turns out to have the most conventional middle-class morals. There's no megalomaniac fantasy here, nothing irregular or transgressive, not even Marlowe's interest in boys. The desire for books certainly shouldn't be a problem, but even there Faustus doubts that he's got what he's asked for—when Mephistophilis produces the books containing all earthly knowledge, Faustus's reaction is 'Oh thou art deceived,' you don't know what you're talking about; and the devil has to reassure him, 'Tut, I warrant thee,' I guarantee it (A 2.2.181–2). But this too doesn't satisfy him; obviously there's got to be more to life than books. So we start again, with less material, more free-floating ambitions: he wants to fly, to go to Rome, to be invisible, to humiliate the pope, to be mischievous without consequences. And then he wants, not to be emperor, but to *impress* the emperor, to get secure employment, to be noticed, successful, admired—by the middle of the play this is what magic can do for you.

It also, however, puts you in mortal danger, not for your soul but for your life. The greatest danger isn't damnation, it's human envy, the other courtiers who resent your success—the attempt on Faustus's life appears only in the B text, but it's implicit in the whole premise of the play. Running parallel with the dream of success, therefore, is necessarily a dream of invulnerability: the magic that damns you is also, quite simply, the only thing that can save your life. The invulnerability is limited in time to the twenty-four years of the contract; but given the dangers of a fantasy life such as Faustus's (and, it follows, such as Marlowe's) a pretty good bargain nevertheless, especially considering Marlowe's other career as a government spy—the career that got him murdered, at the age of twenty-nine, presumably on orders from someone with real power. If Marlowe had made Faustus's deal he would have lived another twenty-four years, and died in 1617, the year after and a year older than Shakespeare. Consider the life expectancy in this period: if you were male and made it past adolescence without succumbing to childhood diseases, smallpox, plague, miscellaneous fevers, wild animals, duels, highwaymen, fires, food poisoning, whatnot, you had a chance of reaching a reasonable age, which in the early seventeenth century was not the threescore and ten stipulated by the Word of God but anything over forty-five—Shakespeare died at fifty-two, and nobody deploring his death claimed that this was especially premature. Obviously it helped a lot if you could make a deal with the devil; it was clear you couldn't make one with God.

For all the play's talk of power, its principal theme is survival. The eventual love scene, conjuring up Helen of Troy to be Faustus's paramour, is unquestionably a triumph; but it isn't really Faustus's triumph. The project is not even Faustus's idea: it's suggested to him by his two scholars—even now, he doesn't know what to ask for. If the initial failure was artistic, lack of imagination, perhaps the ultimate failure is scholarly, lack of originality. But Marlowe rescues him with some of the greatest verse in the language:

> Was this the face that launched a thousand ships . . . (A 5.1.91)

All the disastrous consequences of epic lust provide the language of love poetry; and there's no indication here that the woman who appears this time, whatever she is, is an inadequate reward for Faustus's pains. He really does, finally, get what he wants. But notice what he wants. Mephistophilis has offered him the most beautiful women in the world, all he can handle, every morning. What he wants instead is a literary allusion, a paragon from his classical education, Homer's ideal. Helen *is* a spirit, the quintessential emanation of humanist passion—for the best book, the best poem, the best text. What's desirable about her is that she *isn't* a woman.

The damnation scene is of course a foregone conclusion, but in its evasions and ambivalences it replicates the movement of the play as a whole. If it is true that, doctrinally, Faustus cannot repent, it is a doctrine that Faustus is either unaware of or denies. What he says, several times, is that he is *afraid* to repent, afraid that the devils will tear him to pieces if he does—as if this were worse than, or different from, being carried off to hell. Is the failure to repent one more failure of imagination, and by the same token one more temptation for the audience? The scene is another love scene, too: '*O lente lente curite noctis equi*' (A 5.2.74), Faustus, trying to survive a little longer, quotes (actually, misquotes) the *Amores*. Ovid, making love to Corinna, implores night's horses to run slowly; but the allusion is more elaborate than this. Ovid is not addressing Night but Aurora, Dawn, and urges her to imagine herself in bed not with her aged husband Tithonus but with her young and handsome lover Cephalus; the line, 'Stay night, and run not thus' in Marlowe's translation (1.13.40), is spoken by Aurora in a love scene within a love scene, and it implores more time with the beautiful youth, not with the mistress—Marlowe's textual arabesque provides Faustus with a boy after all. In the final moment of frustration, seeing Christ's blood stream in the firmament and convinced that 'One drop would save my soul,' Faustus calls out 'I'll leap up to my God: who pulls me down?' (77). The answer might be obduracy, pride, despair, or even Calvinist doctrine; but as Edward Snow once mischievously remarked to me, it could also be simply gravity.[15] The play still tempts us to smart-aleck comebacks.

Tobacco and boys: by 1593 tobacco was already big business, and boys really weren't a problem unless, as was claimed in Bacon's case, they were extorting bribes or stealing from the exchequer. Thomas Beard and Francis Meres found in Marlowe's death an epitome of God's justice, but the moral and moralizing George Chapman completed—and moralized—*Hero and Leander*, the most openly licentious of his poems. In the same year that Beard was deploring Marlowe's 'epicurism,' Shakespeare's Rosalind could cite him as an expert on true love: 'Dead shepherd, now I feel thy saw of might: / Who ever loved that loved not at first sight'—this Marlowe is the epitome of pastoral innocence and natural wisdom. Most striking perhaps is the posthumous history of what is certainly Marlowe's most politically transgressive play, *Edward II*. Given the obvious parallel between Edward's treatment of Gaveston and Hugh Spencer and James's of Somerset and Buckingham, one would expect the play to have disappeared from sight after 1603, but in fact it was reissued in 1612 and again in 1622, and performed publicly in that year. In 1621, moreover, in an inflammatory Parliamentary speech, Sir Henry Yelverton had made the analogy of King James and Buckingham with King Edward and Spencer explicit. James, furious, demanded a retraction, and Yelverton was imprisoned, forced to apologize, and fined five thousand marks, to be paid to Buckingham—Buckingham at once graciously remitted the fine, thereby adding nobility of spirit to his other newly minted titles. This incident alone could well have made Marlowe's play libelous; instead it only made it profitable again: so much for transgressiveness. Indeed, ironically, *Edward II* is the play that finally got Marlowe where he wanted to be: the title page of the first octavo, published in 1594, the year after his death, identifies him as 'Chri. Marlowe *Gent.*'

15

THE AUTHENTIC SHAKESPEARE

In 1985 Gary Taylor, then a young American scholar living in England, reported a remarkable discovery: he had found in an early seventeenth-century manuscript collection of poems a hitherto unnoticed poem ascribed to Shakespeare. The ascription seemed to him trustworthy largely because of the nature of the manuscript itself, which contains a number of known poems almost all of which are correctly identified by the scribe, and he also noted a number of verbal parallels between the manuscript poem and other works by the playwright.

Several well-known Shakespearean scholars who were shown the evidence before it was released to the press agreed with Taylor that there was good reason to believe the poem was authentic. But as soon as the story appeared in the papers, the objections were loud and almost universal. For the most part they were based on the manifest inferiority of the poem, and indeed Taylor admitted that it is a pretty awful piece of writing. Here, for example, is a particularly un-Shakespearean stanza:

> A pretty bare, past compare,
> Parts those plots which besots
>   still asunder.
> It is meet naught but sweet
> Should come near that so rare
>   'tis a wonder.
> No mishap, no scape
> Inferior to nature's perfection;
> No blot, no spot:
> She's beauty's queen in election.

I am not concerned here with either the authenticity of this text or with its quality but with certain assumptions that seem to me prior to any judgment about such matters. To begin with, the verse simply does not *sound* like Shakespeare. This is a more complex claim than it may appear, and I want to post-pone considering it for the moment in favor of a simpler claim: we can prob-ably all agree that the poem really is very feeble. We would have a harder time, however, agreeing about what we mean by "really": are we sure we know what constituted a good poem in 1600? Are our standards the same as those of Shakespeare's contemporaries? And even if we decide that the poem is a bad one by any standards, is its badness an argument against its authenticity? Do we believe that Shakespeare was incapable of writing a bad poem? Were there no false starts, no rejected pages, no lines tossed off in ten minutes and then thrown away, perhaps to be rescued by some admirer? If so, then Shakespeare was different from every other writer who ever lived.

Shakespeare either published, or allowed to be published, or failed to pre-vent from being published, a relatively small number of nondramatic poems. Is it conceivable that what made its way into print was everything he wrote? Was there nothing he chose not to publish, or succeeded in keeping from publication? We know in fact of two lost Shakespeare plays, *Love's Labour's Won* and *Cardenio*, and a lost occasional poem written to accompany a heraldic shield borne in a pageant by the Earl of Rutland: are these really the only works of Shakespeare's that have been lost?

The notion that a bad poem cannot be by Shakespeare is a very old one, and it involves a strategy of definition: it defines Shakespeare as the best poet, and then banishes from the canon whatever is considered insufficiently excel-lent. The Shakespeare canon has, therefore, undergone a number of changes over the centuries as critical tastes have changed: quality has always been in the eye of the beholder. But the real issue, if it is authenticity that concerns us, is not the question of quality. Obviously the fact that we do not admire the poem is not evidence that it is inauthentic. And if that is so, then the authen-ticity of the text here is not a function of the poem at all; it is a function pre-cisely of *the text*, in the most limited and literal sense: of the manuscript through which the poem is transmitted.

Taylor took the ascription to Shakespeare seriously because he correctly considered the manuscript to be the crucial piece of evidence, and he judged its testimony to be reliable. In the course of the voluminous correspondence about the poem that followed its publication, very few of his critics, who saw themselves as Shakespeare's defenders, perceived that the manuscript, the medium of transmission, had any relevance all—that is, that it was the man-uscript that needed to be attacked, not the poem.[1] Taylor's judgment on this essential point was, however, energetically confirmed by a British scholar of unquestionable expertise, who agreed that the manuscript was crucial and declared this particular manuscript to be an unusually trustworthy source. Even this, of course, does not make the poem authentic; it only means that a trustworthy witness *said* it was authentic: this is as close as we get to authenticity with this sort of evidence (and it should perhaps be added that people have been hanged on weaker evidence). But three weeks later an American scholar, also unquestionably expert, contradicted the British scholar on every point, ending by declaring the manuscript particularly *un*reliable.[2] And here my story stops: who shall decide when doctors disagree? I am concerned with the issues, not with their solutions, and the issues here are precisely authenticity and evidence. What do we mean by authenticity, and what will we accept as evidence of it? This is my subject, and it is a historical one: what, from Shakespeare's time onward, has constituted an authentic text of Shakespeare?

We might begin by observing that we mean a number of different things by "Shakespeare." For example, the music for Desdemona's "Willow Song" is preserved in a manuscript lute book of 1583.[3] This is good evidence that Shakespeare did not write the song; indeed, he included it in *Othello* precisely because he wanted Desdemona to sing an *old* song, the song of her mother's maid Barbary. All this is perfectly well known; nevertheless, the "Willow Song" is invariably ascribed to Shakespeare, and the editor of the Arden *Othello* does not even mention the evidence that the song is borrowed. Quite simply, it is Shakespeare's because it appears in a Shakespeare play and, more important, because we like it.

On the other hand, a less famous and less attractive song, "Orpheus with his lute made trees" from *Henry VIII*, is generally ascribed to John Fletcher, as is a good deal of the rest of this play. There is no evidence whatever that the song is not by Shakespeare, and the only evidence that the play is a collaboration is that critics have for the past hundred years or so considered a number of its scenes un-Shakespearean—they do not sound like Shakespeare, or at any rate they do not sound the way we want Shakespeare to sound.

But how do we know what Shakespeare sounds like? How do we know that Gary Taylor's discovery doesn't sound Shakespearean? We know because we have a body of works by Shakespeare that have a reasonably determinate range of sounds. But how was that body determined? It was determined initially through contemporary ascriptions, or a citation in the Stationers' Register, or the inclusion of a play in the first folio, or the publication of a work during Shakespeare's lifetime with his name on it. But even these can seem to us questionable evidence. Critics are always removing bits of plays from the canon: the masque in *The Tempest*, Posthumus' dream in *Cymbeline*, more than half of *Henry VIII*, much of the *Henry VI* plays, and for about a hundred years, until relatively recently, all of *Titus Andronicus*. These have the impeccable testimony of the folio behind them, but to one expert or another they have not sounded right.

Such texts may, of course, be inauthentic, but they may also be evidence that Shakespeare had a greater range of styles than we care for. There is really no way of adjudicating the debate here: arguments about the sound of Shakespeare are essentially circular. The question of authenticity, like the question of what constitutes evidence, is profoundly time bound, and different texts have sounded right or wrong at different periods, without much regard to evidence of any sort. Moreover, the fact of a contemporary ascription to Shakespeare is particularly difficult evidence to assess. In the case of Gary Taylor's manuscript poem, most critics felt free to dismiss the ascription as simply an error, and they saw little need to argue questions of motivation. The scribe, they contended, was misinformed. Very few of them gave any attention to the source of the error: why did anyone call the poem Shakespeare in the first place? For a printed poem, on the other hand, the question of motivation is usually felt to be paramount: it is easy for a modern reader to see in an ascription to Shakespeare an unscrupulous publisher trying to cash in on a popular name. This is clearly the case with at least some of the poems in the 1599 volume called *The Passionate Pilgrim*, all of which is credited to Shakespeare on the title page, and which went through two more editions in the poet's lifetime with his name still on the title page—though the implication of immorality on the publisher's part is probably anachronistic. But both these cases might also indicate that contemporaries knew something we do not know, and saw things in Shakespeare that we no longer see or have edited out. It does not require a very large leap of the historical imagination to suggest that to ears trained in Renaissance England Shakespeare sounded different, and that some verse sounded Shakespearean to those ears that does not sound Shakespearean to ours.

Shakespeare's sonnets may serve as a prime example. They look to us quite different from all the other Elizabethan sonnet sequences, and we find them a great deal more complex and interesting as poems. They seem to us to imply an intensely dramatic narrative and to express a complex psychology; far more than the plays, they have been taken as a key to Shakespearean biography. All this, however, is a phenomenon of modern criticism: though Shakespeare's sonnets are praised in 1598 by Francis Meres and two of them appear in *The Passionate Pilgrim*, the publication of the whole sequence in 1609 went almost unnoticed; there is scarcely a reference to them until they reappear, in thoroughly revised versions, in 1640. This strikes us as so inconceivable that we have invented a drama in which the manuscript of the sonnets was pirated and the edition successfully suppressed. There is no evidence whatever to support such a claim, and, as Sir Sidney Lee persuasively argued as long ago as 1905, it is exceedingly unlikely: Thomas Thorpe, the publisher, was perfectly respectable and had no history of piracy.[4] It is much more likely that the sonnets went unnoticed because there was little interest in them. In fact, their status as transcendent works of the poet's genius dates from the late eighteenth century at the earliest. In their own time, it was Sidney's sonnets that were praised for the psychological intensity (and biographical revelations) that we find uniquely present in Shakespeare; what sonnets of Shakespeare's Meres had seen by 1598 he praises for their "sugared" quality. Indeed, sweetness was a characteristic that reappears significantly in contemporary evaluations of Shakespeare—"O sweet Mr Shakespeare! I'll have his picture" (1600);[5] "Sweetest Shakespeare, fancy's child" (1632).[6] Analogously, an anonymous elegy for Richard Burbage (d. 1619) cites his particular excellence in the role of "kind Lear,"[7] singling out as the old king's characteristic quality not the blindness, madness, rage, and despair that have seemed to us so central to the play but his benevolence and affection. As critical assessments, these will strike us as sentimental and reductive, and we are confident that, with our access to the texts and our expertise as readers and scholars, we see Shakespeare more accurately than such contemporaries did. No doubt we do. But we ought also to be aware that they noticed and valued things that we have taught ourselves to ignore.

2

The establishment of a canonical text, whether of Shakespeare or anything else, is only incidentally an objective and scientific matter. It involves much more basically doctrinal and political elements: the debates over which apocryphal books of the Bible, if any, were to be accorded scriptural status provide an enlightening model for the critical history of the Shakespeare canon. Moreover, when the Council of Trent, rejecting Luther's Bible, declared that the authentic scripture was not only the Hebrew and Greek texts but the Vulgate as well, it separated the authentic from the original. It also declared thereby that authenticity was a matter of authentication, something bestowed, not inherent. What was authentic about the Vulgate was that it had the church's *imprimatur*: even God's word was authentic only as mediated through the church—literally mediated in this case, since the Vulgate, no less than Luther's Bible, was a translation. Luther similarly had argued for the sole authenticity of his version over all other vernacular versions.[8]

It is worth pausing to consider how Shakespearean drama became canonical at all. The repertory of a public theater company in Shakespeare's England made no claims to literary status, and even the very few serious defenders of the moral probity of the enterprise never argued that popular theater would make for good reading. On the other hand, the publication of the Shakespeare folio is ample evidence that by 1623 there was a literate and wealthy audience that wanted not only to read Shakespeare in authoritative texts but also to have the plays in a handsome, expensive, and thereby permanent format. Oxford provides a good index to the change in attitude: in 1612 Sir Thomas Bodley, fourteen years after founding his library, wrote his librarian warning against the purchase for the collection of "idle books, and riff-raffs," among which he included books of plays.[9] But the library's accounts for 1623 record the acquisition of a copy of the Shakespeare folio in unbound sheets, and an order for a special binding with the university's arms stamped on the cover. The library was, indeed, the first collector of whom we have a record—this binding order constitutes our earliest evidence that the book was actually in existence. It required only eleven years, and more important the publication of the folio, for Shakespeare's plays to become suitable reading for Oxford's scholars.

The relation between the theatrical repertory and the development of a dramatic canon in this period is a complex and shifting one. The company revised its repertory every season, scheduling a majority of new plays, with some popular works remaining from the previous year and a very small number of perennial favorites—for Henslowe's company, of which the best records survive, the perennials include some plays we might think of as classics, such as *Doctor Faustus* and *The Spanish Tragedy*, but among the most popular revivals were *The Seven Days of the Week* and *The Wise Man of Westchester*, of which (no doubt fortunately) only the titles remain. Since the actors owned the plays that they produced and believed that publication was not in their interests—that an audience that could read a play was less likely to come to see it, that a printed play could be performed by rival companies—plays initially, unless they were pirated, became available for inclusion in a literary canon only when they had stopped being viable in the repertory. Even then, plays were published in the relatively ephemeral form of unbound quartos. The notion of drama as a literary category to be collected, edited, studied, and cherished depended on an analogy with ancient drama, and Ben Jonson's decision to include his plays in the 1616 folio of his *Works* also involved a conscious and repeated allusion not only to the Greek and Roman playwrights but also to the great humanist folio editions of classical drama published in the previous century.[10] The allusion did not save him from the ridicule of critics to whom the notion that plays were works was novel and preposterous. Jonson is the first English playwright to present himself as a classic, and the Jonson folio was the essential model for the authorized collection of Shakespeare's plays in 1623.

3

But even when we have a Shakespeare in an authorized text and a Shakespeare that we believe sounds right, do we really know what we mean by the text of a Shakespeare play—what that authentically Shakespearean text represents? What modern editors usually mean by an authentic text is one over which the author has had full control, either a printed edition that the author oversaw, such as the Ben Jonson folio, or preferably a manuscript in the author's hand. We like to claim that our scholarly texts come as close as possible to that original manuscript, even if it is an entirely hypothetical document, as it almost invariably is. Is that what a Shakespeare text was in Shakespeare's own time? One indisputable fact about the plays is that they were written not for publication but for performance: they are, in their inception at least, not books but scripts, designed to be realized on the stage. So the authentic text in this case is the acting text, at least if we are going to take Shakespeare's intentions into account. The autograph manuscript was where Shakespeare started, not where he ended, the first step, not the final version. This is a respect in which an authentic Shakespeare text would differ from an authentic Ben Jonson text: Jonson rewrote his plays for publication.

And if we look at early performing texts of the Shakespeare plays with this in mind, we learn something very interesting about them. In the earliest acting version we have of a Shakespeare play, a transcription of the quarto text of the two parts of *Henry IV* made around 1622, there are a great many cuts and a number of revisions. This was a text prepared for a private production, but there is every reason to believe that it reflects the normal practice of the professional stage as well. There are two other surviving pre-Restoration promptbooks, of *Macbeth* and *Measure for Measure*, which are marked-up copies of the folio text, and they too are heavily cut, apparently by a professional hand.[11] Indeed, with very few exceptions, every printed Shakespeare text is far too long for the two to two-and-one-half hours that is universally accepted as the performing time of plays in the period; the exceptions are *The Comedy of Errors*, *Macbeth*, and *The Tempest* and in the surviving example, even *Macbeth* was considered too long.[12] Private performances tended, if anything, to be longer than those in the public theaters.[13] Every play, that is, would normally have been cut for production, and the *Macbeth* of the folio certainly seems to be not only a cut but a revised text, including demonstrably non-Shakespearean sections.

What is it that is being realized in the production of such a text? To ask this question is not merely to ask what is being added to the written text by actors and directors, elements like tone, stage action, interpretation. The point is that the acting text of a play always was different from the written text. This means not simply that it was different from the printed text, though it certainly means that, but that it was different from the *script*, what the author wrote. It also means that this was the situation obtaining in Shakespeare's own company, of which he was a part owner and director—it was a situation he understood, expected, and helped to perpetuate. And it implies as well that Shakespeare habitually began with more than he needed, that his scripts offered the company a range of possibilities, and that the process of production was a collaborative one of selection as well as of realization and interpretation.

The realization of a Shakespeare text, then, historically speaking, involves a considerable departure from the text. It is not, that is, what we would call a faithful representation of the text, or of the author's intentions as embodied in it. The text is the basis of the performance, but the performance is an independent entity; indeed, in Shakespeare's time its dependency on the text was often in doubt. Hamlet complains of the clowns obfuscating "some necessary question of the play." One could press very hard there on the implications of "necessary"—necessary to whom, and for what end? Whose interests are served by extemporizing, and by departures from the text generally?

This does not mean that the performing tradition was simply anarchic. Performances had their own kind of consistency and continuity. Figure 15.1 shows a striking early example: in 1635 Inigo Jones designed a masque for the queen called *The Temple of Love*, with a text by Sir William Davenant. It includes four magicians; this is a preliminary sketch of their costumes. The figures are supposed to be Persian, but Jones's outfits for them are utterly eclectic. His notes on the drawings, moreover, show a number of changes of mind. In particular, the second or "fat mago," at the bottom right, was originally to be dressed as an oriental grotesque, and then as a Venetian clown; but Jones finally crossed out these instructions and wrote in the margin that the mage was to be "like a Sir John Falstaff."

For Inigo Jones in 1635 to describe his magician as "like a Sir John Falstaff" implies a clear and consistent tradition of Falstaff's appearance. The earliest representation we have of Falstaff, in the frontispiece to *The Wits* (1662; figure 15.2), shows what looks to us simply like a fat man in military dress. Jones's concept of the character may, of course, have included visual elements that were not part of the costume, such as characteristic gestures and facial expressions, but whatever they were, they must have been sufficiently specific to convey something precise—more precise than the phrase "like a fat soldier."

The independence and self-determination of the performing tradition have important consequences for our reading of Renaissance plays. To begin with, they mean that the text was not the play. Moreover, when Hamlet criti-

Figure 15.1. Inigo Jones, sketch of four magicians for *The Temple of Love*, 1635. Devonshire Collection, Chatsworth. Reproduced by permission of the Duke of Devonshire and the Chatsworth Settlement Trustees.

Figure 15.2. Frontispiece to *The Wits*, 1662. By permission of
the Huntington Library, California.

cizes the clowns for improvising, it is not at all clear what side Shakespeare is
on or, more to the point, intends his audience to be on. This Hamlet is the
same theatrical critic who attacks the taste of the groundlings, half the paying
spectators at the Globe. Perhaps this is not an assertion of community with an
ideal audience, as has always been claimed, but an alienating device: Hamlet
the playwright is not one of us, but an elitist and a snob. Whether this is a correct interpretation of the lines or not will depend entirely on where one
stands (or sits) in Shakespeare's audience. The meaning, in this case, is dependent on the audience, and is not uniform or constant within it.

If performances in the period were characteristically fluid or unstable in
relation to the text, differing from day to day and season to season, so were the
texts themselves. The three texts of *Hamlet* obviously embody many others, all
of them palimpsests of revisions and alternative versions. Indeed, one way of
dealing with the ambiguities of Hamlet's attack on the groundlings is to argue
that it is inserted for one of those performances in Oxford or Cambridge
attested by the title page of the first quarto (figure 15.3), and through which,

THE

Tragicall Hiſtorie of

HAMLET

Prince of Denmarke

By William Shake-ſpeare.

As it hath beene diuerſe times acted by his Highneſſe ſer-
uants in the Cittie of London : as alſo in the two V-
niuerſities of Cambridge and Oxford, and elſe-where

At London printed for N.L. and Iohn Trundell.
1603.

Figure 15.3. Title page to the first quarto of *Hamlet*, 1603. By permission of
the Huntington Library, California.

as Gabriel Harvey notes, the play came to "please the wiser sort."[14] (The note
seems to be pre-1603, and would therefore allude to performances, not reading texts.) The elitism, the scorn for the taste of the public would be perfectly
appropriate before an academic audience. The passage about the War of the
Theaters and the damaging popularity of the children's companies, the "little
eyases," might be a vestige of the same version, an in-group joke explaining
why the Lord Chamberlain's Men were performing on tour in the university
towns rather than at the Globe in London, where business was bad. It is a joke
that would also work for a London audience, but its point would be a different one, a slightly rueful assertion of solidarity and a compliment on that
audience's good sense and good taste.

On the other hand, the special point of Hamlet's exchange with Polonius
about his youthful acting career would have been fully comprehensible only
at the Globe. Polonius says that in a play about Julius Caesar he played Caesar
and was killed by Brutus "in the Capitol." Shakespeare's *Julius Caesar* was new
in 1599, about a year before *Hamlet*, and this passage surely implies that the
actor playing Polonius also played Caesar in Shakespeare's play the previous
season. Polonius *must* be referring to Shakespeare's play, because it is only

there that Caesar is killed in the Capitol. In the standard version of the story (or, as we could have put it in an earlier critical climate, "in fact") he was killed in Pompey's Theater, where the Senate was meeting, which is near the present Piazza Navona, half a mile from the Capitol.[15] This is a joke for the Globe's regulars, those patrons who came to see the company perform every season and were familiar with the repertory and the personnel. It would make no particular sense to the learned spectators of Oxford and Cambridge, anymore than it does to us.

The fluidity of the written text, the divergence between published and performing texts are, then, historically authentic, if not historically determined. And the claim of textual authenticity as a function of the author's hand—the folio's claim to preserve "the true original copies"—becomes an issue only when the plays are printed, and are then claimed to be authors' plays, not actors' plays. In fact, the degree to which the authority of a theatrical text *is* that of the author will be all but impossible to determine: what kind of true original can the folio text of *Macbeth* have been? In this case (and the case can hardly be unique) *true* and *original* mean that the copy used is the one belonging to the company, the authentic text on which performances are based the *authorized* text, which is not necessarily a text in the author's hand. Even authorial texts would have been far more fluid, far more unstable, than most of us, with our yearnings toward final and authoritative versions, will wish to allow. We believe that texts develop and evolve toward publication, and that publishing texts fixes them; we expend great efforts on "establishing" texts that we can then call "authentic." The claim is historically inaccurate, and blinds us to the true nature of the phenomena we are dealing with.

Indeed, it is not even correct to say that printed books in the period fix or preserve "a" text. Because of the practice of making proof corrections during the course of printing, and of assembling the finished book using both corrected and uncorrected sheets indiscriminately, every copy of the Shakespeare folio is different from every other copy; the same is true, to a greater or lesser degree, of all Renaissance books. To the literary historian the differences may appear insignificant, but to anyone interested in the history of the concept of the book, the fact that such variability was not only acceptable but built into the system is of the essence.

4

With the reopening of the theaters at the Restoration, Shakespeare became both a classic and out of date, and the royal license to produce plays carried with it a stipulation that Shakespeare be updated, adapted to the modern theater. This has been represented as more of an innovation than it was: we have seen that the revising of Shakespeare was in progress in the 1620s and before, and in fact the *Macbeth* promptbook, c. 1625–30, makes a number of the notorious rationalizing changes that Davenant later incorporated into his version. The real difference is that after the reopening of the theaters, Shakespeare was a *text*; the revised versions, "as presently performed," were published and could be compared with the plays in the folio, and critics from Dryden's time on observed, with varying degrees of regret, that the revisions weren't the same as the originals. Charles Gildon, in a critical essay appended to Nicholas Rowe's Shakespeare (1710), was especially hard on the Restoration version of *The Tempest*. Davenant and Dryden's play is, he wrote, both "less perfect" and "more extravagant" than Shakespeare's, and the characters and incidents are much less believable. "The alteration," he concludes, "has been no benefit to the original."[16]

This is quite different from arguing that what is wrong with the Davenant text is that it is inauthentic. The issue is performability or readability, and Gildon's claim is that Shakespeare's text is a better play. We will sympathize with this claim, but it is belied by 150 years of theatrical history (Davenant's was the standard performing text of *The Tempest* until 1832), and in any case it reveals no prejudice in favor of Shakespeare. Gildon in the same essay finds Dryden's *Troilus and Cressida* and Nahum Tate's *King Lear* superior to the originals; there is nothing in the argument privileging authenticity.

A decade later Pope, revising the plays to make them more rational (i.e., more comprehensible), mystifies Gildon's straightforward claim by arguing that he was thereby restoring the *real* Shakespearean text, removing what was inauthentic. Pope's edition was declared amateurish and ill informed by the textual scholars, which it certainly is, but the attitude it embodies is nevertheless still firmly embedded in a great deal of very respectable editorial practice. For example, Camillo in *The Winter's Tale*, furiously expostulating with Leontes, has the elliptical line "I have loved thee—" (1.2.321). A number of eighteenth-century editors were disturbed by this, arguing that a courtier could not address the sovereign in the second person singular. J. Dover Wilson duly emended the line to the vague and blandly inoffensive "T'have loved the—." The emendation did not become standard, but many modern editors continue to see the line as problematic, and several assign the line to Leontes instead of Camillo. Here notions of etiquette (quite anachronistic ones at that) are assumed to constitute the reality of the text, trumping a moment of great dramatic intensity. I have elsewhere cited a similar point in Frank Kermode's Arden edition of *The Tempest* where the emendation of a folio reading is defended with the explanation that the original "is disagreeable, being grotesque in a context which does not require grotesquerie,"[17] and therefore cannot be correct. And editors in the tradition running from, say, Johnson to

George Lyman Kittredge—editors whose notion of the editorial task was the translation of the obscurities of Shakespearean verse into clear, rational prose—are also arguing against the authority, if not the authenticity, of the text. The *meaning* lies, in these cases, in the translation, as the "true" text lay, for Pope, in the revision. The assumption is that behind the obscure and imperfect text lies a clear and perfect one, and the editor's task is to reveal it.

The play is conceived here as a platonic idea, only imperfectly represented by its text. The conception is implicit in critical history, and even occasionally explicit. John Dennis argued in 1712 that Shakespeare wrote in haste and without the benefit of learned and tasteful advice, and that editors ought to produce the texts that Shakespeare would have written had he been able to revise.[18] Most editors have subscribed in some measure to the first half of this proposition, and few have been untouched by the second. Pope, for example, assumes that the infelicities and obscurities were imposed on the text by actors or early printers, and it is these that he undertakes to remove or revise as inauthentic. Pope is thus able to claim, unlike Dennis, that the improved and rationalized text is not what Shakespeare *ought* to have written but what he actually wrote, but Pope's editorial practice of rewriting whatever does not seem to him "Shakespearean" implicitly endorses Dennis's claim that the ideal text is the authentic one. The claim sounds outrageously condescending to modern ears, but in fact it is at heart also a very modern claim: the text is not a function of the author; the author is a function of the text. "Shakespeare" is, to these eighteenth-century critics, the supreme playwright, the most perfect exemplar in English of the art. It is the texts, therefore, that must be perfect. Shakespeare's perfection derives from the perfection of the text, and that is supplied by Pope.

Modern claims are much more modest, but, as the Kermode example indicates, they often share Pope's basic assumptions—for Kermode, Shakespeare must be rescued from grotesquerie. Stanley Wells, the general editor of the new Oxford Shakespeare, recommends that we emend in the case of palpable errors, by which he means not simply printers' errors but places where "it may be assumed that Shakespeare would have acquiesced in the correction if the need for it had been pointed out to him."[19] Our editions are to preserve, that is, not what Shakespeare wrote but what he ought (or "really intended") to have written. Wells has in mind what we might call trivial cases—confusions in characters' names, for example—though even here what is trivial to one generation or group of readers may be of the essence to another. Ben Jonson apparently talked Shakespeare into making just such a change in *Julius Caesar*, pointing out the illogic of a line of Caesar's that he gives as "Caesar did never wrong, but with just cause."[20] The line as it appears in the printed text is "Know, Caesar doth not wrong, nor without cause / Will he be satisfied"

(3.1.47–48). Few modern readers will prefer the revised version, which seems to us to have edited out the point of the line, the ambiguities of the concept "Caesar." In the same way, Wells's simple errors might turn out to be of the essence to a psychoanalytic critic, a crucial key to the mind behind the text.

5

But what does a play represent? However authentic our texts are assumed to be, they clearly represent something more than the playwright's mind. Plays have most often been held to be transparent, vehicles for the representation of, say, human nature or history; what is authentic in them—Shakespeare's perfection—lies in what is represented, something behind the play and beyond it that the play brings to life. The ability of Shakespearean texts to realize a recognizable version of human psychology has generally been felt, from the earliest commentators onward, to be beyond praise; but in fact the plays have always required a good deal of help in this department, whether from revisers and elucidators or from actors, directors, and stage designers. Indeed, Shakespearean texts, as we have seen, have been found inadequate to the demands of theatrical representation as far back as our evidence goes, and they have always required, in varying degrees at various times, revisions, cuts, and additions.

In fact, one of the most remarkable aspects of the theatrical medium is its ability to comprehend the widest variety of versions of a dramatic text within the concept of a single play. Davenant's and Dryden's *Tempest* doesn't look much like *The Tempest* of the folio: it has a male ingenu parallel to Miranda named Hippolito, a young man who has never seen a woman; Miranda has been supplied with a sister, Dorinda; Sycorax has become Caliban's sister; Ariel has a girlfriend named Milcha; and only about a third of the dialogue bears any relation to the original text at all. This, as I have said, in one form or another was the standard performing version of *The Tempest* until 1832, and, despite howls of protest from Gildon to Hazlitt, both it and the scholarly text on the bookshelf of every literate household were Shakespeare's *Tempest*. Nor is the situation significantly different today: modern directors feel no less free than Irving, Kemble, Cibber, or Davenant to cut or rewrite the masque, assign Miranda's attack on Caliban to Prospero, or replace the epilogue with "Our revels now are ended. . . ." Clearly the concept of *The Tempest* has never been limited to the original text.

A Shakespeare play on the stage has always involved other intentions than the author's, and it really does not need to be argued that, despite editorial claims for textual authenticity, editions of the plays, from the earliest quartos on, embody nonauthorial intentions as well. These are performances too, concerned with fixing the text, in both senses, in the interests of particular interpretations. The history of realizations of the text, that is, is the history of the text. I want to turn now to the question of what is being realized in such representations.

6

I shall consider three kinds of examples illustrative of embedded attitudes toward the text, each of which makes a different sort of claim to authenticity. These are drawn from a group of related eighteenth-century images deriving initially from David Garrick's 1744 production of *Macbeth*. I have included them because they are, to begin with, convenient and informative pieces of evidence about a critical moment in the performing history of Shakespeare that is crucial to my subject: the moment when Garrick asserted that his performances recovered, for the first time, the authentic Shakespeare. But they are more than that: like our surviving texts, they are versions of performances that both amplify and edit the work they represent. Even more than the texts, they insist on the essential elements of realization and performance in these works, whether imaginative or theatrical. And finally, they provide a contextual world, both social and theatrical, for those texts, and as such they constitute essential cultural documents in the history I have been tracing.

Macbeth was one of Garrick's greatest successes, revived several times, and one of its most original and interesting aspects is the assertion of authenticity Garrick made for it: the play was advertised as being performed for the first time "as written by Shakespeare."[21] The claim was not even approximately true; all that was true was that Garrick took as his working text Lewis Theobald's recent edition of Shakespeare rather than the standard stage version of Davenant. But he cut more than ten percent of the play, including the drunken porter, the murder of Lady Macduff's son, and the dialogue in which Malcolm tests Macduff by imputing monstrous vices to himself. The concept of authenticity in these cases was trumped by an unwillingness to distress the audience. Garrick also retained some of Davenant's most popular bits for the witches, and wrote a whole new dying speech of his own for Macbeth. The original text, in fact, was only marginally more satisfactory to Garrick's sense of the play than it had been to Davenant's. Why then the claim of authenticity? Twenty years earlier a producer could have expected to attract audiences by advertising a wholly new *Macbeth*, bigger and better; Garrick's assertion, the invocation of the author to confer authority on the production, marks a significant moment in both theatrical and textual history.

Figure 15.4 is Henry Fuseli's sketch of the scene immediately after the murder of Duncan. This is Garrick and Mrs. Pritchard in the revival of 1766. Mac-

Figure 15.4. Henry Fuseli, *Garrick and Mrs. Pritchard as Macbeth and Lady Macbeth after the Murder of King Duncan*, 1766. Kunsthaus, Zürich.

beth has mistakenly brought the daggers away with him, and is terrified to return to Duncan's chamber with them. What is being represented here? There is, to begin with, a strong sense of theatrical immediacy; flats are visible, and even a suggestion of footlights. These are particular performers at a particular moment in a particular production. Fuseli's title is *Garrick and Mrs. Pritchard as Macbeth and Lady Macbeth After the Murder of King Duncan*, and he inscribed on it the dialogue of the instant depicted, recorded as if spoken: "My husband . . . I've done the deed." The tension and terror of the moment are rendered with great intensity, but despite the insistence on the actualities of performance, the depiction is not at all naturalistic, and indeed is distinctly reductive. Garrick and Mrs. Pritchard are caricatures, mere expressions of their inner states; neither could be taken as a portrait, and even the stage space around them is radically compressed.

Figure 15.5 is a painting by Johann Zoffany of the same scene in the same production. Garrick and Mrs. Pritchard are now quite recognizable, even to their relative heights (about which there was much joking in the period): these *are* intended as portraits. But the sense of a theater has all but disap-

Figure 15.5. Johann Zoffany, *Garrick and Mrs. Pritchard in Macbeth*, first version, 1768.
The Garrick Club, London. Photo: The Art Archive, Ltd., London.

peared, and the contextual conventions of portraiture have replaced those of
the stage. The figures address each other in highly histrionic attitudes, but the
action takes place in the hall of a Gothic mansion full of medieval detail. They
wear, moreover, not stage costume but formal evening dress, impeccably
arranged and showing none of the disarray that their exertions have produced
in the drama and in Fuseli. It is especially instructive to compare the costumes
in the two paintings. Fuseli shows Garrick in a military uniform and Mrs.
Pritchard in a hoopskirt. The hoopskirt to begin with is anachronistic but
correct: it was the standard female costume for the tragic stage, but by 1760 it
was decidedly out of fashion outside the theater, except as formal court attire.
The extraordinary Amazon in figure 15.6 is a 1770s Joan la Pucelle—Joan of
Arc—in 1*Henry VI*: by this time the style was a generation out of date, but it
was still the proper costume for the tragic actress. Zoffany's Mrs. Pritchard is
dressed in a modishly romantic gown—dressed, in fact, as Mrs. Pritchard
might have dressed had she been going to a reception rather than performing
in *Macbeth*. The title of the painting, *Garrick and Mrs. Pritchard in Macbeth*,
is hardly less explicit than Fuseli's, and the two figures certainly seem to be

Figure 15.6. *Mrs. Baddeley in the Character of Joan la Pucelle,*
from Bell's Shakespeare, 1776.

acting. The iconography implies, however, that this is not the play but the
world of real action that the play represents, and that Garrick and Mrs.
Pritchard do not impersonate but realize the central figures of that action.

In Fuseli's version of this scene, as we have observed, Garrick wears the
costume of a Hanoverian officer. This is in fact what he wore in the production. But Zoffany here puts Garrick in elegant civilian dress. Zoffany also,
however, did a second, rather more formal version of the painting (figure 15.7)
in which Garrick is wearing his proper costume, and in which Mrs. Pritchard
is now dressed in a dignified black gown. I shall return to what I think are the
reasons for this double representation, but here I want to observe that though
the second version is marginally truer to the facts of the production, it is no
closer to the realities of the stage.

Nevertheless, despite the suppression of the immediate theatrical context
in both paintings, Zoffany's presentation of the two performers is deeply and
obviously theatrical. The Gothic setting is appropriately medieval, but there is
no sense of historical reconstruction in the scene as a whole, nor would we be
likely to take the figures, given their poses, for anything except actors performing roles. In fact, the formal eloquence of the attitudes suggests precisely
the old declamatory style of acting that Garrick's naturalism was credited
with revolutionizing. "If this young fellow is right," said the old tragedian

Figure 15.7. V. Green after Zoffany, *Garrick and Mrs. Pritchard in Macbeth,*
second version, 1768. Mezzotint of the painting in the collection of the Maharaja
of Baroda. Private collection.

James Quin, "then we have been all wrong."[22] What is most striking about the pictures is their juxtaposition of the conflicting realities of setting, action, and performers.

What then is being represented here? The reality, in fact, probably lies far behind the action. Garrick almost certainly commissioned the first version of the picture, as he did a number of other paintings of himself in his most popular roles, and of himself at home and in his park, living the life of a country gentleman. The substitution of the elegant attire of high society for the costumes of the stage makes a clear and very new assertion that has nothing to do with *Macbeth*: that actors and actresses are gentlemen and ladies. This must be relevant to Garrick's claim to be presenting authentic texts, authorized by Shakespeare himself: the claim of authenticity is here extended to the persons of the actors and their physical surroundings. But the play, ironically precisely because of the claim of authenticity, has become even more definitively an actor's, not an author's, text, with Garrick assuming the mantle of Shakespeare.

Figure 15.8. Fuseli, *Garrick and Mrs. Pritchard in Macbeth*, 1812.
Tate Gallery. © Tate, London 2002.

The differences between the first and second versions of the painting are instructive. The second was done for Mrs. Pritchard—the production had been a benefit for her, and she retired shortly afterward.[23] The changes in dress doubtless reflect differences in the actor/patrons' respective tastes, as well as in the relative functions they saw the paintings serving. Mrs. Pritchard's sober gown advances her in dignity and grandeur, but Garrick wears his costume from the play. For Mrs. Pritchard, the painting is a memento as well as a performance.

Zoffany's depiction of his subjects here reflects a perfectly traditional relation between artist and patron, a relation that is as old as artistic patronage itself. Fuseli's attraction to Garrick is of quite another order. Near the end of his life, nearly fifty years later, he did another sketch of the same moment in the same production (figure 15.8), a ghostly memory of remarkable intensity. It is worth pausing to compare Fuseli's versions of Garrick with what were universally perceived as the innovative aspects of Garrick's art: a break with the formality and stylization of the tragic stage, the development of an easy and natural style, and through it a new range of expressiveness, a fuller humanity in theatrical representation. Garrick was praised as a notably realistic actor; Fielding testifies to the excesses of the claim as well as to its accuracy when in *Tom Jones* he sends the naive Partridge to see Garrick play Hamlet and Partridge cannot perceive that Garrick is acting at all: he behaved, the countryman says, as anyone would who had met his father's ghost. That naturalistic acting should have been seen as producing realistic performances is hardly surprising, but if that is how Fuseli saw Garrick, it is not how he represented him. What is conveyed in both the Fuseli sketches is the emotional power of the performance, and the expression of this power limits rather than extends its humanity: the two figures are shown as caricatures.

Let us now turn to another set of realities behind the realization of this scene. Fuseli returned to the subject eight years later, in Rome in 1774, where he had gone at the suggestion of Reynolds to study classical art and painting. The sketch in figure 15.9 is entitled *Macbeth and Lady ("Give me the daggers")*, but there is no hint of Garrick and Mrs. Pritchard or of the eighteenth-century stage. It is a classical fantasy: Macbeth, an idealized nude in an eloquent posture of renunciation, acts out "I am afraid to think what I have done: /

Figure 15.9. Fuseli, *Macbeth and Lady ("Give me the daggers")*, 1774.
© The British Museum.

Look on't again I dare not." Lady Macbeth, possessed and demonic, clutches the daggers in an ecstatic dance.

What is this extraordinary version of the scene expressing? The revulsion and ecstasy are certainly present in the text, but they have here in a sense been isolated from it. And what is the significance of the classical context? This is a case in which the search for sources yields especially rich results. Macbeth's gesture is part of the standard bodily rhetoric of the eighteenth-century stage. It appears, for example, among several hundred "Complex Significant Gestures" in Gilbert Austin's codification of body language *Chironomia* (figure 15.10). But the gesture has a history reaching back to antiquity. Fuseli, looking at ancient art in Rome, would have seen it on the Orestes Sarcophagus in the Vatican (figure 15.11): Orestes' old nurse flees in horror as Orestes murders Clytaemnestra and Aegisthus. This is cited by Gert Schiff as Fuseli's immediate source,[24] and when I tracked it down the connection at first struck me as tenuous. But as I pursued it I found that the gesture really was quite special for Fuseli: he used it, so far as I can determine, only once again (figure 15.12), three

Figure 15.10. *Complex Significant Gestures*, from Gilbert Austin, *Chironomia*, 1806.

Figure 15.11. The Orestes Sarcophagus, detail. From Karl Robert, *Die antiken Sarkophag-Reliefs*, vol. 2 (Berlin, 1890), p. 173, fig. 157.

Figure 15.12. Fuseli, *Oedipus Curses Polyneices,* 1777. Nationalmuseum, Stockholm.

years later in 1777, for a drawing of Polyneices recoiling from Oedipus' curse. Schiff missed another much more obvious source also visible in the Vatican, Michelangelo's figure of Adam expelled from paradise on the Sistine ceiling (figure 15.13). As a sequence of allusions this is so intensely private as effectively to exclude the viewer. With the exception perhaps of the Michelangelo, they are allusions designed not to be recognized (and Michelangelo was no exception for Schiff), but the association of Orestes, Oedipus, and the fallen Adam with *Macbeth* in Fuseli's mind really is of the essence of his vision of the play, and in this context the use of the gesture can hardly be accidental.

Lady Macbeth, who has become a bacchante with daggers instead of castanets, derives from another ancient sculpture, the figure of a dancing maenad in a Bacchic revel depicted on a marble vase from the Borghese collection, now in the Louvre. Figure 15.14 shows a detail from Piranesi's engraving of the vase.[25] The maenad looks on as, immediately behind her, a faun supports the drunken Silenus, who has dropped his cup and is about to sink to the ground. Fuseli's classical context again is strikingly relevant, an index to how deeply textual his imagination is: "That which hath made them drunk," says Lady Macbeth as the scene opens, "hath made me bold, / What hath quenched them hath given me fire."

Figure 15.13. Michelangelo, The Expulsion of Adam and Eve,
from the Sistine Ceiling.

Figure 15.14. Giambattista Piranesi, relief of a vase from the Borghese Collection
(detail). From *Coupes, vases . . .* (Paris, 1805), no. 84.

The moment here involves no sense of terror, nor of the evil of the act that
has been committed. Macbeth, both murderer and witness, withdraws in dismay; Lady Macbeth pursues the action with ecstatic energy. The romantic
intensity, the suppressed violence that Fuseli saw in Garrick and Mrs.
Pritchard are here replaced by a balanced elegance and a Flaxmanish decorum. The two versions of the scene are, on the surface at least, diametrically

opposite; and indeed there is no obvious reason why this classical vision should be attached to *Macbeth* at all—the subject would be unrecognizable without its title. And yet the classic prototypes really are of the essence: Adam expelled from paradise; the guilty Orestes pursued by the furies; Oedipus afraid to think or look on what he has done; Polyneices cursed by his aged father for his attempt to occupy the old man's throne; and, perhaps most striking of all, Lady Macbeth as part of a sacred ritual, possessed and demonic. Fuseli's realization here looks beyond the stage, the actors, the text to a complex of other texts, visual, poetic, dramatic. And the sources of Fuseli's realization become the sources of Shakespeare's imagination. The play has become, in the most literal sense, a *locus classicus*.

7

We have concluded by considering five performances of the same Shakespearean scene. Each in its way makes claims to authenticity but means something quite different by the concept. Each also includes an embedded attitude toward the text that conditions, and ultimately determines, the terms of its realization. We could have looked at other, even more obvious, examples of what we might call the authenticity topos: Macklin in 1773 costuming his Macbeth in kilts, Irving in 1888 reproducing an archaeologically accurate eleventh-century Dunsinane Castle, Orson Welles speaking a Scottish brogue —or editors from Dover Wilson to Fredson Bowers yearning after Shakespeare's handwriting. What is authentic here is something that is not in the text; it is something behind it and beyond it that the text is presumed to represent: the real life of the characters, the actual history of which the action is a part, the playwright's imagination, or the hand of the master, the authentic witness of Shakespeare's own history. The assumption is that texts are representations or embodiments of something else, and that it is that something else which the performer or editor undertakes to reveal. What we want is not the authentic play, with its unstable, infinitely revisable script, but an authentic Shakespeare, to whom every generation's version of a classic drama may be ascribed.

NOTES

Notes to pages 8-22

2: What Is a Character?

1. "The Horrors of *King Lear*," *The Kenyon Review* 11:2 (spring, 1949), pp. 348–50.
2. See *Impersonations* (Cambridge, 1996), pp. 53–7.
3. C. M. Ingleby et al., *The Shakspere Allusion Book*, New Edition (Oxford, 1932), 1:272. Proposals to emend "kind" to "King" are obviously misguided, as the context makes clear: each of Burbage's roles includes its defining adjective, "young Hamlett, ould Hieronymoe/ kind Leer, the Greued Moore. . . ."

3: What Is an Editor?

1. Published as *The Aeneid of Thomas Phaer and Thomas Twyne*, ed. Steven Lally (New York: Garland Publishing, Inc., 1987).

4: Acting Scripts, Performing Texts

The extracts that appear in this essay have been printed with permission from the following sources: Extracts 2–10 (from the facsimiles in G. Blakemore Evans, ed., *Shakespearean Prompt-Books of the Seventeenth Century*, Vol. I, *The Padua "Macbeth"* [Charlottesville, 1960]; and Vol. II, *The Padua "Measure for Measure"* [Charlottesville, 1963]) have been reprinted by permission from the Bibliographic Society of the University of Virginia. Extracts 19 and 20 (two short sections of three pages from two manuscripts of Middleton's *A Game at Chesse*), and extracts 21 and 22 (from Middleton's *A Game at Chesse*, STC 17882, sig. E4r; and STC 17884, p. 31), are reprinted by permission from the Huntington Library.

1. See below, pp. 231–56
2. *On Editing Shakespeare* (Charlottesville, 1966), 112; my italics.
3. Quoted by E. K. Chambers, *William Shakespeare: A Study of Facts and Problems*, 2 vols. (Oxford, 1930), I:97.
4. Shakespeare quotations are my own modernizations of the 1623 folio. Line references are keyed to the Riverside edition (Boston, 1974).
5. G. Blakemore Evans, ed., *Shakespearean Prompt-Books of the Seventeenth Century*, Vol. I, *The Padua "Macbeth"* (Charlottesville, 1960); Vol. II, *The Padua "Measure for Measure"* (Charlottesville, 1963); *The History of King Henry the Fourth as revised by*

Sir Edward Dering, Bart., ed. George Walton Williams and G. Blakemore Evans (Charlottesville, 1974).

6. *Padua "Macbeth"*, General Introduction, 10. Reproduced by permission of the University Press of Virginia.

7. The film Virginia used for p. 135 of the Padua folio *Macbeth* had been damaged, with the result that what was printed from it is nearly illegible in places. For text on this page I have supplied a facsimile.

8. *Padua "Measure for Measure"*, Introduction, 1–2.

9. Forman's account is reproduced in the Arden *Macbeth*, ed. Kenneth Muir, 8th edition (Cambridge, Mass., 1953), xvi–xvii.

10. The account is reprinted in my Oxford *Winter's Tale* (1996), p. 233.

11. Raphaell Holinshed, *The Firste Volume of the Chronicles of England, Scotlande and Irelande* (London, 1577), *The Historie of Scotlande*, 243 (for the woodblock) and 243–44 (for the quotations, below).

12. As an editorial argument, however, this is not inconceivable, and the combination of Forman plus a source has been used to argue both for and against emendation. Wells and Taylor, in the Oxford Shakespeare *Cymbeline*, emend the name "Imogen" to "Innogen," noting that the name is so given both in Forman's report of the play and in Holinshed, and that Shakespeare elsewhere once—for a ghost character in *Much Ado*—uses the name Innogen. It would, of course, be as logical to argue that the unique, ghostly Innogen is the erroneous form, that Forman got his version of the name from Holinshed, and that Shakespeare was not controlled by his sources in this matter, anymore than he was in numerous others.

13. The passage, and the implications of its rearrangement, are discussed in Paul Bertram, *White Spaces in Shakespeare* (Cleveland, 1981), 28–30.

14. *Ralph Crane and Some Shakespeare First Folio Comedies* (Charlottesville, 1972), 36.

15. Thomas Middleton, *A Game at Chesse*, ed. R. C. Bald (Cambridge, 1929).

16. Salzburg, 1980.

17. From the Huntington ms, fol. 53r; this section is in Middleton's hand. Reproduced by permission of the Huntington Library.

18. *Ralph Crane*, 37.

19. From the Huntington ms, fols. 22v–23r.

20. *A Game at Chesse*, n.d., (STC 17882), E4r; n.d., (STC 17884), 31.

21. See Alan Brissenden, *Shakespeare and the Dance* (Atlantic Highlands, NJ, 1981), 97.

22. Both are cited in the Variorum *Tempest*, 78.

23. Stanley Wells, Gary Taylor, John Jowett, and William Montgomery, *William Shakespeare: A Textual Companion* (Oxford, 1987), p. 614. The editing of this play (and the note) is by John Jowett.

24. The setting is discussed and reproduced in J. M. Nosworthy's Arden *Cymbeline* (London, 1955), 220–22.

5: The Poetics of Spectacle

1. "Of Masques and Triumphs," *Essayes* (London, 1625), p. 223.

2. *Love's Triumph through Callipolis*, lines 1–3. Texts of the Jonson masques are those of the Yale edition, ed. Stephen Orgel (New Haven and London, 1969).

3. From *Tempe Restored,* by Jones and Aurelian Townshend, in *Aurelian Townshend's Poems and Masks,* ed. E. K. Chambers (Oxford, 1912), p. 83.

4. *Ibid.,* p. 99.

5. Jonson's usage is comparable not to the medieval *speculum,* but to, e.g., Spenser's in the Proem to *the Faerie Queene,* III, v.

6. "Poet and Architect," *Journal of the Warburg and Courtauld Institutes,* XII (1949), 152–78.

7. The text of *Timber, or Discoveries* cited throughout is that of C. H. Herford, P. and E. Simpson, *Ben Jonson,* VIII (Oxford, 1947). Numbers in parentheses are line references to this edition.

8. See, for example, De Anima, 431a, b.

9. Not, of course, in any simple way: it is also true that for Ficino the Word was higher than the Image. One could not express Platonic Ideas merely by drawing pictures of them.

10. *The Tempest,* IV.i.59.

11. *In librum Aristotelis de arte poetica explicationes* (1548), p. 57. A detailed analysis of the commentary by Bernard Weinberg is in *Critics and Criticism,* ed. R. S. Crane (Chicago, 1952), pp. 319–48.

12. The best general discussion of the place of wonder in Renaissance drama is J. V. Cunningham's "Woe or Wonder," in *Tradition and Poetic Structure* (Denver, 1960).

13. See the analysis by Bernard Weinberg in Crane, *Critics and Criticism,* pp. 349–71.

14. Bernard Weinberg, *A History of Literary Criticism in the Italian Renaissance* (Chicago, 1961), p. 685.

15. *The Ten Books on Architecture,* trans. M. H. Morgan (Cambridge, Mass., 1914), p. 150.

16. *Ibid.,* p. 282.

17. *The First (etc.] Book of Architecture . . .* (London, 1611), fol. 24 (N1r) . The translation, the first in English, was based on a Dutch version.

18. Ibid., fol. 24 (N1r)-fol. 26 (N[=O]1r).

19. Lines 10–14.

20. Subsequently published as *The Queen's Arcadia.*

21. Nichols, *Progresses,* I, 548.

22. A full account of the visit is given (in Latin) by Isaac Wake, *Rex Platonicus* (1607), and in Nichols, *Progresses,* I.538ff. Jones's stage for the productions is discussed by Allardyce Nicoll, *The Development of the Theatre* (London, 1927) p. 127.

23. Nichols, *Progresses,* I.558.

24. The suggestion was first made by Lily B. Campbell in *Scenes and Machines on the English Stage* (Cambridge, Eng., 1923), p. 87, and subsequently by Frances Yates in *Theatre of the World* (London, 1969), pp. 31–2.

25. In contrast, for example, the Teatro Olimpico at Vicenza, designed by Palladio and Scamozzi for an academy of social equals, has five perspectives running back from a stage wall along the radii of the circular hall. It thus provided every spectator with a perfect perspective.

26. E.g. Dryden, *Prologue . . . at the Opening of The New House* (1674), lines 34ff.

27. The account is in Nichols, *Progresses,* I.558.

28. 1632, A3r–v.

29. Line 63.

30. 1655, A4r.

31. Cited by Alfred Harbage, *Cavalier Drama* (New York, 1936), p. 152.

32. *A Short Discourse of the English Stage* (1664). The passage is cited by Campbell, *Scenes,* p. 236.

33. Chambers, *Elizabethan Stage,* III, 377.

34. See, e.g., *Theataetus* 155d, though of course the wonder produced by dramatic spectacles is immediately excepted.

35. *Ode to Himself* ("Where dost thou carelesse lie") lines 21–6.

36. Lines 159–60.

37. Lines 21ff.

38. Quoted by Herford and Simpson, X, 448.

39. *Ibid.,* 410–11. The account must be second-hand, since Wood was three years old in 1636.

40. *Hymenaei,* lines 15–17.

41. *News from the New World,* lines 318–27.

42. *Platonic Theology,* trans. Josephine L. Burroughs, in *Journal of the History of Ideas,* V (April, 1944), 235.

43. From *Eikonoklastes,* in *Complete Poems and Selected Prose,* ed. M. Y. Hughes (New York, 1957), p. 784.

6: The Spectacles of State

1. See Roy Strong, *The Cult of Elizabeth* (London, 1977), pp. 17–55.

2. See *The Triumph of Honour* (Leiden, 1977), and "Henry VII and the Origins of Tudor Patronage," in *Patronage in the Renaissance,* ed. Guy Fitch Lytle and Stephen Orgel (Princeton, 1982), Chapter 5.

3. The best account of the politics of the incident is by Jonathan Goldberg in *James I and the Politics of Literature* (Baltimore, 1983), Chapter 1.

4. See the summary in the Arden edition of *Richard II,* ed. Peter Ure (London, 1956), p. lix.

5. E. K. Chambers, *The Elizabethan Stage* (Oxford, 1923), 4:500.

6. Conversations with Drummond, in *Ben Jonson,* ed. C. H. Herford and Percy Simpson (Oxford, 1925), 1:141, lines 330ff.

7. Chambers, *Elizabethan Stage,* 2:419.

8. J. E. Neale, *Elizabeth I and Her Parliaments* (New York, 1958), 2:119.

9. C. H. McIlwain, ed., *Political Works of James I* (Cambridge, Mass., 1918), p. 43.

7: The Renaissance Poet as Plagiarist

1. Stephen Orgel and Roy Strong, *Inigo Jones* (London and Berkeley, Calif., 1973) 2:706, lines 1–12.

2. Enid Welsford, *The Court Masque* (Cambridge, England, 1927) p. 236.

3. *The Jacobean and Caroline Stage* (Oxford, 1956) 3:209.

4. Orgel and Strong, *Inigo Jones*, 2:505–35. For Fidamira's costume and the Knole portrait see nos. 261–63 and figure 91.

5. Don Cameron Allen, *Francis Meres's Treatise, "Poetrie"* (Urbana, Illinois, 1933).

6. E. W. Talbert, "Current Scholarly Works and the 'Erudition' of Jonson's *Masque of Augurs*," *Studies in Philology* 44 (1947), pp. 605–24; and see also the earlier article "New Light on Ben Jonson's Workmanship," *SP* 40 (1943), 154–85. The argument was called to account by Percy Simpson in *Ben Jonson* (Oxford, 1925–52), 10:640. Talbert implicitly recants in D. T. Starnes and E. W. Talbert, *Classical Myth and Legend in Renaissance Dictionaries* (Chapel Hill, N.C., 1955), p. 212; but see the amusingly self-defensive piece of scholarly gobbledygook in note 69, p. 432.

7. British Library MS Harley 6057, fol. 30. The poem is transcribed in *Ben Jonson*, 11:385–86.

8. *An Essay of Dramatic Poesy*, in *Essays of John Dryden*, ed. W. P. Ker (Oxford, 1900), pp. 43, 82.

9. Quoted in *Ben Jonson*, 11:542.

10. *Ben Jonson*, 11:534.

11. Preface to *The Works of Shakespear*, 1725, in D. Nichol Smith, *Eighteenth Century Essays on Shakespeare*, 2nd edition (Oxford, 1963) p. 49.

12. Preface to *The Plays of William Shakespeare*, 1765, in Nichol Smith, pp. 124, 126–27.

13. *An Essay on the Learning of Shakespeare*, 1767, in Nichol Smith, p. 156.

14. *Timber or Discoveries*, in *Ben Jonson*, 8:638, lines 2466–71.

15. *Timber*, lines 2479–80.

16. Julius Caesar Scaliger, *Poetices libri septem* (Lyons, 1561), p. 83; and cf. also pp. v and 113.

17. *Letters of Peter Paul Rubens*, trans. R. S. Magurn (Cambridge, Mass., 1955), pp. 76–7.

18. *Albrecht Dürer* (Princeton, 1955) p. 284.

19. P. 26. The book is a translation of Giovanni Lomazzo, and in the original this passage is about religious images.

20. Quoted in Roy Strong, *Portraits of Queen Elizabeth* (Oxford, 1963), p. 39.

21. *Leviathan* 1.16.

22. J. Ferne, *The Blazon of Gentry* (1586), p. 82.

23. "To . . . Sir Peter Lilly" [i.e., Lely], line 27.

24. Quoted in Helmut Gernsheim, *The History of Photography* (London, 1969), p. 70.

25. *Timber*, line 2353.

26. *A Defence of Poetry*, in *Miscellaneous Prose of Sir Philip Sidney*, ed. K. Duncan-Jones and Jan van Dorsten (Oxford, 1973), p. 102.

27. § 472 d–e.

28. The best general discussion, including a brilliant analysis of the situation in the Renaissance, is Jonas A. Barish, *The Antitheatrical Prejudice* (Berkeley, Calif., 1981).

29. *Idea*, trans. Joseph S. Peake (Columbia, S.C., 1968), Chapter 2.

30. P. O. Kristeller, *The Philosophy of Marsilio Ficino* (New York, 1943), pp. 95–6.

31. The fullest discussion is still that by Harold Ogden White, *Plagiarism and Imitation during the English Renaissance* (Cambridge, Mass., 1935). Richard Bern-

heimer's *The Nature of Representation* (New York, 1961), posthumously published from an unfinished manuscript, is intermittently helpful, though it suffers from serious methodological and theoretical problems. John D. Boyd's *The Function of Mimesis and Its Decline* (Cambridge, Mass., 1969), though it does not deal directly with the question of plagiarism, is an indispensable guide. And W. A. Edwards' *Plagiarism* (Cambridge, 1933), an undergraduate prize essay, is still worth a look for its genial and intelligent overview.

32. *The Civile Conversation*, trans. George Pettie, 1581 (London, 1925), 1:153.

33. *Pseudodoxia Epidemica*, ed. G. Keynes (London, 1964), 1:43–4.

34. *Timber*, lines 745–47.

8: Gendering the Crown

1. According to the epigraph engraved on the pedestal of the *Daphne*; see Jean Seznec, *The Survival of the Pagan Gods* (New York, 1953), p. 271.

2. *Ovids Metamorphosis Englished* (Oxford, 1632), p. 35.

3. *The xv. Bookes of P. Ouidius Naso*, ed. (as *Shakespeare's Ovid*) by W. H. D. Rouse (London, 1904), p. 206.

4. *Metamorphosis*, p. 361.

5. William Caxton, *Ovyde Hys Methamorphose* (1480), 10:6.

6. The most thorough discussion of the iconography, though one I disagree with on some central points, is by Raymond Waddington, "The Bisexual Portrait of Francis I," in *Playing with Gender*, ed. Jean R. Brink et al. (Urbana, 1991), pp. 99–132.

7. For a general discussion of the satirical iconography of the reign, see Keith Cameron, *Henri III, A Maligned or Malignant King* (University of Exeter, 1978). The two images considered here are plates 7 and 8, discussed on pp. 78–84.

8. From Sebastian de Covarrubias Orozco, *Emblemas Morales* (Madrid, 1610), II, no. 64; the emblem is discussed in Paul Julian Smith, *The Body Hispanic* (Oxford, 1989), pp. 9, 16–7.

9. The drawing is now in Stockholm; in the catalogue of the 1989 Giulio Romano exhibition in Mantua it is reproduced and discussed on p. 283.

10. *Dictionarium Historicum, Geographicum, Poeticum* (Paris, 1596), p. 26.

11. *A Choice of Emblemes* (London, 1586), p. 93.

12. *Gloriana* (London, 1987), p. 99.

13. *Gloriana*, pp. 113–14, and figure 112.

14. In the Vulgate, the psalm is numbered 84.

15. See the anonymous pamphlet addressed to Edward VI, *Al Serenissimo Re d'Inghilterra Edoardo Sesto, De portamenti di Papa Giulio III*, 1550, cited by Alessandro Nova, *Artistic Patronage of Pope Julius III* (Garland, 1988), p. 48 n. 57. A photograph of the Villa Giulia stucco is reproduced in figure 28.

16. Neither Hind (I, 285) nor Strong (*Portraits*, p. 113) sees an allusion to the Armada in the print; Yates (*Astraea*, p. 58) does. I am indebted to Peter Hammer for calling my attention to the Cadiz allusion. Hind incorrectly claims the birds are both versions of the phoenix.

17. Cited by Strong, *Gloriana*, p. 96.

18. W. Milgate, ed., *John Donne, The Satires, Epigrams and Verse Letters* (Oxford, 1967), p. 212.

19. *The Forest* 10, lines 17–18.

20. *Underwood* 88, line 1.

21. Philip Sidney, *The Countess of Pembroke's Arcadia*, ed. Albert Feuillerat (Cambridge, 1912), p. 176.

22. *The Discovery of . . . Guiana*, ed. Sir R. Shombergk (Hakluyt Society, 1848), p. 115.

23. *A Relation of the Second Voyage to Guiana* (London, 1596), sig. F2v.

9: The Play of Conscience

Note: I am indebted to the late David Sachs, who first called my attention to Gerald Else's reading of the catharsis passage and persuaded me that it was worth taking seriously. For guidance through the classical minefields, I am grateful to Andrew Ford, Jay Reed, David Halperin, and especially to Francis Sparshott's excellent essay "The Riddle of Katharsis," in Eleanor Cook et al., eds., *Centre and Labyrinth* (Toronto, 1983), pp. 14–37. Thanks are due for suggestions and enlightenment on various points to Randall Nakayama, Peter Stallybrass, and the late Bradley Rubidge. Finally, a timely and thoughtful question from Jonathan Arac helped to clarify the argument.

1. *Aristotle's Poetics: The Argument* (Cambridge, Mass., 1963), pp. 225–32, 423–47.

2. A brief summary of the arguments against it is in Stephen Halliwell, *Aristotle's Poetics* (London, 1986), p. 355.

3. This is not, however, Else's argument. He suggests, on the contrary, that the passage from the *Politics* is not relevant at all, that it is something Aristotle believed when he wrote it but changed his mind about when he came to write the *Poetics* (pp. 442–3). I find this as unpersuasive as everyone else has found it—critics do tend to put their worst feet forward in dealing with catharsis.

4. And indeed, Jonathan Lear rejects the reading precisely because it is formalistic, accusing it of deriving from "a misapplication of a principle from new criticism" ("Katharsis," in A. O. Rorty, ed., *Essays on Aristotle's Poetics*, Princeton, 1992, p. 336), but this is not really correct: Else argues only that an internally consistent interpretation of catharsis in the *Poetics* cannot be refuted "*merely* by appealing to a reference in another work which seems to imply another concept, especially if that reference is obscure or controversial in itself" (p. 441). In fact, Else's own explanation of the difference between the uses of the term in the two works, far from being new critical, is based on quite romantic assumptions about Aristotle's intellectual biography (see above, note 3). I describe Else's reading as "new critical" below simply because it undertakes to keep catharsis within the limits of the text. A more particular objection to the argument as a reading of the Greek, raised by both Stephen Halliwell (*Aristotle's Poetics*, p. 355) and Elizabeth Belfiore (*Tragic Pleasures*, Princeton, 1992, p. 264), is that it requires us to take pity and fear, *eleos kai phobos*, to mean not the emotions of pity and fear, but events producing these emotions, and Aristotle specifically refers to them as *pathemata*, emotions. Else

anticipates this objection, and cites a parallel usage earlier in the essay which does support his reading (pp. 228–9, ignored by both critics); but even without this, the objection seems excessively narrow. As indicated below, *pathemata*, the word normally translated "emotions," means literally "sufferings"; it includes both what the hero undergoes and how he feels about it. Indeed, to use emotional terms in this way is so commonplace that it is the criticism that seems eccentric: when Horatio at the end of *Hamlet* promises to satisfy his hearers' appetite for "aught of woe or wonder," he is promising a narration about events that will evoke these emotions, not about the emotions themselves.

5. *Tragic Pleasures* (Princeton, 1992), pp. 257–336.

6. 1455b15.

7. 1341b39–40.

8. The indispensible guide to the material is Bernard Weinberg, *History of Literary Criticism in the Italian Renaissance*, 2 vols., Chicago, 1961, hereafter cited as Weinberg. In cases where passages I discuss are included in Weinberg's survey, I have for convenience given the citation to his text, though I have occasionally revised his translation in the interests of clarity. An excellent brief overview is given by Halliwell, *Aristotle's Poetics*, pp. 290–302.

9. Weinberg, 1:358.

10. The Latin is, "de miseratione & pauore terminans talium disciplinarum purgationem" (Weinberg, 1:372).

11. "per misericordium uerò atque terrorem perturbationes huiusmodi purgans" (*ibid.*).

12. Aristotle's *ton toiouton pathematon*, "such emotions," is similarly ambiguous, and many critics have taken it to be equivalent to *ton touton pathematon*, "these emotions," which would clearly limit the emotions to pity and fear.

13. *Grundzüge der verloren Abhandlung des Aristoteles über Wirking der Tragödie* (Breslau, 1857), in many ways the originary modern treatment of the subject.

14. *Sopra la purgazione della tragedia . . .* (1586), discussed in Weinberg, 1:626–8; the passage cited is discussed on p. 627.

15. Weinberg 2:927.

16. *Discorso intorno à que' principii, cause, et accrescimenti, che la comedia, la tragedia, et il poema heroico ricevono dall philosophia . . .* (1586); the argument is summarized by Weinberg, 1:621–6. The passage about military training is discussed on p. 625. Compare John J. Winkler, "The Ephebes' Song: *Tragôedia* and *Polis*," *Representations* 11 (summer, 1985): 26–62.

17. *Poetices libri septem* (Lyons, 1581), p. 29.

18. Weinberg, 1:571.

19. 1448b4–19.

20. For a detailed discussion of the argument, see my essay "The Poetics of Spectacle," above.

21. *Poetica d'Aristotele vulgarizzata et sposta* (1570/76); Weinberg 1:502ff. The passage cited is on p. 506.

22. For the marginalization of catharsis in Aristotle, see Andrew Ford's essay "*Kathar-*

sis: The Ancient Problem," in *Performativity and Performance*, ed. Andrew Parker and Eve Kosofsky Sedgwick (New York: Routledge, 1995), pp. 109–32.

23. *In Aristotelis librum de Poetica paraphrasis* (1572); Weinberg 1:519–23; the passage cited is on p. 521.

24. *An Apology for Poetry*, ed. Forrest G. Robinson (New York/London: Macmillan, 1970), p. 45.

25. Book 1, chapter 24 (ed. G. D. Willcock and Alice Walker, Cambridge, 1936, p. 48). I have modernized the passage.

26. Stephen Gosson, *Playes Confuted in Five Actions* (1582), sig. C7r–v; Phillip Stubbes, *The Anatomie of Abuses* (1583), sig. L7r; William Prynne, *Histrio-Mastix* (1633), p. 448–9 and elsewhere.

27. Prefatory note to *Samson Agonistes*, lines 1ff.

28. *Ibid.*, line 1758.

29. *An Apologie for Actors* (1612), sigs. G1v–G2v.

10: Shakespeare and the Kinds of Drama

1. Samuel Johnson, *Preface to Shakespeare*, in *The Works of Samuel Johnson*, 9 vols. (Oxford, 1825), 5:109–10.

2. See Diderot's *Essai de la poesie dramatique* (Paris, 1758).

3. Johnson, 5:112.

4. Sir Philip Sidney, in *English Literary Criticism: The Renaissance*, ed. O. B. Hardison, Jr. (New York, 1963), p. 138.

5. Thomas Rymer, *Critical Works of Thomas Rymer*, ed. Curt A. Zimansky (New Haven, Conn., 1956), p. 132.

6. *Ibid.*, pp. 164 and 173.

7. T. S. Eliot, *Selected Essays* (New York, 1950), pp. 128–29.

8. Lionel Trilling's review first appeared in *Columbia Varsity* in 1926; it was reprinted (by me, to his chagrin, when I was editor) in *Columbia Review* 35 (February 1955), p. 46.

9. Scaliger, *Poetices Libri Septem* (Lyons, 1581), pp. 28–29; here and elsewhere, my translation. All further citations to this work appear in the text.

10. Gerald Else, *Aristotle's Poetics: The Argument* (Cambridge, Mass.: Harvard University Press, 1957), pp. 224–32, 423–47.

11. The summary is by Bernard Weinberg, *History of Literary Criticism in the Italian Renaissance*, 2 vols. (Chicago, 1961), 2:658.

12. Sidney, quoted by Hardison, *English Literary Criticism*, p. 120. His later objection to "their mungrell Tragy-comedie" derives not from the mixture of genres but from the failure to observe decorum, "mingling Kings and Clownes . . . Horn-pypes and Funeralls" (pp. 139–40). This is not to say that there were no critics who deplored the mixture of comedy with tragedy; but they were, in the main, those critics who scorned drama as a form precisely because it depended for its effect on an audience.

13. *Ibid.*, p. 140.

14. Samuel Pepys, *The Diary of Samuel Pepys*, ed. G. Gregory Smith (London, 1905), p. 287; all further citations appear in the text.

15. Thomas Platter, quoted in E. K. Chambers' *Elizabethan Stage*, 4 vols. (Oxford, 1923), 2:365.

11: Macbeth and the Antic Round

1. The assumption is that the inclusion of the Middleton material dates from the revision printed in the folio. The complete text of the songs is printed in the Oxford, Norton and New Pelican editions of *Macbeth*.
2. Quotations are from my edition of the play in the New Pelican Shakespeare.
3. "Jonson and the Amazons," in Elizabeth D. Harvey and Katharine Eisaman Maus, eds., *Soliciting Interpretation* (University of Chicago Press, 1990), pp. 119–39.
4. "The Early Scenes of *Macbeth*: Preface to a New Interpretation," in his collection *Making Trifles of Terrors* (Stanford, 1997), pp. 70–97.
5. The book tabulates seven allusions, but in fact includes eight. *The Knight of the Burning Pestle* and a play called *The Puritan* refer pretty clearly to Banquo's ghost, and *The Two Maids of Mortlake*, a parodic play by Robert Armin, the principal clown in Shakespeare's company, recalls Macbeth's "Will all great Neptune's ocean wash this blood / Clean from my hands?" Since Armin's play was published in 1609, this must be a recollection of *Macbeth* on the stage. Sir Thomas Browne in 1642 saying that he begins "to be weary of the sun" is more likely a recollection of the printed text.
6. *Spectator* 45 (1711).
7. Described in *The Dramatic Mirror*, quoted in Gamini Salgado, *Eyewitnesses of Shakespeare* (Sussex University Press, 1975), p. 299.
8. Davenant's *Macbeth* is quoted from Christopher Spencer's edition, *Davenant's Macbeth from the Yale Manuscript* (New Haven, 1961).
9. *Bell's Edition of Shakespeare's Plays* (London, 1774), 1:71.

12: Prospero's Wife

1. Line references throughout are to my Oxford edition. In this instance, I have restored the folio punctuation of line 59, which adds to the sense of ambivalence.
2. Edited by Murray M. Schwartz and Coppelia Kahn (Baltimore: Johns Hopkins University Press, 1980).
3. *The New Yorker*, March 1, 1982, p. 53.
4. "So Rare a Wonder'd Father: Prospero's *Tempest*," in *Representing Shakespeare*, p. 48.
5. Coppélia Kahn makes this point, following a suggestion of Harry Berger, Jr., in "The Providential Tempest and the Shakespearean Family," in *Representing Shakespeare*, p. 238. For an alternative view, see the exceptionally interesting discussion by Joel Fineman, "Fratricide and Cuckoldry: Shakespeare's Doubles," in the same volume, p. 104.
6. The charge that he was David Rizzio's child was current in England in the 1580s, spread by rebellious Scottish Presbyterian ministers. James expressed fears that it would injure his chance of succeeding to the English throne, and he never felt entirely free of it.

7. C. H. McIlwain, *Political Works of James I* (Cambridge, Mass.: Harvard University Press, 1918), p. 24.

8. From the 1603 speech to Parliament; *ibid.*, p. 272.

9. *Metamorphoses* 7.197–209, apparently at least partly refracted through Arthur Golding's English version.

10. Most editions (including my own) read "entertained," but the folio reading is not clearly incorrect, and makes a particular sense in the context of this argument.

11. "'Wife' or 'Wise' *The Tempest l.* 1786," *University of Virginia Studies in Bibliography* 31 (1978).

12. Introduction to the 2nd ed. of the Norton Folio facsimile (New York: W. W. Norton, 1996), p. xxxi.

13: Marginal Jonson

1. *The S[c]hoole of Abuse* (London, 1579), sig. A2v.

2. B text, 2.1.534–5.

3. *Conversations with Drummond* in C. H. Herford and P. Simpson, *Ben Jonson* (Oxford, 1925), 1:139.

4. Cited in C. H. Herford, P. and E. Simpson, *Ben Jonson*, vol. 10 (Oxford, 1950), p. 448.

5. *Ibid.*, p. 447.

6. *Ibid.*, p. 449; the writer is identified only as 'Vincent,' and may not be the herald Augustine Vincent.

7. The remark concerned the diplomatic squabbles over invitations to *The Masque of Beauty*, in which the queen countermanded the king's orders; see *Ben Jonson* 10:456.

8. *Letters of John Chamberlain*, ed. Norman E. McClure (Philadelphia: American Philosophical Society, 1939), 2:286–7.

9. *Ibid.*, p.294.

10. See Graham Reynolds's discussion of the painting in *Costume of the Western World: Fashions of the Renaissance*, ed. James Laver (New York: Harper and Brothers, 1951), p. 146: "The lace of the ruff and cuffs and round the yoke of her bodice is dyed with saffron."

11. See Ania Loomba, *Gender, Race, Renaissance Drama* (Manchester: Manchester University Press, 1989), esp. Chapter 2; Lynda Boose, "The Getting of a Lawful Race," in Margo Hendricks and Patricia Parker, eds., *Women, "Race," and Writing in the Early Modern Period* (London: Routledge, 1994), pp. 35–54; Margo Hendricks, "Managing the Barbarian," *Renaissance Drama* n.s. 23 (1992), pp. 165–88; Ruth Cowhig, "Blacks in English Renaissance Drama," in David Dabydeen, ed., *The Black Presence in English Literature* (Manchester: Manchester University Press, 1985), pp. 1–25; Gretchen Gerzina, *Black England* (London: John Murray, 1995); Peter Fryer, *Staying Power: The History of Black People in Britain* (London: Pluto Press, 1984); Kim Hall, *Things of Darkness* (Ithaca: Cornell University Press, 1995).

12. Cesare Vecellio, *Habiti Antichi et Moderni di tutto il Mondo*, 1598, p. 429.

13. Boose, "The Getting of a Lawful Race," p. 44.

14. See "The Getting of a Lawful Race," pp. 42–5.
15. Richard Hakluyt, *The Principal Navigations . . . of the English Nation* (Glasgow, 1904), 6:176, 200, 284.
16. *Tudor Royal Proclamations, 1588–1603*, ed. J. L. Hughes and J. F. Larkin (New Haven: Yale University Press, 1969), p. 221.
17. "Jonson and the Amazons," in Elizabeth Harvey and Katharine Eisaman Maus, eds., *Soliciting Interpretation* (Chicago, 1990), pp. 119–39.
18. W. Milgate, ed., *John Donne, The Satires, Epigrams and Verse Letters* (Oxford, 1967), p. 212.
19. *Ben Jonson* 7:279.
20. Leeds Barroll, an honorable exception, has recently mounted a strong defense of her acumen in *Anna of Denmark, Queen of England* (Philadelphia: University of Pennsylvania Press, 2001).
21. *John Florio* (Cambridge, 1934), p. 248.
22. *The Golden Age Restored* (Manchester: Manchester University Press, 1981), p. 42.

14: Tobacco and Boys

1. *Corpus Association Newsletter* 45 (1966), pp. 24–6.
2. A facsimile and transcription are in A. D. Wraight, *In Search of Christopher Marlowe* (New York: Vanguard Press, 1965), pp. 308–9.
3. "Sodomy and Society: The Case of Christopher Marlowe," in *Staging the Renaissance*, eds. David Scott Kastan and Peter Stallybrass (New York: Routledge, 1991), pp. 75–82.
4. Quotations are from my own edition of Marlowe's *Complete Poems and Translations* (Penguin, 1971).
5. See David Halperin, *One Hundred Years of Homosexuality* (New York: Routledge, 1990), p. 134.
6. *Marlowe's Counterfeit Profession* (Toronto: University of Toronto Press, 1997).
7. Cited in Tucker Brooke, *The Works of Christopher Marlowe* (Oxford, 1910), p. 114.
8. *The Reckoning* (London: Cape, 1992), p. 68.
9. Cited in Brooke, *Marlowe*, p. 114.
10. Lisa Jardine and Alan Stewart, *Hostage to Fortune* (London: Gollancz, 1998), p. 17.
11. *Ibid.*, p. 465.
12. *Times Literary Supplement*, June 19, 1998, p. 12.
13. Cited in Jardine and Stewart, *Hostage to Fortune*, pp. 464–5.
14. Quotations from *Doctor Faustus* are from the edition edited by David Bevington and Eric Rasmussen (Manchester University Press, 1992); the 1604 text is A, the 1616 text B.
15. Snow's brilliant essay on the play is "Marlowe's *Doctor Faustus* and the Ends of Desire," in Alvin Kernan, ed., *Two Renaissance Mythmakers* (Baltimore, 1977), pp. 70–110.

15: The Authentic Shakespeare

1. Both the excitement and the outrage had more to do with the press-agentry atten-

dant on the poem's discovery than with the poem itself, and in one respect, at least, revealed an embarrassing lack of research on everyone's part: the poem had already been included, thirty years earlier, in the old Pelican edition of Shakespeare's *Narrative Poems*, edited by Richard Wilbur under the general editorship of Alfred Harbage, and had raised no hackles at all. Harbage apparently lost faith, or interest, in it, and it was deleted, without comment, from the poems when the Pelican *Complete Works* was issued. It currently survives as Shakespeare's in the Oxford and Norton editions.

2. Peter Beal, *Times Literary Supplement*, 3 January 1986, 13; Donald W. Foster, *Times Literary Supplement*, 24 January 1986, 87–88.

3. E. K. Chambers, *William Shakespeare*, 2 vols. (Oxford, 1930), 1:462.

4. Lee's discussion appears in his introduction to the 1905 Oxford University Press facsimile of the *Sonnets*, pp. 26–53. Katherine Duncan-Jones has extended the argument, observing that there are no real grounds for assuming that the publication was even unauthorized; see "Was the 1609 Shakespeare's Sonnets Really Unauthorized?" *Review of English Studies*, n.s., 34 (May 1983): 151–71.

5. From the *Parnassus* plays; cited in Chambers, *Shakespeare*, 2:200.

6. John Milton, "L'Allegro," line 133.

7. *The Shakespeare Allusion Book*, 2 vols. (London, 1909), 1:272.

8. For an excellent analysis of the issues involved in the publication of Luther's Bible, see Jane O. Newman, "The Word Made Print: Luther's 1522 *New Testament* in an Age of Mechanical Reproduction," *Representations* 11 (Summer 1985): 95–133.

9. The letter is quoted in G. E. Bentley, *The Profession of Dramatist in Shakespeare's Time* (Princeton, N.J., 1971), 52.

10. Nicholas Barker has pointed out to me that in the hands of humanist editors and publishers, classical drama went through a similar progression in the previous century, starting as the Aldine octavos in 1502 and 1503, becoming small quartos in the next decade, and only beginning to appear in folio in the mid-century, in annotated editions modeled on those of Herodotus and Augustine. Only Terence was published in folio from the beginning, in Strasburg in 1470 and Venice in 1474, illustrated and in a format that imitated manuscripts.

11. G. Blakemore Evans, *Shakespearean Promptbooks of the Seventeenth Century* vol. 1, part 1, *The Padua "Macbeth"* (Charlottesville, Va., 1960), 10. I have discussed these in detail in my essay "Acting Scripts, Performing Texts" in this volume.

12. To observe the disparity between the performing time and the length of the surviving texts is a critical commonplace, but its implications are rarely considered and never taken into account. For example, to read through the full standard text of *Hamlet* takes four-and-one-half hours; an uncut *Lear* takes three-and-one-half; and even "the two hours traffic" of *Romeo and Juliet* can scarcely be gotten through—briskly—in under three hours. These figures do not, of course, allow for any scene breaks or intermissions. In fact, there is some evidence that *The Tempest* originally had breaks between the acts, and the three-hour figure given within the play for the duration of the fictive action (5.1.223), if it is intended to coincide with the length of the performance, may be including time for the intervals. Ben Jon-

son apologizes for the length of *Bartholomew Fair*, which he says will take an unprecedented two-and-one-half hours to perform. The text of *Bartholomew Fair* is as long as *Lear*, but we know that Jonson revised and augmented his plays for publication. The most precise bit of hard evidence for the time of performance is in a note from Lord Hunsdon to the lord mayor of London dated 8 October 1594, asking permission for his company to play in the city and assuring him that the performance will "begin at two and have done betwene fower and five"—this figure would include everything, including music, intermissions if any, and the indispensable final jig; the document is quoted in Peter Thomson, *Shakespeare's Theatre* (London, 1983), 21.

13. University performances lasting from four to five hours were not uncommon, and Walter Montagu's *Shepherd's Paradise*, originally planned to take eight hours, though in the event performed in a cut version, became notorious as much for its length as for William Prynne's prosecution in connection with it.

14. Chambers, *Shakespeare*, 2: 197.

15. The only other place I have found in which Caesar is killed in the Capitol is Chaucer's "Monk's Tale." This has not previously been cited as a source for the play. Shakespeare clearly knew his Chaucer, but he was primarily following North's *Plutarch* (1579), where the murder takes place in Pompey's theater. Does the decision to follow Chaucer rather than Plutarch reflect a preference for poetic justice? Or was Shakespeare deliberately moving the violence of history away from the theater to the world of politics?

16. Nicholas Rowe, ed., *The Works of Mr. William Shakespear*, 9 vols., 2nd ed. (London, 1714), 9:240, 249.

17. *The Arden Shakespeare*, note to *The Tempest*, 1.2.379. The emendation is discussed in more detail in "Acting Scripts, Performing Texts" above.

18. John Dennis, "On the Genius and Writings of Shakespear," letter 3, in D. Nichol Smith, ed., *Eighteenth-Century Essays on Shakespeare*, 2nd ed. (Oxford, 1963), 39–42.

19. Stanley Wells, from *The Oxford Shakespeare Editorial Procedures*, November 1978, 15. This is a mimeographed handbook supplied to the editors of volumes in the series.

20. From Ben Jonson, *Timber; or, Discoveries*; the passage is reprinted in Chambers, *Shakespeare*, 2:210.

21. George C. D. Odell, *Shakespeare from Betterton to Irving*, 2 vols. (New York, 1920), 1:340. Odell greatly understates the extent of Garrick's revisions.

22. W. Moelwyn Merchant, *Shakespeare and the Artist* (Oxford, 1959), 59.

23. Victoria Manners and G. C. Williamson, *John Zoffany, R. A.* (London, 1920), 177.

24. Gert Schiff, *Johann Heinrich Fussli*, 2 vols. (Zurich, 1973), 2:452, no. 456.

25. Piranesi engraved the vase and its frieze for his two volumes of *Vasi, candalabri, cippi . . .* (in the Paris edition of 1905, nos. 83 and 84). These were not published until 1778, though it would of course have been possible for Fuseli to see individual plates before their appearance in book form. Certain details in the drawing, however, seem closer to the vase itself than to Piranesi's version of it.

INDEX